BOUNTY
• Beyond • the • Voyage •

BOUNTY

• Beyond • the • Voyage •

Julie Pearson

First published in 1989 by
TRUSSON PUBLICATIONS
9b Park Rise, Leatherhead,
Surrey KT22 7HZ
in association with
The Self Publishing Association Ltd
Lloyds Bank Chambers
Upton-upon-severn
Worcestershire WR8 4HU
England

A MEMBER OF

British Library Cataloguing in Publication Data

Pearson, Julie,
Bounty: Beyond the Voyage
1. Great Britain. Royal Navy. Sailing vessels:
Bounty, (Ship). Mutiny
I. Title
359.1'334

ISBN 1-85421-045-9

A proportion of the profits from the sale of this book will be donated to H.O.P.E.

Designed and produced by the SPA Ltd, Upton-upon-Severn
Printed and bound in Great Britain by Billings & Sons Ltd, Worcester

This book is dedicated to my daughters, Emma and Alaine, my husband Bill, my mother Joyce Trusson, my aunt Meme and especially to my late father, Herbert Trusson. He was the last in a long line of Trusson printers; family tradition would have us believe there was one in every generation since the days of Caxton though I have only been able to prove, through my genealogical researches, this theory back to 1804.

Originally I had intended to publish under my maiden name in memory of my father – that way I would not have severed the family printing connections entirely, but my mentor Tony Harold mercenarily told me to use the name I am most commonly known by. His convincing argument was that more local recognition should result in more sales. It was my first lesson in becoming a ruthless business woman; I do believe I have a long way to go!

Finally, it is with much gratitude that I thank Peter Gibbs of Wallington Seafoods, 46 Springfield Road, Wallington, Surrey, SM6 OBB (01-647 7128) for his sponsorship and faith in me.

Christian Family

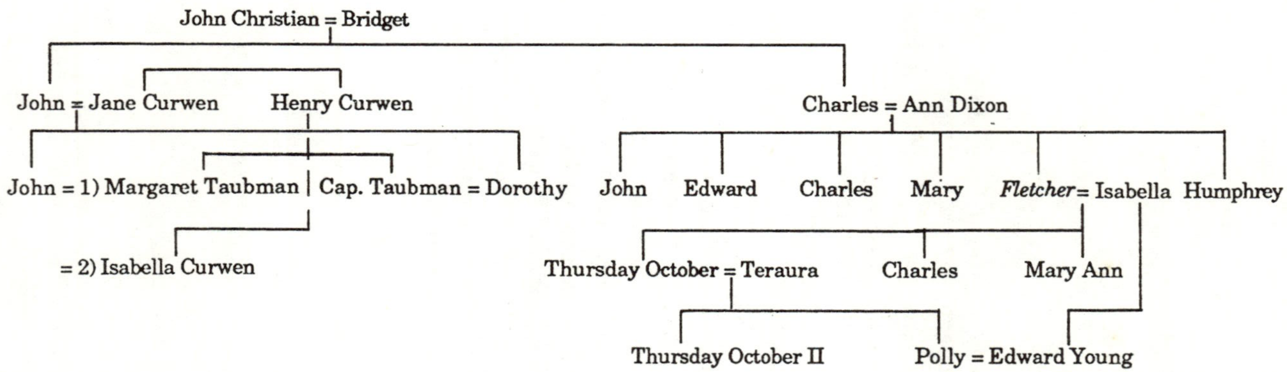

Bligh Family

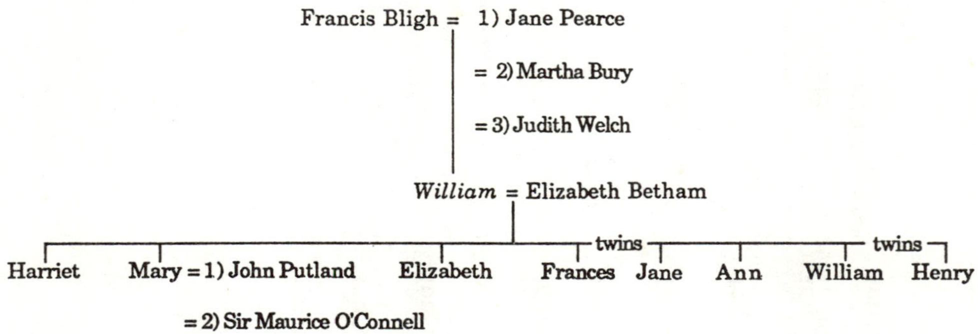

CONTENTS

Breadfruit

The breadfruit itself seems to be something of an enigma, with a tangled web of theories woven around its harvest. I had come to understand that they were grown into plants solely by seed, but discovered later, although that is definitely the case in some parts of the world, the Tahitian variety collected by *Bounty* propagates itself by giving out suckers, which meander just under the earth's surface, sending up new shoots at indiscriminate intervals.

Confusion has reigned over how *Bounty's* nursery was originally augmented, and Bligh himself appears to be the perpetrator by referring to 'seeds' in his log during their long stay in the South Seas, but eventually it is he who clears up the matter. Whilst staying at Coupang on Timor after his long boat voyage, he 'desired to see the seed breadfruit' and made a point of remarking, 'the tree . . . is to all appearance the same as that which bears the fruit without seed or the Otaheite kind.'

For those who share my interest in cultivating herbs, you may have noticed how tarragon reproduces itself, sending out shoots from its large and probing roots. So it would seem to be with this stoneless strain of breadfruit.

INTRODUCTION

If you thought there was nothing new to say on the subject of *Bounty* and her momentous voyage, you are in exactly the same position as I was two years ago. Most of us have watched at least one of the three famous films based on this tale, believing after only two hours viewing, we can lay claim to knowing all the glorious details about the mutiny on the *Bounty*. I have been proved wrong, and now pass the excitement of fresh discoveries over to you.

Many people have asked why I, a woman, chose to delve into such a male dominated story. I can only answer it is because I am a nice girl – and what do all the nice girls love? With a lifelong, casual interest in history, I could not resist the lure of a story based around forty-six sailors who lived in the eighteenth century.

I can remember the exact day and place my interest was first aroused; my 28th birthday treat to see a good friend in the musical "*Mutiny*"*!* For some unfathomable reason, as my husband Bill and I sat cushioned between those two monuments to the boy-meets-girl syndrome, the famous Eros and infamous Raymond's Revue, the love story unfolding before us took over my life. I have always had the ability to keep my feet on the ground, well knowing the difference between fantasy and reality. I indulge in both and enjoy both but do not allow the two to become confused, though now I was coming dangerously close. I consoled myself with the knowledge that *Bounty's* tale was factual.

Hereby hangs the crux of the matter. Obvious inconsistancies contained within the stage show perplexed my pedantic mind and I was compelled to search them out. The images of brightly clad natives cavorting and whirling to pulsating rhythms, dusky maidens coupled with randy English sailors pushed me on in my quest to discover how something so seemingly superfluous could still demand such attention. I began to search for the reasons why such a private quarrel could provoke so varied an aftermath.

My personal researches became the foundation for a programme for the charity H.O.P.E. (Hospital Orientated Programme Enterprises). As a director of the organization I am involved with making shows for Hospital Radios to play to their patients and my two consuming hobbies came together.

My first interview came entirely by accident. A news report caught my attention regarding the First Fleet, including a replica of *Bounty*, lying in Portsmouth Harbour. I organized an interview with her owner and on Sunday 10th May 1987, stood with Bill and our daughters on the dock alongside the exact reproduction of *Bounty*. In company with four other sailing ships, she was due to commemorate the Bicentennial of the first cargo of British convicts to be transported, by re-enacting the voyage of the 'First Fleet' to sail to Australia with a human cargo. The original *Bounty*, of course, had nothing to do with this important event, though nor did the others. However they all looked so superb it really did not matter.

Bounty was absolutely beautiful, partially painted blue and yellow with the rest of her timbers keeping their natural hue, and around the back and side windows were the most exquisite decorations of scroll-like arabesque work, which made her so much more exciting than the plain white and dull brown vessels laying beside her. But she was so small! I found it difficult to believe she had been built exactly to the original Admiralty specifications and plans; therefore the first *Bounty* was the same 90 feet 10 inches in length and 24 feet 3 inches wide. She was actually made a bit longer by the long pole jutting out at the pointed end but, as most of this extra room was already taken up by the figurehead of a woman dressed in a very fetching blue riding habit, they probably forgot about it, unless trying to park in a tight space.

Once on board (treading the same hallowed decks as the definitive Fletcher Christian, Mel Gibson) and witnessing the compactness of it all, I began to realise how unbearable and difficult life must have been. There was obviously no privacy, every crevice, every niche openly visible, and two years of constant supervision, walking the same boards, tripping over the same ropes and clambering up the same precarious rigging, which I never before realised actually hung over the edge of the hull, must have strained every nerve and contributed towards the eventual outcome of her maiden voyage. Standing next to the ship's wheel, the gentle breezes quietly ruffling my hair, the silent, subtle yet definitely noticeable sway as the deck tilted below my feet, the tender lapping of the Solent waters softly caressing her coloured hull, I was transported back through the past two hundred years. I could hear the eighteenth century sailors battling against storms and throwing complaints, William Bligh berating his men, turning more and more frequently against Fletcher Christian. *Bounty's* long dead crew came very much alive for me.

During another interview I was invited to hold out my hand. The top of a small container was prized open and the contents shaken on to my palm; a rusty nail and a small, green encrusted, jagged piece of metal. I was holding two minute pieces of *Bounty*.

By then I was eager to gather more information and arranged to meet Colonel John Blashford-Snell, leader of Operation Raleigh, who had just returned from an expedition at the site of the wreck of *Bounty*-related ship, the *Pandora*. I had to reschedule the appointment as I was ill with chicken pox; my interest in *Bounty* plummeted to zero, but the eventual meeting with Colonel Blashford-Snell re-fired me. I asked one question, he finished answering twenty-five minutes later. The detailed facts and information intrigued and lifted me and I once again picked up on my own particular adventure.

It was one I could pick up and put down at my leisure, spending many happy hours in the Public Record Office at Kew, a luxurious modern building housing musty documents that keep our nation's heritage alive. It was here that I actually held *Bounty's* original muster list, turning the pages that once lay clean and white before William Bligh, now covered in his practical distinctive handwriting, the corners almost black with time.

Bounty's Log is one of the most prized possessions at Kew, so only microfiche copies are available to mere mortals such as myself, and no amount of enthusiasm can prepare you for the headaches peering at the small screens produce. But once I became used to the formation of the writing, a whole new world opened up before me. William Bligh took me half way round the world on a voyage of discovery. I battled to circumnavigate Cape Horn, explored Tahiti with him and lay sleeping beside him when three armed men disturbed us and cast us away. We fought, we bickered, but survived a harrowing journey. I then left him and headed for the cafeteria and treated myself to a much deserved meal.

As my individual crusade to dispel the 'Hollywood myth' became more intense, I gradually realised how totally opposite the two main protagonists in *Bounty's* story, Bligh and Christian, could be. Bligh was an only child, born in Plymouth and seemingly always destined for the sea. Christian came from a large family, living at the other end of the country in Cumbria, with no apparent seafaring ties. Bligh was descended from a long line of social climbers, four of his ancestors having served as mayors of Bodmin between 1505 and 1588. John Blygh, also of Bodmin, diligently oversaw the dissolution of the local monasteries, necessitated by Henry VIII's desire to fulfil his Tudor lust for an unwilling woman. Power crazed minds find revolting methods and the snakes crawl out of their pits to dumbly do their master's bidding. I suddenly realized the over zealousness of which Bligh has often been accused was due to an inherited trait of characteristics bequeathed by his forefathers. Fletcher Christian however was born into the landed gentry, the grandson of the then present Deemster of Man, and could even boast a genealogical link with Edward I.

Bligh began his Naval career at the tender age of twelve. Strange though it may appear to me as a twentieth century humanitarian, there actually was nothing unusual in his lack of years in the mid seventeen hundreds. In fact my own mother started work at the 'tender' age of fourteen, and that was not so very long ago. It is only recently the blessings of an uninterrupted childhood have fallen upon us – long may it remain so.

What *was* unusual was Christian's decision to join the Navy at the unconventional age of eighteen, due to a fall from grace following his father's death. As William Bligh rose in reputation, so Fletcher Christian fell. They were destined to meet in the middle on board His Majesty's Armed Vessel, *Bounty*.

The whole story of this tiny ship and the one voyage she made which affected so many different people, started in August 1787. It is not finished even now, and is still creating repercussions that have reverberated around the world.

CHAPTER ONE

'A proper ship to be purchased for His Majesty's Service'

In the late summer of 1787 William Bligh was appointed commander of an expedition that was to sail to Tahiti, barter for breadfruit plants and drop them off at the West Indies on his way home. The matured trees would supply cheap rations for the slaves, who were currently living on expensive bananas and therefore quite literally eating away a substantial proportion of the Plantation owners profits. Bligh was chosen because of his intimacy with the people of the South Seas, having visited them as master of Captain Cook's *Resolution* at the time these esoteric, plentiful 'loaves' of bread were first discovered by Europeans hanging tantalizingly from heavily burdened boughs, and because of his soaring reputation as a navigator extraordinaire. In those days influential people acted as sponsors, and Sir Joseph Banks (who originally put forward the idea of transporting the breadfruit, and easily obtained the full support and blessings of King 'Farmer' George III for his venture) had, before becoming a knight of the realm, also been a member of Cook's earlier expeditions, though he was a civilian on *Endeavour*. He therefore knew Tahiti well and, having long held a high opinion of Bligh's capabilities, had no hesitation in recommending William for the job.

Bligh was only too happy to have such an important task and was delighted with the ship the Admiralty had chosen from a final five they had whittled down from the flood of offers received in answer to their advertisments, necessitated due to war with France being considered an imminent certainty for which every reasonable ship was being held in readiment. Their eventual choice was the *Bethia*, a two and a half year old coastal trader sturdily built at number two dry dock, Wincolmlee, Hull, purchased for £1,950, a far cry from the £2,600 the vendors Messrs Wellbank, Sharp and Brown were asking. Probably in anticipation of the rewards her voyage might bring, she was renamed *Bounty*, after all, every previous voyage to the South Pacific had been one of discovery and they were now preparing to grasp the 'Bounty' for their own advancements. The 230 ton, three-masted, square-rigged with single top sails and top-gallant sails ship lying in Wapping Old Stairs was deemed 'A proper ship to be purchased for His Majesty's Service'.

William embarked upon a marathon correspondence with his newly acquired sponsor; every problem and complaint was referred to him, including a desire to be promoted to Captain. Sir Joseph willingly obliged and petitioned the Admiralty on his behalf, but the powers on high were unimpressed and *Bounty* was destined to eventually set out on her historic voyage commanded by a disgruntled Lieutenant.

Bounty had acquired a new owner, a new name and a new commander, now she had to be made ready to serve all three. William Bligh personally oversaw the refit that transformed her into a floating nursery. Working with a dedicated vengeance he supervised the sheathing of her hull in copper to combat the effects of ships' worms on her outer wooden casing; not even endowing these nuisances with the Latin name *Toredo Navalis* helped lessen the awful amount of damage they could wreak. He ordered the masts shortened, making her less top heavy which could cause havoc in problematic seas. The main cabin was extended from eleven feet to thirty feet – tight up to the aft hatchway, which prevented them from going any further, and turned it into a conservatory, with five rows of racks running its full length plus more acting as shelving around the walls, all interspersed with neat holes (totalling 629), each large enough to hold a pot which would eventually contain the precious cargo of young breadfruit trees.

So the whole of the master cabin, which is normally used by the commander, was turned into an indoor garden and Bligh had to make do with a minute room next door; not only was he denied his promotion but also the luxurious quarters that should have accompanied it.

He also had to pick his crew, which was fraught with problems. He now found himself in a position to grant favours instead of soliciting for them, but in a way was too eager to please and ended up overburdening himself. The Heywood family from Douglas on the Isle of Man were close neighbours of his wife's family (he had met Betsy while staying on Man and they had lived there in the early years of their marriage) and he was unable to refuse when asked to take the youngest Heywood, Peter, on his first ever sea voyage. Again, William had stayed with the Stewarts in the Orkneys and was now able to take their son George with him, as a midshipman. Other men who had previously sailed with him applied to join again; even though he possessed a wicked turn of phrase he was esteemed a superb foul-weather tar. Presumably he was delighted when a past companion of his signed on (or perhaps he even invited him aboard), not having the slightest notion he would one day bitterly regret meeting Fletcher Christian once more.

The final muster list contains 68 names, but of course not all of them finally sailed; there were lots of changes, with the pressed men defiantly going, leaving a final tally of 46 men. They consisted of the following roles:

1	Lieutenant in command	1	Boatswain's Mate
1	Master	1	Gunner's Mate
1	Boatswain	1	Carpenter's Mate
1	Gunner	1	Carpenter's Crew
1	Carpenter	1	Sailmaker
1	Surgeon	1	Armourer
2	Master's Mates	1	Corporal
2	Midshipmen	1	Clerk and Steward
2	Quarter Masters	23	Able Seamen
1	Quarter Master's Mate		

There we have 44 sailors; the missing two were the botanist and his assistant appointed by Sir Joseph Banks. Bligh had also been given the position of purser, so had the added burden of taking on provisions. Unusually for those days, his ideas were mercifully enlightened and he cared very much for the well being of his crew and instigated many new methods of hygiene, picking up on several of the concepts of his hero, Captain James Cook. In the vittles line he made sure there were stores to last for eighteen months and included some of the very latest in convenience foods; a lovely sounding concoction that went by the name of 'portable soup', a solidified mass of boiled vegetables. As every schoolgirl in an Home Economics kitchen knows, such concentrated stewing soon rids the food of any goodness it could once lay claim to, but Bligh's contemporaries were of the opinion that this was the answer to keeping perishable goods fresh. New innovations such as sour krout, malt, barley and wheat were included as well, but there were also plenty of the usual rations to be found aboard a Navy ship of those days – the infamous biscuits, (sometimes referred to as hard bread), salt pork and beef, beer and grog.

The newly installed departures from the accepted norm were surely eyed with suspicion and distrust by the average hardened sailor, and were probably ignored as much as possible; the preference remaining with the almost imperishable ship's biscuits. If they were consumed in a dark corner, along with a healthy measure of rum, extra meat rations provided by squiggling, squirming weevils were hardly noticeable, even if one was accidentally chomped in half.

Progress of the very expensive re-fit (costing a further £4,000) was hindered by extremely leisurely carpentry work, but on the 4th October 1787 all was ready for the pilot to take her down river; she who was once *Bethia* wove totally unrecognisably on her proud and stately passage down the Thames under the new banner of *Bounty,* to Long Reach. Here all the guns and ammunition were taken on board. During his woeful correspondence with Sir Joseph Banks, Bligh had requested the installation of marines, whether to quell the natives or crew is hazy, but the request was denied as the marines were busy with other duties, either escorting prisoners to New Holland (Australia) or being held in readiness for the imminent fracas with France. However he was allowed one solitary marine, Master at Arms Corporal Charles Churchill, a hard-bitten man he would well have been better off without.

Very unfavourable weather dissuaded them from heading on to Portsmouth until 4th November. The seas continued to be so troublesome that a great deal of damage was wrought during the short journey upon the freshly installed 23 foot launch, 18 foot cutter and 16 foot jolly boat. The launch suffered mostly and had to be replaced by a new model which was supplied by the yard of John Samuel White, residing across the Spithead in Cowes, on the Isle of Wight.

They sat a further twenty days awaiting final orders, affording Bligh plenty of time to supervise the installation of his recent acquisition and pen a complimentary letter of thanks to Mr White. Could he have had a premonition as to how important this boat was to become? He was certainly very grateful to White's for the stout vessel they had built. As is often the way, those three weeks spent loitering in port brought forth the most clement of conditions but when they were finally given permission to leave, the waves were pounding yet again. The 29th saw them valiantly trying to make their way out of the Channel but all to no avail, and they had to limp ignominiously back into Portsmouth.

Several more attempts were made, with changes still occuring on the lower deck as pressed men grasped God given chances to run (new recruits were signing on as late as 6th December), until two days before Christmas 1787 a completely voluntarily manned *Bounty* glided away at the start of her exotic cruise. It is doubtful they were waved off with a fond farewell by their loved ones, presumably all wives, girlfriends or ladies of the night had bid a passionate adieu a month previously and already headed home to begin their lonely struggle without their menfolk. Perhaps the conflicts of the years ahead were lessened by the proportion they were given of the two months wages that had already been paid, and surely the wanton women who had earned their share did not grieve quite so hard.

In his biography of Fletcher Christian, *Fragile Paradise*, Glynn Christian informs us of one fortuitous occurance that came through the delays, namely the meeting between Fletcher and his elder brother, Charles. While *Bounty* resided in Portsmouth Harbour awaiting her original orders to leave England, the East Indiaman, the *Middlesex,* arrived home with Fletcher's surgeon brother aboard.

So eager was the younger-by-two-years Christian to be reunited with the older one that he hired a boat to take him from *Bounty* to the *Middlesex,* before she even had a chance to dock. Charles had been away for nearly two years so they had much to catch up on and did so by spending all night ashore. Fletcher imparted the sad news that their only sister Mary had died, but Charles' revelations were to eventually dominate the conversation. He had taken part in a mutiny! He had been extremely lucky though that the *Middlesex* was a merchant ship, meaning that no threat was actually made against the King's own person. Although he was tried by the East India Company, and banned from sailing with them for two years, the court refrained from passing a harsher sentence as they regarded the intended victim, Captain John Rogers, negligent and partly accountable for the mutiny he successfully scuppered. Therefore Charles found himself at liberty to discuss the subject openly with his brother, and was later to be paid his full wage of fifty-two pounds, twelve shillings and twopence, which he had the effrontery to sign for and accept.

What thoughts possibly ruminated through Fletcher's mind when he finally rejoined his ship? He must have been reeling!

CHAPTER TWO

Onward to discordant glory

Bounty ploughed a trough through the choppy waters of the Solent, passed the Channel Islands and carried along her course due west. By the most northwestern tip of France (a little further along the coast from Brest) she turned into the Atlantic Ocean, running straight into a squall, which roughly tossed and threw them about but luckily did not unduly hinder progress. Christmas passed by quietly, with William providing a celebratory dinner of beef, plum pudding and rum, but the New Year was a soggy affair. Waves tumbled uninvited over her sides and stole away the store of beer that was sloshing around in casks lashed to the deck, while other multitudes of droplets crashed through her bows straight into the bread room, causing no end of trouble. The people on board fought hard with the elements and ultimately won; their greatest victory being the securing of the small boats which the wild seas had valiantly attempted to set free.

Once Neptune recalled his angry warriors, all hands set about repairing the damage. Sailmaker Lawrence Leboque busy with needle and thread renewing rent canvas, William Purcell and his team of carpenters making good the battered and splintered timbers, maybe from within the jolly boat hoisted over the side by strong, muscular arms, and bobbing to and fro on top of the enervated ocean. Bligh especially ordered a team of able seamen to pick over the ruined biscuits amongst the flotsam in the bread room and rescue anything they deemed still edible and unspoilt by salt water. *Bounty* was in good shape when they finally pulled into the Tenerife port of Santa Cruz for an unscheduled stop to re-stock. In this bustling harbour *Bounty* kept company with many other ships, including an American brig and a Spanish packet.

Here on this Canary Isle was the first definite piece of favouritism bestowed upon Fletcher Christian by William Bligh. With implicit faith in his abilities, *Bounty's* commander sent his master's mate to acquaint the island's governor, the Marquis de Bracheforté, with details of their arrival and plight. Stickler-for-protocol Bligh also included the message that he would be prepared to salute the Marquis with *Bounty's* guns, and obviously expected to receive a similar greeting, but was to be disappointed. The reply Fletcher brought back was unwelcome; the governor was only prepared to fire a salute for officers of an equal rank to himself. Bligh even had the audacity to record how 'extraordinary' he felt this answer to be and declined from fulfilling his original intent. But the Marquis was quite amiable and invited William to dine with him. Bligh readily accepted and obtained permission for the purchasing of new provisions to go ahead and for botanist Mr Nelson to roam the island in search of any curious flora he may happen upon. So, while David Nelson explored on shore, Bligh bartered for replacement goods and engaged local boatsmen to ferry them out to him, not trusting his own boats after the battering they had so recently taken.

Five shillings for a ton of water was agreed upon and £10 each pipe of wine, which Bligh considered 'very good'. Corn, pumpkin, potatoes, very ill quality fruit, beef in a poor condition and fresh livestock were all taken on board within four days, and soon after they were back at sea again.

Fully repaired and re-stocked, *Bounty* slid through the deep waters. Bligh was of the opinion that all was well with his crew, but he failed to record an incident picked up by a probably insignificant sailor at the time, but definitely a very significant person to the modern day *Bountyologist;* James Morrison, the boatswain's mate, was a most articulate and lucid diarist. Educated way above his position, he seemed to have a somewhat deep rooted hatred of his commander and delighted in recording every embarrassing moment in the journal he was to compile during the voyage. Therefore we have two versions of the journey; what Bligh carefully omitted from his official account, James Morrison detailed in glorious technicolor terms.

Just after leaving Tenerife, when the casks of cheese were opened to the air, it was discovered that some were missing. The cooper, Henry Hillbrant, laid his back on the line by declaring that Bligh's clerk and steward, Mr Samuel, had ordered the food to be taken from Deptford to Bligh's own home. William answered this malicious slur by stopping the rations of all the men forthwith until the shortage was made up, a move that did nothing to ingratiate him with his 'happy' (according to his log) crew.

Up to that point the men had absolutely no idea where they were going, so on 11th January 1788 all were mustered and informed they were headed for the tropical isle of Otaheiti, hopefully via Cape Horn. William pointed out this was the route his instructions from the Admiralty ordered him to take (being by far the quicker way on paper), but as their departure from Portsmouth had been so desperately delayed, due to bad weather and mismanagement from their hierarchy, there was a possibility they might not round the Horn, the season being much more advanced than originally allowed for. All these theories that Bligh wanted to circumnavigate the globe appear to be pure nonsense. He was a Naval commander through and through, knew his place exactly and blindly followed orders, expecting everyone else to unquestionably be of the same mind.

Anyone who survived the treacherous journey ahead could almost certainly look forward to promotion once their voyage was completed. William must have believed that this promise induced the cheerfulness that flooded through his crew, but more likely the thought of reaching the nubile lovelies most had only heard about, but not yet witnessed, made them want to arrive as quickly as possible, and if that entailed facing the Horn, then so be it.

The third watch was instigated on this same day and given to Fletcher Christian to command, a job not new to him as he had been put in charge of men at the young age of nineteen whilst on board the *Eurydice* in India. Even so, this was a very unusual occurence, and a month later was followed up by the even stranger development of Fletcher's promotion to the rank of acting lieutenant, on Sunday 2nd March. Some say that master John Fryer was annoyed at his mate being raised above him, but a convincing argument has to be contained within the fact that a master cannot be replaced. Assigned to *Bounty* by the Admiralty (and NOT Bligh) he had very special duties to adhere to and no self respecting commander would withdraw a fully qualified man and replace him with someone inexperienced just for the sake of face. There would be plenty of opportunities for Fryer to be promoted once they arrived in England, as had indeed happened in Bligh's own case after his spell as James Cook's master. Unfortunately for him, Fryer did not join this school of thought, and spent the rest of the voyage moving in and out of events as an extra cross for William to bear.

Also of course the feelings of the gunner, the carpenter, the boatswain and the surgeon have to be considered – all of whom were ranked above Fletcher, but each highly trained in his own specific sphere and therefore irreplacable on account of a mere whim (death was a somewhat different circumstance). The only one who perhaps could be sympathised with for feeling overlooked would be the other master's mate, William Elphinstone.

There is a strange aside to this promotion; the only document in existence bearing the autograph of Fletcher Christian is a report by Fryer explaining the loss of a barrel of oil, and is countersigned by

Christian and Elphinstone, both identified as 'Master's Mates'. But it is dated 16th April, 1788, well over a month after Fletcher was upgraded. Crosses my mind to question how seriously any changes of circumstance were treated.

And this not even the first alteration in ranks. Already Thomas Hayward was raised from an able seaman to a midshipman, Thomas McIntosh swapped places with Charles Norman; McIntosh having initially been the carpenter's mate became an ordinary member of his crew, and George Simpson was assigned to assist the quartermaster.

All things come in threes and on this momentous day of 11th January 1788 (William gives the date in his log as Saturday 12th January, but his days ran from noon to noon instead of midnight to midnight as ours do, so I have tried to bring his timing into civil reckoning), he ordered rations cut to two thirds as he observed that was as much as the men usually ate. Although the logic is clear, perhaps the reasoning was not very understandable; grown men like to be able to decide for themselves how much they consume and not have their choices made as if they were children. This is only one example, but Bligh seemed to be of the opinion that his crew had to be treated like youngsters. As the voyage went on, so his theory deepened.

Determined to run a kindly ship, William hoped not to have to inflict any form of punishment during their time at sea. Then, just over two months after leaving home waters, he instigated the third watch. Usually a ship's crew were divided in half, either on duty or asleep apart from exceptionally dire circumstances when all hands could be called on deck. In these cases men would be on duty for long, protracted periods, but Bligh felt a third watch gave them greater opportunities to rest and therefore be much more useful in an emergency. It is a policy still in use today in the British Navy, but in those developmental days no allowance was made for the tedium that would accompany such inactivity by bored illiterates riding peaceful oceans. Idle hands found unacceptable employ, and the lash had to be dusted down.

Another notion of William's was to hold daily dancing sessions to provide his crew with regular exercise and for this reason took on board a near blind able bodied seaman, who could nevertheless play a mean fiddle, Irish born Michael Byrne. The now famous horn pipe was in its formative stages here, but that is basically what this miscellaneous gang of seasoned matelots were ordered to participate in, feet rhythmically pounding *Bounty's* toughened timbers while arms were reverently crossed in front of them. Probably some of the men enjoyed this new pastime and some didn't, but no question of choice was involved, if the Lieutenant believed dancing was good for you, you danced!

As the knots flew past life was uneventful and routine. The seas behaved themselves and the weather was pleasant enough, apart from the moistness in the air which covered everything with mould, especially the sails. It would appear William had a high regard for vinegar; Thursday 7th February was spent washing 'the beams and between decks with vinegar', the next day the crew were drinking it.

On the 9th February they crossed the equator, and celebrated in the inimitable style only the Navy could condone, tarring, shaving (with an iron hoop), dancing and the paying of a forfeit of rum. Bligh's promise to make good their losses could only have enhanced the overall joviality, although he refused to allow that most famous of traditions, ducking, to befall the twenty-seven first timers, a tradition he beheld as 'the most brutal and inhumane'. Good for him! 'The people', as the officers called the able seamen, worked hard and the ship handled and ran well; William was very pleased with his crew, noting that it was not until the 10th March, 1788 (well over two months since they had left home) that he had to hand out his first punishment. Poor Matthew Quintal's back was laid bare as he found himself on the wrong side of two dozen lashes, after a complaint by Fryer about his 'insolence and contempt'. It is interesting to note that in the narrative Bligh wrote two years after the mutiny, the description of Quintal's misdemeanour had changed to 'insolence and *mutinous behaviour*'. Over a year before the real thing did he, with hindsight, think that Matthew had indulged in a dress rehearsal?

During the initial period fresh friendships were surely forged and ancient acquaintanceships reaffirmed, while curiosity must have overflowed about unknown faces, and probably old diehards were soon filling in the gaps of the newcomers gossip. The man most information flew around about could not have been anyone other than William

Bligh, a man to be placated and pandered to by all. He was born in Plymouth on 9th September, 1754 (and baptized at St Andrew's, the church his parents were married in, on 4th October), the only child of custom's officer Francis Bligh and his first wife, widow Jane Pearce, born of the Balsam family. (Francis was to show a definite penchant for widows before leaving one of his own on 27th December 1780.)

William had an impressive record of seafaring accomplishments behind him, since joining the Navy at the age of twelve. Some reports say he was eight, others profess he was as old as sixteen – as I have seen no documentary evidence on this point at all, the middle theory seems to be the most probable and acceptable.

After his first taste of active service, he embarked upon an interval without a ship, when he stayed on the Isle of Man, married a local Manx girl, Elizabeth Betham on 4th February 1781, delighted in the arrival of four daughters and accepted the post of Captain on a merchantman belonging to his bride's great-uncle, Duncan Campbell. By 1785, William was in command of the *Britannia,* sailing with supplies to the West Indies, where Campbell owned a vast area of sugar plantations. It was in the latter half of this year that he received a letter from a prominent member of Man society, Captain Taubman, supplicating for a young kinsman to be taken on board *Britannia,* but Bligh's quota of midshipmen was full and he reluctantly declined. This ambitious young man took it upon himself to follow up the good Captain's lead and wrote directly to William asking to be taken on as an able seaman, his only wish to be allowed to mess with the gentlemen. Otherwise he was quite content to work before the mast so long as he could be instructed by William Bligh.William agreed and Fletcher Christian sailed with him.

So now the *Bounty's* men knew how their Lieutenant first met Christian, who had joined Bligh twice on the *Britannia* and now ate at his table regularly and was generally the most well favoured amongst them. The funny thing being though, that none of them could find any reason to dislike this extremely genial shipmate, including John Fryer! Fletcher's life was a sad tale (and susceptible sailors are always ripe for a ripping good yarn), yet he always had time for his fellow comrades; he listened to their grievances, worked alongside them and willingly passed on his ever increasing knowledge to those who wished to learn. Many hours, for instance, were spent instructing the young Peter Heywood, a distant relation on whom Fletcher kept a friendly eye.

As *Bounty* shot through the South Atlantic, the old tars enjoyed whistling anecdotes through rotting teeth about their officers to those who were inclined to listen with rapturous attention, and so the sorry story of the likeable young gentleman must have toured through the ships company. Fletcher Christian was twenty-three years old, born into the landed gentry on 25th September 1764. The seventh child of Charles and Ann Christian, only four were still alive when he joined them at the family home of Morland Close, Cockermouth, Cumbria; Ann Dixon's dowry to her new husband was this farmstead, an inheritance from her mother's side, the Fletcher's. In the Christian sector though, for decades long since disappeared, his ancestors had been Deemsters of Man; his grandfather holding the position as his father settled into life as a farm owner, and passing, during Fletcher's childhood, into the hands of an uncle, John Christian.

A strange chain of events started to link around this brother of Charles Christian, which were to affect the young Fletcher's future. John married Jane Curwen and they managed to produce seven children, including a son, named John after his father, and a daughter, Dorothy. John junior wed Margaret Taubman, sister of the captain Dorothy married, and it was this mysterious husband without a known first name who approached the person he and his wife used to socialise with on the Isle of Man, William Bligh, on behalf of his cousin-in-law.

Margaret was to die after only a few short years of marriage and her husband decided to take another wife, again within his family circle. His second bride was his cousin, Isabella Curwen, daughter of his mother's late brother, Henry. A wealthy heiress, orphaned at the age of thirteen, and left in the care of two more of his sisters, Bridget and Jane, she was an enviable catch with many hopeful suitors left distraught. Yet in true romantic fashion they eloped, due to her trustee (the Lord Chancellor no less) having refused them permission to wed, and they married in a secret ceremony in Edinburgh on 9th October 1782. A honeymoon in Paris followed, the twenty-six year old groom, his blushing bride of seventeen – and her guardians, Bridget and Jane!

However, before these rapturous nuptials occured Isabella would often have visited the Christian ancestral home of Ewanrigg, Cumbria. It is thought that Fletcher was frequently here too and used to silently bask in her beauty.

But why did Fletcher want to go to sea? His was a wealthy family and he was more than likely destined to follow his two eldest brothers into the law. He started out on the right lines, attending several local schools, and should probably have gone on to university (maybe even acquiring the style of a gambling, debauched rake typical of the eighteenth century).

His father Charles died in March 1768, three months after the birth of another son, Humphrey, leaving a none-too-thriving farmstead behind, together with several bad debts. His widow turned to her wealthy brother-in-law, John Christian of Ewanrigg, Deemster of Man, for financial assistance and he heroically came up trumps for her. But the silly woman and her feckless eldest sons, John and Edward, did not learn any lessons; loans were taken out and secured against their home, other monies were borrowed from cousin John, until their financial commitments were so pressing that Morland Close had to go. Again John Christian came to the rescue and softened the blow by handling all the details and taking over the Close himself, but the outcome was that Ann had to take her two youngest sons, Fletcher and Humphrey, to live in Douglas, Isle of Man and forget about providing any advancement for them.

His inheritance lost forever, Fletcher's standing in life must have taken a drastic nosedive. No one knows what careers he may have considered; the Army might have come to mind, but in those days it took a healthy income to raise oneself up from one rank to another, and that was the one thing sadly lacking in his position. All the breeding and connections were there, the necessary cash wasn't.

We discover his final verdict three years after the unexpected upheaval from his place of birth – he joined the Navy, signing on board the *Eurydice* on 25th April 1783. A leisurely decision? We know from the example of William Bligh he was not waiting to fulfil any age limits, but – go back six months; Isabella Curwen eloped with his mother's saviour the previous October. Did Fletcher run away to sea to escape a broken heart?

A quixotic notion, but the more sensible theory is gained by looking at the structure of Georgian society. Fletcher had been born into a higher class than the one in which he now found himself, but once in the gutter, you were supposed to stay there. It was not in his make-up to accept such things though, and the Navy offered the way out; no matter who he was or where he came from, the Navy was the only institution where advancement was gained through personal merit, as opposed to personal wealth. Determination (maybe to a point of selfishness) surged through him, and he sought to put his foot on the first rung of the ladder that should have taken him back to where he, by extraction, belonged.

The idle chatter had to stop. *Bounty* stood at the latitude of 55°59'S, longitude 67°16'W. She was upon Cape Horn.

A thirty one day up-hill battle ensued, with respites very few and far between. To think that William would put the lives of any of his men at risk during that time is ridiculous, he was determined to keep each and every one of them safe and sound. All his energies were devoted towards the continuing health and welfare of his crew, as they battled against northwesterly winds which would viciously whip round and attack again from the south west. He ordered fires to constantly burn and allowed hammocks to hang in the unused great cabin to dry and air. A member from each watch was appointed to sit before the blaze, holding forth his companions wet clothes in an attempt to allay any discomforts.

During the stinging hail, driving sleet and turbulent snow (which settled onto the frozen decks, shrouded the rigging and stiffened the sails) the crew threw out baited hooks and caught not fish, but birds; albatrosses, petrels and pintadas, which they caged, fattened with corn, slaughtered, cooked and ate. From being on the skinny side and fishy to taste, they quickly became very acceptable substitutes for duck and geese. As few of their livestock were managing to survive the terrible ordeal, these birds were a fortuitous blessing indeed.

Casualties started to add up though, the cook was knocked off his feet during one of the rougher patches in the gale and broke a rib, another sailor was knocked over by the squall and dislocated his shoulder. The final tally on the sick list was only eight from a possible forty-six men (the gunner William Peckover was also there suffering with rheumatism), but the worst invalid was *Bounty* herself; she creaked and groaned and finally could not take any more, leaking so badly that the pumps were in hourly usage. The last straw was the realisation they were just drifting with the wind, and instead of making any headway were actually losing ground, so William made the only sensible decision and 'ordered the helm to be put a weather'; they were heading for serener waters and the Cape of Good Hope.

Our exhausted heros were an ill assorted bunch; ranging in ages from 15 to 40. They consisted of experts, assistants, apprentices and labourers. Lieutenant William Bligh was in charge of:

William Brown	Assistant botanist
Thomas Burkitt	Able seaman
Michael Byrne	Able seaman
Fletcher Christian	Acting lieutenant
Charles Churchill	Master-at-Arms
William Cole	Boatswain
Joseph Coleman	Armourer
Thomas Ellison	Able seaman
William Elphinstone	Master's mate
John Fryer	Master
Thomas Hall	Able seaman
John Hallet	Midshipman
Thomas Hayward	Midshipman
Peter Heywood	Midshipman
Henry Hillbrant	Able seaman
Thomas Huggan	Surgeon

Robert Lamb	Butcher
Lawrence Leboque	Sailmaker
Thomas Denman Ledward	Able seaman
Peter Linkletter	Quartermaster
Isaac Martin	Able seaman
Thomas McIntosh	Carpenter's crew
William McKoy	Able seaman
John Mills	Gunner's mate
John Millward	Able seaman
James Morrison	Boatswain's mate
William Muspratt	Able seaman
David Nelson	Botanist
Charles Norman	Carpenter's mate
John Norton	Quartermaster
William Peckover	Gunner
William Purcell	Carpenter
Matthew Quintall	Able seaman
John Samuel	Clerk and steward
George Simpson	Quartermaster's mate
Richard Skinner	Able seaman
Alexander Smith	Able seaman
John Smith	Able seaman
George Stewart	Acting master's mate
John Sumner	Able seaman
Matthew Thompson	Able seaman
Robert Tinkler	Able seaman

James Valentine	Able seaman
John Williams	Able seaman
Edward Young	Midshipman

A long list of mere names (and not quite fulfilling the inital roles declared, several of the original twenty-three able seamen had stepped into other positions, leaving only nineteen to attend to all the menial tasks), but each possessed of an individual temperament, a being who contributed towards the eventual, even eventful, outcome of what was never exactly a pleasant trip on the high seas. Time spent on shore however was a completely different matter.

Hollywood thrice got round the problem of the similarity between the surnames of Thomas Hayward and Peter Heywood by ignoring the existence of either one or the other, and bestowing both sets of faults and virtues on to the one character, but however did they manage with the original pair? We can almost visualise both jumping to attention when Bligh boomed, 'Mr Hayward, Sir!'

Another problem was Alexander Smith; two Smith's on board (him and John) may have caused greater mayhem than our young friends Peter and Thomas, but it was not even necessary – Alexander suddenly decided to admit that his real name was John Adams. He had jumped from another ship to join the *Bounty,* making him the only one with anything near a sordid (and interesting) past, yet he ended up being famous.

Tempestuous seas gave way to discordant harmonies while *Bounty* lay convalescing in Simon's Bay, the inner part of False Bay near Cape Town. She was cosseted and pampered, life saving operations constantly in progress as she was completely overhauled, her open wounds recaulked. Thirty-eight days spent recuperating at this Dutch colony were industriously spent by Bligh, making good the damage wrought yet again on their supplies and purchasing some seeds and plants he trusted would be useful to negotiate with in Tahiti. He delighted in recounting old local fables and intrigues and describing the neighbouring geography in minute detail. But what of the bickering and uneasiness that abounded. Why else did John Adams say in the latter years of his life that the 'original quarrel' between William and Fletcher happened here? And why oh why did Bligh himself, on a subsequent visit to the Cape of Good Hope four years later in the *Providence,* remark, 'During my stay at this place nothing intervened of a material nature . . .'? Was he remembering a stay at that place when something of a material nature DID intervene? Bligh's personal papers have revealed that he lent Fletcher money, so was it (as Glynn Christian has provokingly suggested) at this last European settlement that Fletcher ever visited, perhaps after much nagging, wheedling and sulking from one used to getting his own way?

William was well pleased with the way *Bounty* was brought back to full vitality after spending over five weeks in port, and even more delighted when the thirteen gun salute he fired, as they resumed their voyage, was returned in an equal number; that was one up on Tenerife! Travelling in an east south easterly direction the weather still hounded them, with all of Bligh's extraordinary talents in navigation and seamanship brought forth once again as he steered them toward Van Diemen's Land; discovered in 1642 by Dutch navigator Able Janzoon Tasman, he named it after the governor of Java, Anthony Van Diemen, who sponsored his journey. Later Taoman was posthumously rewarded when his island became known throughout the world as Tasmania.

Clever management of the *Bounty* brought them safely through more storms, except in one instance when 'the man at the steerage was thrown over the wheel, and much bruised', until they edged (by cautious degrees) into Adventure Bay on 21st August 1788. Wood and watering parties were sent out under the guidance of Mr Christian and Mr Peckover, and at least one man was occupied laundering all the crew's clothes, while Lieutenant Bligh inspected the land, noting signs of past visits from English ships, including his own with Captain Cook. Other duties his people had to perform were to dig a huge pit, lay a freshly felled tree across it and saw the timber into planks. Some of the men experimented with fishing; could they gain the best catch from the lake or the sea, from on shore or onboard ship? All were usefully employed as William and botanist David Nelson mulled over the question of how a deceased male opossum (a small marsupial possessed of a monkey-type tail, and with a natural inclination to play dead) came to his genuine expiration.

Happy in the knowledge he had left explicit orders behind, William took leisurely strolls around the immediate area, taking in the delightful sights of beautifully coloured birds, bringing his log up to date, and making overtures of friendliness to the aborigines by throwing nails and small beads at them. (Friendship might not have come readily to mind.) He appears to have been a loner, comfortable only in the company of tried and trusted companions who shared mutual interests, as is often the way with the only child. He had an immaculate eye for detail and revelled in nature, so obviously the man he suffered most gladly while on shore was the botanist.

Meanwhile, back at the ship, sailors were silently seething; 'the seeds of eternal discord were sown between Lieutenant Bligh and some of his officers' – boatswain's mate James Morrison, quietly working in the background, was noting all. One instance Bligh recorded for posterity was when William Purcell was reprimanded for his behaviour whilst with the wooding party, and soon after he refused to assist in the general duties he had been assigned to as punishment. Insubordination at its highest was defused when his rations were stopped, and rather than starve, the shamed carpenter toed the line. Should William have taken a harder line with him? He answers that very question by explaining in his log, 'I could not bear the loss of an able working and healthy man.' That remark could have been connected with the recent illness of the until then very hale able seaman James Valentine, who was bled to ease his indisposition. One man out of action might be accomodated, two may be construed as the top of the slippery slope.

Planks stowed aboard along with overflowing water casks heralded the end of their stay and once again they embarked on their voyage. Valentine's complaint had improved greatly by the drainage of his bad blood, but when out at sea, the arm which had suffered the full brunt of the surgery flamed up and thrust seering pain through him. A hollow cough, troubled respiration and on Thursday 9th October James Valentine shuffled off this mortal coil.

His one hundred per cent record of running a completely healthy ship irreversibly dented, William did not need John Fryer to add to his problems, but with a deplorable lack of tact the master chose that very same day to make a stand against his despotic commander. It boded well for neither of them; if Fryer had a grievance then common sense should have told him to wait for a more opportune moment, but suddenly he demanded a referral of his good and blameless conduct during the *whole* expedition, a certificate signed by Bligh, before he would co-sign the expense books of a couple of the warrant officers, as his station demanded. The short fuse was lit and Bligh duly exploded. After a second refusal from the master, all hands were summoned up on deck and the articles of war read out, for all to take heed of the drastic recourse he could effect upon those who crossed him. Fryer signed.

The entire ship's company endeavoured to keep out of his way. The surgeon, Dr Thomas Huggan, already having endured Bligh's terrible wrath over the death of Valentine, sank deeper and deeper into his cups, drinking his misery away. The problem with a flourishing crew was you then had a very inactive doctor, and this one already whiled the time away by keeping too much company with a bottle, so when a patient needed his attention, his reactions and skills were not entirely competent.

A silly drama revolved around the surgeon in the middle part of that October. Bligh thought it necessary to look after four men with rheumatism personally, as Huggan was constantly inebriated. Thomas appeared on the sick list himself, having taken to his bunk with the same complaint, but Bligh was to discover that Thomas Ledward, the doctor's assistant, had covered up for his master, as Huggan was only drunk again. After being left to languish in his cabin for four days Bligh finally took action; the tiny room was stripped and searched for any alcholic beverages, which were taken from him. 'The operation was not only troublesome but offensive in the highest degree,' says Bligh; poor Huggan must have used some form of inner defence system as his sanctuary was ransacked. The next sick list included the doctor again, this time suffering from 'paralytic affection'; though, despite claiming to have lost the use of his body right down one side, was found perfectly well enough to roam the ship in search of more liquor. Eighteen hours on the wagon and he was back up on deck, perfectly sober and in full, but weak, control of his faculties; William appeared rather sarcastically incredulous at his rapid recovery.

Saturday 25th October 1788 Tahiti blessedly came into sight, leaving Huggan with one last duty to perform, one which no-one could blame him for being drunk whilst completing. He had to physically check that none of *Bounty's* men were suffering from a delicate disease that could be lovingly transmitted to the native women, thus increasing the probability of eventually infecting the whole adult population and sending all the island mad. Bligh knew that this blight had existed on Tahiti eleven years before but, rather naively, hoped that during the intervening years the absence of contact with white men would have resulted in its disappearance. He therefore did not want to be responsible for giving them another resounding round of applause, so it was backs-against-the-wall-boys time. Dr Tom gave them all a clean bill of health, a relieved William recorded this finding in his log and let his men loose on the enchanting tarts that were clambering aboard long before he even had a chance to anchor; the only stipulation was nobody was to mention the death of Captain Cook – who could talk with his mouth full anyway?

As he could not see any of his crew within ten minutes and hopefully with an intrinsic understanding for the feelings of a British sailor newly arrived in paradise, William deferred mooring until the next morning, when all their visitors were very firmly asked to vacate the ship. *Bounty* was gently coaxed through the surrounding canoes that afforded an extravagant splash of colour, into Matavai Bay and brought to a final halt. Everybody made friends; white men were considered as gods by the islanders, who scrambled back on board in order to attach themselves to one of these manifestations. The men offered strength and loyalty and became *tyos* (blood brothers) while the ladies offered just themselves and became used.

Structured classes were in evidence even then on Tahiti and the different castes effortlessly fell in with the equivalent rank of sailor. At the very top were the *Ari'i*, the class from which all chiefs great and small came; the ruling bodies were somewhat like England boasted before the Norman conquest – different areas (like Mercia, Wessex and Northumbria) under the guidance of a separate King; another example would be that of the varied Scottish clans. The *Ari'i* were so keen to preserve their pure blood line that cross-breeding incestuously was the only form of relationships the unattached could look forward to, so not even the officer gods would have been welcome amongst their footloose maidens, disproving the theory that Fletcher Christian married a chief's daughter. However, William alone was on a par with the chiefs and eligible to bed one of their wives (she had probably already done her bit to contribute towards the thoroughbred *Ari'i,* and was allowed to be more dispensable with her charms!).

Fletcher Christian, along with his fellow officers, would have the pick of the *ra'atira* girls, daughters of the landowning sector. With passion unbridled he sought their company with a little too much enthusiasm and ended up on William's venereal list. Despite Bligh's precautions, the dreaded Western malaise was still around. Fletcher's behaviour on the *Britannia* prompted an ex-shipmate to later remark of him: 'One of the most foolish young men I ever knew in regard to the sex.' Obviously he was not going to improve.

The ones who really gave Tahiti her reputation for rampant raptures were the *manahune* girls, the lowest denomination reserved for the lowliest seamen. For the price of a few nails, they sold their favours with a most beguiling smile and musical laugh; the story is told of how one of Captain Cook's ships was stripped almost bear of her hardwear by over enthusiastic matelots.

The men were happy sampling the Polynesian delights, while Bligh enjoyed entertaining the chiefs, accompanying them ashore as he sought the gratitude and indulgence necessary to the successful completion of his job. Minor chiefs visited first, then Bligh was reunited with his old friend, the highest ranking man in the northern territories of Tahiti, Otoo. On his arrival at the shore Mr Christian was despatched to collect him in the launch. Bligh discovered Otoo was ruler of Oparre no longer and neither was he Otoo any more. Since William's last visit one of Tahiti's stranger customs had come into force; it would seem anything was a welcome divergence that interrupted their languid, though well ordered, lives. Otoo's son was now *Earee Rahine,* the most powerful and revered person on Tahiti, majestically carried on the shoulders of his subjects to avoid anyone ever standing taller than him. As this six year old boy was also called Otoo (abbreviated to Tu), Dad became known as Tynah.

During William's next visit to them, in the *Providence,* Tynah and his wife Iddeeah were both called Pomarre, a winsome name bestowed upon the pair of them due to yet another tradition. When a child died the grieving parents would take upon them the name of the disease that had finished off their offspring, and as their eldest daughter had passed over from the illness pomarre, their names had automatically altered. This happened in all families, and should anyone have the misfortune to lose several children they could build up quite a long list; as the last one was usually used, their names could be constantly changing. Should things get out of hand though, they just passed them amongst their relatives. (Makes me doubly appreciate the modern day miracle of vaccination and antibiotics; following the epidemic last summer which affected both my girls, I can't say I have a desperate longing to be called Chicken or, even worse, Poxy!)

Perhaps Tynah was passed over in deference to his son because he had become too portly; there was surely some method behind the madness of replacing the adult chief with his young son. Bligh described him as, 'a very large man, much above the common stature, being not less than 6 feet 4 inches in height, and proportionably stout' - it was surely easier, and more comfortable, to transport a small boy than someone too obese to be hoisted upon anybody's shoulders, and, as Tu was still a minor, Tynah remained very much in charge of state matters as regent, probably functioning better for being less hindered by protocol.

As soon as his regal friend stepped on board *Bounty* with his huge entourage William was presented with a present; with a touch of the Cleopatra's, 'a woman that was usual to Captain Cook and others came wrapped up in a very large quantity of cloth'. Coyly, he says he spent, 'a few minutes' below with her (how long can we construe 'a few minutes' to be?) before returning to shower his esteemed guests with gifts of their own; 'hatchets, small adzes, files, gimblets, saws, looking-glasses, red feathers and two shirts' were presented to Tynah and 'ear-rings, necklaces and beads' were given to his wife Iddeeah, but she (canny woman) wanted the same as her husband and received as much, without returning what she had already got! Under the thinly disguised excuse of a guided tour, they set off on a pillaging expedition, while

Bligh could only pray they would quickly tire of plundering his abode. Eventually they turned their attention to the cannons, wanting to witness one in action, so William ordered Mr Peckover to be about his duty. A great gun was fired, the booming racket as a shot thundered far out to sea startling the innocent natives.

Dinner followed. There were two sittings held, roughly an hour apart, as the women were not allowed to eat with the men. So Tynah and his companions (including his constantly drunk brother Whydooah, whom Bligh observed was often unable to stand) ate their fill first, then when it was the turn of the ladies Tynah joined in with them. The women could not eat with the men, but the men could eat with the women. *What's the difference?*

David Nelson had been roaming the island and reported back that their mission would be easily accomplished, but still Bligh continued to court Tynah's royal family, slowly ingratiating himself with them. Visits to Tynah's home, breakfast onboard *Bounty*, presents given and received, sojourns to visit Tu (when Bligh was told he would have to strip to the waist before being allowed into the young master's presence, but William declined stating that he would be welcomed by his own King in his present state of dress so Tu should not be any different. Tynah compromised by pulling William's hat off and placing a piece of material round his shoulders). All this subterfuge was thought necessary, along with the strict instructions to *Bounty's* men not to divulge the reason for their visit, so as not to raise the worth of the breadfruit plants; as far as Tynah was concerned William had brought forty-four of his friends half way round the world especially to meet him. It was not too long however before Bligh forced the issue by telling Tynah that he intended to visit some of the other islands. The chief instantly protested – they would be much safer staying with him as those natives would rob them. William wanted some sign of good faith, telling him that after all the gifts he had received from his King, it would be an idea to send something back. A long list of possibilities poured forth from Tynah's lips until he happened upon breadfruit, to which Bligh, with an Oscar winning performance, nonchalantly replied that King George would appreciate them most. Probably Tynah couldn't believe his luck; no sooner said than done.

The paradisical era of Fletcher Christian's life was about to begin. He was sent with a party to erect a tent within a previously agreed area on Point Venus, Matavai, where the breadfruit nursery was to reside. Boundaries were fixed and only those natives employed in helping with the labour were allowed to step over them, and the Tahitians did everything possible to help their visitors do them the honour of taking breadfruit back to the *Earee Rahie no Britanee,* King George. Bligh had so manipulated the situation, they never realised that they were doing him the favour, but rather believed it to be the complete opposite.

David Nelson and assistant botanist, William Brown, set up the garden with the aid of seven unnamed men, except Fletcher who remained in charge and from then on lived ashore. John Fryer tells us in his narrative (like Bligh's, written when safe back in England) that only two of the men, George Stewart and James Morrison, had regular girlfriends, so possibly they were also of the shore party. As a matter of fact, Fryer unintentionally clears up a very favoured misconception, when looking for his own reasons why the mutiny occurred, by saying *'Christian was not particularly attached to any woman at Otaheiti . . .'!*

The next six months were weird. Bligh spent most of his time fraternising with chiefs of different importance, but always came back to the supreme Tynah. His details of the ceremonies and customs indulged in by the Tahitians positively make your eyes pop out in amazement; his steady, sloping, fluent hand recorded the time he witnessed a sordid tribal dance by the *Arreoys,* a kind of exclusive club found amongst the island's hierachy. They were made up of strong young men who were kept, away from most of the others, in readiness for war. Therefore the best part of their time was spent in idleness, generally connected with procreation. Membership of this club was not hereditary, as their children were instantly killed at birth. As they had to remain fit and ready for any outbreaks of fighting they were not allowed to be tied down or hindered in any way; it would seem that children were too much of a nuisance. Poor Tynah's first child was immediately slaughtered, her neck twisted as she left the womb, so before any more fruits of his loins could be claimed he handed in his resignation from the selfish *Arreoys.* His sister was not quite so lucky, bearing eight children only to hand them over straight away to these ritualistic sacrifices.

William would have put many a Fleet Street hack to shame as he relentlessly pursued the most intimate details of life on Tahiti with his penetrating, probing questions. It took him ages to finally arrive at the truth behind the fate of Tynah and Iddeeah's first born, delving deeper when decency and respect would have long since stopped even one of today's News of the World reporters! He did however discover a delicious piece of information from Iddeeah; talking to her on the subject of having children, she was curious as to how English women gave birth. He told her all that he knew on the subject (not that he tells us how much he knew). Following her lead he enquired after Tahitian childbirth and, delicacy apart, she gave him a graphic description, complete with an action packed replay, of a Tahitian lady in labour.

Squatting on her heels an assistant sat behind, straddling her with both arms and legs, his hands resting on the upper part of her tummy. Come a contraction, he pushed down with her until the baby was, relatively painlessly, born. She laughed on hearing how much the English mothers suffered, and told him to advocate her version to them. Why is it that something recommended two hundred years ago, is suddenly being heralded as an innovation?

However much the Tahitian's may have been thought of as unsophisticated savages, they certainly had a way with logical thinking. Not only was childbirth effortlessly sorted out, they laughed in amazement at Bligh's religious doctrine. Yes, he told them, he believed in a God, who had a son, but this God had no wife, nor a mother or father; that one was beyond their unpretentious way of understanding.

He formed a kind of routine, dictating work on the ship in the morning, feeding various local dignitaries in the early afternoon, then visiting the breadfruit nursery on shore before being wooed with wine, women and song during the evening. Many of the spectacles are recorded in his log, but the one I took a particular liking too is where he describes the girl performers' apparel thus (the punctuation, grammar and spelling are all his), 'the dress of the girl I think was really becoming and pretty it was all of white cloth, the neck shoulders and arms were only bare. The petticoats spred with much ellegance and the waist is short on each side, tied in with the petticoat and falls over it on the hips are many folds of platted cloth in the appearance of a ruff.' It sounds a great shame, but this elegantly attired young lady spoilt the effect by pulling the most hideous of faces by way of entertainment.

Every day David Nelson, with a little help from his friends, gathered more and more shoots and transplanted them into the pots brought specifically for this purpose. Things were going so well that William set the carpenters about constructing even more racks and stands, because it was becoming apparent that a greater number of plants would be available for them to take home than was originally allowed for. Others still based on board ship busily tarred and turpentined the hull and spruced up the figure-head with a coat of fresh paint, inbetween being allowed to visit on shore in pairs. The only man not to take advantage of this concession was the surgeon, Dr Thomas Huggan, who never set foot on deck all the time they were docked in Matavai Bay, except for one last attempt on Wednesday 10th December, 1788, to alleviate the difficulty he was experiencing with his breathing. It was all to no avail though and within an hour the poor man was dead; Bligh's sympathies remained constantly non-existent right to the end, still bemoaning Tom's lack of exercise, cleanliness and sobriety.

Supposition is the only recourse we can turn to for a picture of what was going on with the land party. The very obliging breadfruits were growing exactly according to plan and therefore desired no real exertions in the caring of them; Mr Nelson would have been amply capable of taking on the whole responsibility, and no doubt revelled in the opportunity solely for the love of his craft, leaving the rest plenty of time free to sample the local delights. We know they did this because the lily white pure skins that left Britain were slowly becoming used as pin cushions, as the local tattooist got to work on their voluntarily bared bodies. Fletcher would have paid more than one visit as first a star appeared on his left breast, followed by the ultimate symbol of a fully-fledged Tahitian, the complete blacking of his hide. Painful and often dangerous, the tattoos undertaken on the Europeans were remarkable; George Stewart went further than his friend Fletcher, along with the star and black bottom, his arms were covered with hearts and darts, while Peter Heywood chose the three legged symbol of the Isle of Man for his right leg. James Morrison gives us another clue to his pretentions of a higher position in life by having a garter tattooed around his left leg, complete with the Knights logo, 'Honi soi qui mal y pense'. Most of *Bounty's* compliment joined in at some point, maybe having already determined to seek out a native versed in the art, after envying the heart and date 1777 on the arm of 40 year old armourer Joseph Coleman, visible every time he set up his forge and wrought yet another miracle, by fashioning a useless piece of metal into a practical item.

William has left us a full description of the mutineers on a 'retribution list' (as I term it) and it is from this that we know the full extent of the designs and pictures permanently impressed upon some of his people, but the question has to be asked, how did he know the vivid details of their exact positions, as some were in such places as should make you blush?! The answer has to be that they were no longer wearing their usual clothing, especially the officers their uniforms. What's the alternative? Having become so enamoured of the Tahitian mode of existing, Fletcher Christian and his commune cohorts were daily becoming more and more native; dressing, eating, singing, dancing, talking, loving, playing, *being*, in an idyllic setting that suited them admirably. Had they been living during the 1960s they would surely have instigated the 'flower power' that abounded.

Bligh found he was an important man amongst the islanders and enjoyed nothing more than being flattered by all the chiefs. Prematurely priding himself on the success of his mission, he was too busy congratulating himself to be bothered with presiding over lowly Britishers. He delegated his responsibilities of running the ship to all the officers left behind. Whether they knew it or not, as he went exploring, is an entirely different matter. He automatically expected them to and to him that was all that mattered. Never mind that delegation should involve supervision, support and praise, his form of deputation was to simply relinquish his responsibility.

Suddenly the tide began to shift. He gave his guests the impression of being Lord and Master of all they surveyed, and to prove his point he ordered William Purcell to cut a stone for the natives to sharpen their axes on. The carpenter point blank refused, not wishing to damage his tools, which were his own personal property. It would appear that, as a warrant officer, this fractious man was exempt from any floggings, so this might explain why Bligh only confined him to his cabin. In this instance I feel inclined to agree with Purcell, but once Bligh was committed he had to chastise him in some way, giving him his freedom the following day to continue with his duties, while telling him he was still under punishment. Unfortunately Matthew Thompson took the brunt of William's smarting ego, receiving twelve lashes the very same day Purcell played up.

The carpenter went back to his duties and it would seem all was forgotten; Bligh certainly doesn't mention it again. He might have kept it at the back of his mind though, as he suddenly acceeded to a request that Tynah had constantly made ever since their arrival, for a chest to be built for him and Iddeeah. Not that this was to be an ordinary sea chest, he wanted it big (and strong) enough for them both to sleep on, and was actually designing a new house to fit around it. Notwithstanding the enormity of the task it was duly constructed and finished in what must be a record time of five days.

It turned out to be just as well it was made so quickly because all of them quite unceremoniously found themselves with more important things to think about. For most of December, storms had abounded in Matavai Bay, gradually increasing in temper until this unsheltered bay turned into a raging cauldron of white horses. Knowing he had to move to somewhere more secluded, William consulted with Tynah, who advised him to sail six miles around the coast to Toahroah Harbour in his own district of Oparre. Bligh walked across the terrain to inspect this site, found it favourable to his requirements and sent John Fryer to measure the depth of the water. Out in his launch the master threw a weighted line in front of him, carefully calculating a safe passage through the reef, and reported back, declaring the shallowest part to be 16 fathoms.

On Christmas Day, one year and two days after leaving Portsmouth, they were on the move again. 774 pots containing precious breadfruit plants were transported to the ship and, in a relatively quiet sea, they edged a cautious way round the corner towards their newly appointed residence. The launch was sent ahead packed to the gunwales with dismantled tents, which were first unloaded before returning to the entrance of the reef to guide *Bounty* in. John Fryer was balancing on the foreyard, rendering him a magnificent view down into the clear sea, Fletcher Christian was in the launch denoting the best passage to take, and so Bligh let her sail on, past the small boat, and run aground.

No damage was done as mercifully the pace had been so slow, but a great deal of time was unnecessarily wasted as she was laboriously kedged off the ridge. The stern anchors were repetitively towed in the long boats further and further away from the hostile coral and thrown into the deeper, safer waters. Sheer brawn then sprung into action as the cables were heaved aboard; the fixed anchors pulling against them in a sweaty game of tug-of-war, sinews versus nature. Exertion applied to the oars of the launches, connected to the ship by ropes, aided the hawsers squad, and the combined team effort dragged *Bounty* bit by bit away from the danger zone. No wonder it took them all day.

With Tynah and his retinue aboard, Bligh had lost face again as a procedure that should have literally been plain sailing encountered the ultimate result of languid management and bad seamanship. Putting a brave face on things, the anchorage and encampment were completed, but every time a large incident occurred someone suffered not long after. On 26th December 1788 two things happened. Bligh announced that the following day was to be considered as Christmas Day, and William Muspratt was flogged.

The dawning of the very momentous 1789 happened without giving the slightest idea of what was to come. 5th January gave the first hint. Still with the scars on his back, William Muspratt, along with Charles Churchill and John Millward stole the small cutter and deserted ship in the early hours of the morning. Bligh was informed of the fact half an hour after the change of watch discovered the boat missing at four in the morning, and he rushed ashore to demand information from the chiefs. The jungle telegraph had already swung into action and it was reported that the cutter had been left at Matavai and swapped for a canoe. The three runaways were headed for the nearby island of Tethuroah.

John Fryer was despatched to collect their valuable small vessel while William turned his nasty, peevish temper on the mate of the watch who, by falling asleep, had inadvertently allowed the escape to succeed. Thomas Hayward was 'disrated' and confined below in irons; he was not to see daylight for another eleven weeks. Meanwhile, Fryer was met half way on his trip to Matavai by a horde of natives returning the cutter to the ship. The return of the disillusioned absconders was not effected quite so rapidly, but eventually Tuesday 22nd January arrived with news that they were back on Tahiti. William set off to the prescribed place, and sure enough there they were, battered and worn by persistent harassment from the none too charming hottentots of Tethuroah. The arms and ammunition they had sensibly thought to take with them were rendered useless by the appalling weather, so they found two courses of action open to them – stay and be slaughtered, or face Bligh's harsh, though familiar, retribution. Who, confronted with such appalling alternatives, would not choose the latter? Certainly our young would-be buccaneers decided to follow that course, and they sailed from the arms of stone-bashing, spear-waving natives into the arms of lash-wheeling, irons-clamping Bligh.

Actually they missed the intended landing site and docked six miles further up the coast. William needed to take the launch to collect them, but in triumph he escorted them back to *Bounty* where punishment awaited them. With a bit firmly clamped between their teeth, Muspratt and Millward were roughly thrown against the raised chequered gratings cover, spread eagled, wrists bound to the frame and given four dozen stinging strokes, while Churchill received only twenty-four – surely Bligh could not have got the impression that his Master-at-Arms was led astray by two able seamen? More than likely, Churchill's rank halved his discomfort. After twelve days spent keeping Hayward company (who must have pouted at being trussed up with the very men who had caused the discovery of his neglect), Morrison's aching arm was flexed again as the punishments were repeated.

This sorry business was not yet over; an epilogue was about to unfold. Hayward had one friend willing to stand up for him, his *tyo,* who promptly sawed through the ship's cable two days after seeing the final punishment meted out on the deserters. According to our weary boatswain's mate (still able to hold a pen after flaying 120 welts across three mates' open spines) he wanted to drive the ship onto the rocks, forcing everyone ashore, so not only would his blood-brother be out of the hold, he would live on the island forever. He was to be disappointed though, as the fraying rope was detected in time with one thread still intact. Immediate action prevented the designed accident, giving Bligh another excuse to burst into ferocious hysterics, sending Tynah's parents, staying onboard with their son, scuttling away into the darkest depths of the mainland, so as to be rid of the fearful tantrum indiscriminately directed at all the Tahitians. William did not know who actually had perpetrated such a heinous deed, but rightly guessed it to be a native. Eventually he was consoled with the idea that a neighbouring islander had wanted to cause a rift between him and Tynah, and the matter settled.

Finally Hayward was brought up out of the bowels of the ship, to lend a hand with preparing her for their return to the northern hemisphere, laden with over a thousand recherché breadfruit plants. As in the beginning, so at the end, their departure was delayed by foul weather. Presents were thrust on board by Tynah for William to take to King George, as a sign of his friendship and Iddeeah was thrust on board for William to feed.

Right to the final hours of their stay the two-way entertaining was still continuing. One of these on shore was followed by the almost obligitory wrestling that William had never enjoyed, being too much of a free-for-all devoid of any skill. Small wonder then that he did not notice it getting too much out of hand on this occasion, but he was suddenly implored by Otow, Tynah's father, to intervene. The usual display of high spirits had been infiltrated by warring factions from other districts on Tahiti, and instead of having to sit through the mundane tussles to which he was regularly treated, he found himself witnessing a full scale battle complete with weapons brandished about. Striking his finest imperious pose, Bligh requested them all to desist, but realising he was being none too efficient, he took refuge behind his men who were armed and ordered them to fire two guns without any shot. The noise was enough to scare the rabble rousers away, and peace was soon restored.

The sad day was finally upon them. 4th April saw Tynah and Iddeeah shedding tears at the imminent departure of their dearest 'Bry', as Fletcher Christian's recent luxurious term of office came to a crashing end. He had bid a fond (and no doubt passionate) farewell to the bewitching ladies, danced his last dance on the water's edge to throbbing drum rhythms, partaken of his last banquet of luxuriant, sumptuous fruit, fresh fish and succulent meat dishes, climbed his last coconut tree in search of delicious white flesh and silky smooth milk, laid aside the aromatic garlands that once adorned his neck, and plucked his last breadfruit from over-laden branches on his final stroll down pathways bordered by leafy palms.

Bare feet scrambled up loosely strung rigging and nimbly edged a sturdy crab-like path along the yard arms. Anchors rose and clattered into allotted resting places, fresh winds billowed out released sails and *Bounty* turned her back on Oparre's dark, volcanic beaches, accompanied by a chorus of wailing woe, uttered by the desolate natives. Were they really such pure and simple, grief stricken souls, or did they lament the loss of useful and heavily armed allies, being now forced to resume their own defences against the local fractious districts? At least a parting gesture from Bligh to Tynah was to leave some firearms; obviously better than nothing.

CHAPTER THREE

'Mr Christian, consider what you are about!'

They were somewhat like young children on their first day back at school, playing exotic and fanciful games of make believe in the playground, but all too soon the whistle blew; the shrieking blast heralding an end to their blissful summer holiday and dragging them back to their desks. Headmaster Bligh fought with them to keep their minds on their lessons, punishing and demeaning the surreptitious glances stealing out of the windows at the glorious sunshine, accompanied by day-dreams of what was once theirs.

Bligh's position was an unenviably difficult one. He must have suffered the most after leaving Tahiti. Having been fawned and adored by the highest ranking people, he was suddenly stranded in the middle of sultry seas with what he devoutly believed were a useless bunch of good-for-nothings. After all the bowing and scraping that came his way unbidden, he was now having to demand respect from those to whom he would never have considered returning it. Even Christian (who used to adhere to his every word; once Fletcher boasted to his elder brother Edward that despite Bligh's temperamental attitude, he knew just how to deal with him) had strayed from the upright clone into which Bligh had endeavoured to mould him. Christian's taste of freedom amongst the Tahitians had provided him with an opportunity to prove it really was possible for him to think for himself. William could not approve of this challenge to his authority and attempted to beat it down the only way he knew how, by lashing out with his salty tongue.

While on Tahiti, discipline had slipped away bit by bit with the ebbing tides. Bligh had noticed what was happening, giving rise to caustic comments in his log about how 'neglectful and worthless' his Petty Officers were in his eyes, and of how he felt it necessary to write down all of his orders, not trusting them to remember the spoken word. He was treating them like children again. On one occasion he even wrote of how he wanted to disrate boatswain Cole and master Fryer but, like so many of us he took his comfort in writing it all down and did not take any practical action. Now, though, his worries and doubts about his crew's abilities were resurrecting themselves in his mind as the passage through the Endeavour Straits loomed ever nearer. Morale was low, abilities even lower and his whipping sarcasm never failed to chastise and ridicule any slight shortcomings (real or imagined, it made no difference to him) detected in his 'subjects'. He allowed his brain to torture himself with dread thoughts of trying to find a safe way through one of the world's most feared channels.

His nerves must have been in shreds as he daily watched more and more evidence of incompetence, his temper increasing as he strove to drive *Bounty*'s men back towards the excellence they originally possessed (and should never have lost), but was now desperately needed to get them through. The only one in his eyes not lacking was himself; the only one in my eyes totally lacking was himself. The argument has often been made, and has to be endorsed, if he had but kept a tighter reign on things from the beginning of their stay at Tahiti they would never have slipped so cruelly low. He was too busy entertaining the chiefs to bother about discipline, probably expecting everyone else to be off exploring the countryside and collecting the local plants, keeping themselves sensibly occupied, exactly the same as he had when there with *Resolution*. Instead, they kept themselves sensually occupied – not quite the same thing.

Thrusting himself back into the rigours of life at sea, he pushed his crew along with him. It can only have been his desperation to show who was in charge of the ship that prompted him to limit the rations to six plantins a day and some pork; when the plantins were exhausted yams took their place. Bligh kept them hard at work, but refused to give them the nourishment needed to keep pace with his orders, and all this after the licence in which they had so recently indulged. Perhaps for the first time in their lives they had had the pick of plenty without limitations. Having eaten their fill whenever the fancy had taken them, these sailors were suddenly near to starvation point again. It is hard to return from whence you came after sampling the better things in life. Probably the hardest part to bear was that the ship was over burdened with fresh food!

On 12th April, while charting a new found island, Aitutaki, John Sumner was unceremoniously stripped to the waist and flogged for neglecting his duty, a favourite expression of Bligh's, usually denoting that he felt the recipient fell short of his standards of hygiene. Sumner was by no means the only one to incur the commander's displeasure, though the stopping of grog was Bligh's preferred reprimand.

They sailed on, finding themselves off the coast of Nomuka, an island 1800 miles from Tahiti. Here they anchored off shore on 23rd April and Bligh went on land to woo and bribe the chiefs with his inexhaustible supply of presents, receiving a few unwanted coconuts in return. Two days later, wooding and water parties were sent ashore, Fletcher Christian in charge of filling the casks with fresh water. He and his party rolled the tubs from the beach inland to the watering hole used by Cook during his visits in those parts of the Pacific. We will see how James Cook's influence becomes surprisingly prevalent soon.

Amidst many tall trees, the men set about ladling the cool water into the receptacles when they increasingly found themselves surrounded by natives, not the friendly, helpful and loving kind they were used to, but chanting and spear waving ones, threatening yet not hurting. The sentries lifted their muskets, warning them not to attack. All the savages did was copy the stance with their spears. Most casks hurriedly filled, Christian ordered everyone back to the ship, post-haste.

He reported to Bligh what had happened, vainly trying to explain why their task had not been completely accomplished. Did he expect understanding from a man he had already had to inform that due to his great abuse he no longer enjoyed doing his duty? The same old story was repeating itself; Bligh had chiefs on board and his officers were letting him down in front of them. Quietly Fletcher told William he was not able to accomplish the job, to which Bligh reacted in what can only be termed as a very characteristic way. He screamed that Fletcher was a 'damned cowardly rascal', demanding to know if he was frightened of a few natives when he had guns to defend himself. The reply was too acute for Bligh – Christian told him the arms were no good, coupled as they were with his orders not to use them.

The following day Christian and party returned to try again and, as soon as they were out of sight, Bligh sent Fryer to check up on them. At the beach the master ordered the boat to wait for him, ready to go, a little away from the shore, and set off into the undergrowth, amidst a throng of locals. Two of them, male and female, took him by the arm and attempted to entice him to join them in a meal. The arrival of Matthew Quintal complete with cask and hordes preoccupied his mind and he accompanied the seaman back to the launch. Having supervised the barrel into the boat, he and Quintal set off for the watering hole, when they came upon the pair of natives he met before, still wanting him to go away with them. He threw a few gifts their way and carried on, when suddenly a horrified Quintal yelled, 'Mr Fryer, there's a man going to knock you down with his club!' Fryer spun round. Sure enough there was the young man brandishing his club over the master's head. A look was all it took, and he ran off. Fryer had no choice but to carry on.

The scene he came upon was frighteningly remarkable. Fletcher Christian was urging his men to fill the barrels as quickly as possible while scores of natives stood about hurling stones and grabbing at shirts; one leader took a particular interest in Christian himself, prodding and poking him with a spear. The sight of muskets with fixed bayonets did nothing to deter them. John Fryer grasped the desperation of the situation immediately and ordered everyone back to the launch, no matter how empty or full the tubs were. Using a few nails to buy extra labour, they all returned to the beach to find the boats lying on the sands, instead of waiting in the water according to his instructions. The sentries had been enticed into playing with some of the children and, while their attention was elsewhere, a grapnel was stolen. Fryer attempted to recover it before having to inform Bligh, but eventually had to go back to the ship and tell his commander that natives from a neighbouring island had taken the grapnel off in their canoe.

This is where the Cook example, constantly bubbling underneath all of Bligh's actions, erupted to the fore. He declared he would keep the chiefs he had aboard prisoners until their property was returned. Cook had taken the old queen on Tahiti captive after the disappearance of a quadrant; it was returned. Fryer felt Bligh's suggestion somewhat excessive seeing as they had other grapnel's on board and plenty of iron to make new ones, and the chiefs were nothing to do with the actual thieves. Now John Fryer was about to make the worse comment of all – 'Our loss is not very great.' Memories of an incident on *Resolution* with Bligh at the heart surely stirred in William's mind; a goat was stolen from the ship as she lay in Matavai Bay and Williamson, a fellow officer in whom William placed no trust, had termed it 'a minor theft'. Cook had taken Bligh's side, both knowing if any theft was allowed to pass by unchecked (no matter what the article in question), respect immediately disappeared. Cook wrought havoc before the animal was returned, ordering the villagers' canoes to be chopped and burnt and their homes razed. Bligh witnessed the terrible ordeal the locals were put through, and saw the goat sent home.

He too was going to exert his authority. The boats were unloaded and hoisted in, souvenirs were purchased from the canoes alongside, then Bligh issued the order to sail. Yelling for Fryer's assistance, he told him to hand out the arms. He was going through with his threat. One chief was sent overboard into a waiting vessel, with instructions to find the grapnel, while four more were detained by uneasy, musket wielding sailors. *Bounty* was gaining speed with canoes full of natives deliberately mutilating themselves, trying to keep up, imploring the return of their leaders. Eventually only one was able to stay the pace.

As if he had not done enough already, Bligh gives us good reason to question his sanity. He turned on his own, armed, men spewing forth a tirade of hate, telling them 'they were all a parcel of good for nothing rascals', while holding a loaded gun to McKoy's head, terrorising him with a warning that he would be killed if he did not listen to this mindless diatribe. Am I alone in jumping to the conclusion of a stunned atmosphere, studded with fearful and bewildered eyes?

The occupants of the canoe still travelling beside them continued to proclaim their innocence, frantically making signs that the grapnel had been taken away to another island. Bligh looked ridiculous enough already; his angelic, baby face did not correspond with the bouts of fury that exploded forth. What was beheld as masterful in a man of Cook's stature and bearing seemed absurd in Bligh, and this time it did not have the expected result. The missing article was not returned, but the chiefs were eventually allowed to leave the ship. Plenty of presents accompanied them and William put on a brave face (yet again) by declaring they parted better friends than they were before. I am convinced James Morrison comes nearer the truth when he wrote, 'they only smothered their resentment,' and he pitied the next ship to land at Nomuka.

Remember that every time something of a magnitude happened to Bligh, someone was made to suffer? This time mental, instead of physical, torture was used. *Bounty* passed slowly through the Friendly Isles, but with little wind to assist did not make much progress. They were not far from Nomuka, northward near the island of Tofua, when Commander Bligh called over Fletcher Christian. The disdained coconuts were heaped on the deck the previous day, and William now felt he detected a shrinking in their numbers, and, without any preamble, accused his officer of the watch (laced with such naughty words as 'damned hound') of stealing his coconuts. Christian admitted straight away eating one of them – they were so prevalent on board (having been purchased for the princely sum of twenty per nail) he was quite stunned at this recrimination, and answering the charge that he was a liar as well as a thief, retorted, 'Why do you treat me thus, Captain Bligh? I hope you do not think me so mean as to be guilty of stealing your coconuts'.

All hands were called on deck, along with their personal stores of coconuts, for Bligh to question everyone about the other missing ones; he was not content to accept the disappearance of just one, he declared at least half were missing. It would be too easy for him to listen to Fryer's protestations that the men walking over them had probably flattened the pile, he was certain everyone aboard was a thief; but no one knew anything about his damned coconuts. Now they became liars en masse and his fury was directed deliberately towards the officers in general, Fletcher Christian in particular. With a trail of cerebal devastation left behind, the hurricane of Bligh's fury subsided with one last cunning reckoning; he would increase their allowance of yams to one and a half pounds but, if the thieves were not found, once through the notorious Endeavour Straits, rations would be cut to three quarters. His final act was to impound the nuts of every officer; he was showing as little regard to others' possessions as did the Polynesians, a trait he despised and passionately believed should be crushed at every opportunity.

Smarting with humiliation, Fletcher and his colleagues gathered together in a mutually sympathetic huddle muttering and bemoaning their lot. Left on his own, he decided upon action; he was at the end of his tether and could no longer put up with the constant unwarranted criticism coming his way. Forming a plan in his mind he consulted Messrs Cole and Purcell, entreating wood, rope and hardware from them. Many times he was seen going into the fore-cockpit, where such things were stowed and the warrant officers slept, although it was completely out of character for him to usually set foot down there. It kept him busy, though, as he fashioned a raft on which to desert ship, while a small pig was roasted on his orders, under the pretence of wanting it for his messmates' supper. Much to the disappointment of some of them, it did not materialise. Thomas Hayward and George Stewart knew why – it was hidden in a bag along with trading nails and beads in Robert Tinkler's hammock, ready for Fletcher to go AWOL.

That afternoon, during the height of his clandestine activities, his resolution was further strengthened by another summons from, and clash with, Bligh. Again he was denounced a thief and a liar, and probably his dependency on Bligh and debts owed to him were regurgitated. The young twenty-four year old wallowed in self pity as soon as he could remove himself from Bligh's presence and allowed the tears to stream down his face. Purcell enquired what was wrong. It was clear that Bligh liked an audience; never would he chastise quietly and in private. He had to be seen doing his duty, and it should therefore follow that the carpenter knew exactly what was wrong. Fletcher seemed just as incredulous, pointing out the 'treatment' he had just received, but Purcell was unmoved. He cited the fact that he had also suffered at Bligh's hands all through the journey, presumably meaning he did not cry every time he was chastised.

Christian now admitted his worst fears by telling Purcell that the carpenter's rank as a warrant officer prevented him from being flogged. From the evidence of this sentiment it looks as if all Christian had between him and the cat was his Lieutenant's good will and favour. Until just recently it had stayed acceptably in check, but the upright and honest person he once knew now masqueraded as a vile and vindictive madman, and Fletcher Christian was scared. Not only was there the pain factor to consider, but also the point that a person born into his position, should never have to even consider experiencing the humiliation of going through punishments meted out to those of the lower classes. If he was flogged, it would symbolise the fact that all the hard work and effort he had put into climbing back up to where he really belonged was all to no effect. So frightened was he of the lash he swore that he would first take Bligh in his arms and jump overboard, so killing them both. It must now be imagined that Christian was a solid and well built man, physically more powerful than Bligh. The worst part of this presumption being that it was social climbing Bligh, a customs officer's son from Plymouth, who would dish out his mortifying disgrace.

Purcell attempted to comfort him, saying it was not for long, but Bligh's constant references to the dangers of Endeavour Straits were implanted in Christian's still impressionable mind; he felt 'the ship will be a hell' going through them.

He was determined to take his chances; he probably tried to convince himself that the Tofuans (the nearest land he could head for) lived up to the title of 'Friendly Islanders', but surely he could not have forgotten the welcome afforded them by the Nomukans, also of the 'friendly' ilk. Bligh's behaviour must have been beyond our imagination for Fletcher to prefer their company to his, unless his silly, spoilt head was exaggerating the situation.

His raft was complete, his provisions ready, he just had to dispose of his personal papers. Whilst sorting them out in his berth, John Samuel sought after him with a message from William Bligh; would Mr Christian care to dine with him tonight? Another insight into the complex Mr Bligh – after venting his spleen he apparently felt that his reprimands once given were all over and done with, the incident forgotten until he chose to resurrect it. In the meantime affability and goodwill should automatically abound. Instead, Fletcher's recorded reply is that he refused, saying he did not feel well. Poor John Samuel touted his errand around the rest of the young gentlemen, being in turn refused until Thomas Hayward accepted. As he left the mess, 'he was hist [sic] by all the rest.' A thought has to be spared for Thomas, though. He had spent eleven weeks in chains due to the displeasure of this man and would not dare defy him again.

Fletcher took his papers up on deck, ripped them to pieces and solemnly threw them overboard, then stalked the ship waiting for an opportunity to activate his idea. Somehow the moment never arose. Maybe too many people were around to witness his actions and stop him from even going over the side; if he did launch his raft how would he get quickly away from the ship? She was hardly moving. He might be seen and hauled back to yet more derisory mocking. Eventually he abandoned his scheme, maybe with the thought in the back of his head to wait for his own watch, and headed down to his hammock. Sleep would not come. While Bligh bid a civil good night to Fryer up on deck, Fletcher's mind raced through all the threats, hardships and punishments the entire compliment of *Bounty's* crew had had to endure.

What was pumping around in his head, directing the cancerous worm deeper and deeper? The incident with the cheeses after leaving Tenerife did not show William up in a very good light, for without investigation or comment he had immediately punished the entire crew. Not long after, expensive pumpkins bought on the same Canary Isle were found to be rotting, so Bligh ordered them to be consumed quickly, at a price. They were expected to exchange two pounds of biscuits for one of pumpkin. The men almost rioted, refusing with one voice such a reduced, monotonous diet. Bligh forced the almost-anarchists into devouring the vegetables, declaring they would be eating grass before he had finished. Cape Town had seen another bone of contention and Van Diemens Land witnessed Purcell coming off worst. The carpenter was right, he had suffered a lot during the voyage, though it would seem he asked for most of what he got by his insolent attitude. The master was never on speaking terms with his commander for very long and had overstepped the mark by wanting a signed certificate confirming his good behaviour. That had brought out the worse in Bligh.

Their time at Tahiti had not been all the wine and roses it initially promised to be; the native inhabitants had scant regard for their own possessions let alone those of uninvited, though welcome, strangers, and were repeatedly flogged and chained up for theft, as were the crew with fearfully increasing frequency. Starting on the journey out with Matthew Quintal receiving twelve lashes just over a year before, the impetus gathered more and more speed on Tahiti. Bligh, who had wished to go the whole voyage without inflicting corporal punishment on anyone, was swinging the lash almost weekly. Alexander Smith on 4th November, Matthew Thompson on 5th December, William Muspratt on 26th December, two days later Robert Lamb, Muspratt again with Charles Churchill and John Mills on 23rd January, the same trio twelve days later, and John Sumner on 12th April. Was Fletcher next? It was not so much the actual floggings (being an accepted, normal part of Navy life) but the reasoning behind them that seemed unacceptable.

The ship ran aground during the move to Oparre, and Bligh again blamed everyone aboard apart from himself, unwittingly goading three of his men into deserting. Fletcher's idea was not particularly original – others had wanted to rid themselves of Bligh and set up home in those seductive lands as well. As the person in charge of the nursery, Christian might have hoped to avoid Bligh's antagonism but he followed him ashore, starting quarrels and criticising his demeanour; in front of all the natives that adored Christian, Bligh belittled him and told his *tyo* in no uncertain terms that he was only one of the people, not second in command. How spiteful and unprofessional to hand out a promotion, only to withdraw it at the first sign of pique.

As Fletcher's memories came nearer and nearer to his present time, so the instances of Bligh's irascibility increased. Did Christian suddenly recall his last conversation with his brother Charles during the night spent in Portsmouth just before *Bounty* sailed, when they spoke of mutiny? It is a fair assumption that is exactly what he thought of as he fought off his insomnia.

At three-thirty a.m. on 28th April 1789 he drifted off to sleep. At four o'clock, his confidant and ally George Stewart disturbed his fitful slumber and roused him for the start of his watch. Troubled at the sight of his friend's anguished countenance, Stewart urged him not to attempt his planned desertion, knowing it could well turn into his suicide, and left to fall into his own inviting hammock. His advice made sure he did not stay there long.

Fletcher admitted himself that the short nap from which he had just woken left him very much out of sorts. Most likely, he was confused and befuddled as he clambered up the hatchway on to the deck, and looking around all must have appeared calm and quiet. Still, with little wind to whisk them away, I doubt if he managed to gain relief from any fresh air; the atmosphere must have hung heavy and threatening over his pounding and troubled head. On the distant horizon a volcano on Tofua was busy throwing a natural firework display for the sailors to enjoy, though most by then had already had their fill and long since retired, leaving only the handful on watch to witness the ferociously red spectacle. How long he took before deciding to activate his course of action is unknown, but certainly within that first hour he witnessed mate of the watch, Thomas Hayward, settle down to another of his illegal snoozes, probably content in the knowledge that he had made amends for the previous occasion by supping with Bligh a few hours before. Charles Norman was leaning against the rail, transfixed by the actions of a shark alongside; John Hallet, the other midshipman, was nowhere to be seen.

As the only officer awake, the ship was temporarily his – why should he take his chances on a makeshift raft? Why not make Bligh go instead? He was not alone in having a grievance against the commander; he was convinced most of the mariners would be with him and *Bounty* could permanently be his.

Furtively he sought out strong, though short, Matthew Quintal and the taller American, Isaac Martin, (both heavily tattooed as a sign of their love for Tahiti, both sufferers from the wrath of Bligh) and clandestinely sought their help in taking control of *Bounty*. Martin was wary, but Quintal's immediate enthusiasm for the idea (plus his own memory of an intimate introduction to the cat-o'-nine tails) won him over, and he was queasily committed. These two able seamen roused the instantly willing corporal, Charles Churchill, and once pushed over the edge by the slightest nudge, the rolling stone of liberty increased in speed. Very soon a hard core of mutineers formed as Matthew Thompson, William McKoy, Alexander Smith and John Williams joined their ranks.

Quickly they sorted out the ground rules; Christian was adamant there would be no killing, all he wanted was to be rid of his tormentor. They agreed that Bligh would be turned off the ship in the small cutter, along with his clerk, John Samuel and the two midshipmen, Thomas Hayward and John Hallett. Hayward's treachery of the previous evening must have still rankled with Fletcher, (perhaps he was worried that Hayward had revealed his planned desertion to Bligh in an effort to regain his good will) and Samuel was probably thought of as the lieutenant's 'man', but it is unclear what Hallet had ever done to upset them.

The first thing to do was arm themselves, so they stole down to Joseph Coleman's cabin and asked the armourer for the keys to the arms chest. He must have been fast asleep, and so, hearing mention of them wanting to shoot at the shark still alongside, handed the desired keys over without thinking anymore of it and drifted straight back to sleep. Jubilantly clutching the keys to success, they made their way up to the main hatchway where the arms chest was stowed (right in the middle of the floor), only to find the missing John Hallet right across it, also asleep. Christian assumed full authority and, disturbing the youngster's slumber, sent him about his duties. He scampered away, not realising the men left behind had other things to worry about that far outweighed his misdemeanour.

Other trustworthies were woken and the chest was opened and raided, with muskets, cutlasses and bayonets distributed amongst the throng of men, some of whom did not even know what was going on and merely followed orders. Leaving Matthew Thompson to guard the arms chest, Christian, having helped himself to a cutlass, a pistol, plenty of ammunition and a musket on to which he firmly fixed a bayonet, led the rest back up on deck. What a fearful sight these stoney, grave-faced men must have seemed to Thomas Hayward, now awake (having been roused by Charles Norman to join him in his shark spotting while everyone was down below), appearing in relays as they came up the fore-hatchway. He rushed forward to find out what was happening, but Christian growled at him to hold his tongue.

Sentries were dotted around, as Fletcher organised the next part of the proceedings; he, Churchill and Burkitt were to pay a visit to William Bligh while Quintal and Sumner kept Mr Fryer out of the way. Back down the fore-hatchway to the two cabins directly opposite each other, Bligh's on the starboard with his door slightly open, a regular habit of his in case the officer of the watch should need him, which was exactly the case now.

The three die-hards, with weapons primed, crashed into the tiny room, their bulks entirely filling the available space. Christian faced his mentor, his aggressor, sleeping the innocent slumber of a baby, and, grabbing at his nightshirt, heaved the inactive body to its feet. The bleary eyes focused on shining metal, made out the distinctive shape of a musket and set his mouth into action. 'MURDER,' he roared, his brain automatically setting his lips into overdrive as that one word repeated unhesitatingly, reverberating around the ship. Across the way, John Fryer woke, hearing the anguished cry of his commander as the door of his cabin swung open to reveal Quintal and Sumner. If they looked for him in his bunk they were to be unlucky, as the strange man preferred to rest on his locker, where he claimed it was much cooler. For a split second, did the thought flit across their minds that he had disappeared, until they spotted his bewildered face peering at them from the top of the furniture? With straighforward bluntness they informed him that he was their prisoner, and so long as he stayed quiet no one would hurt him. On the other hand, one false move and he was dead. How Quintal could have enjoyed the dramatic irony of it all, as his first flogging had come about due to a complaint from the very man he now held captive.

Noises were coming from outside, Churchill's voice booming above it all, demanding a length of rope to be sent down. Those still up on deck heard, but only one man, John Mills, moved to do his bidding. Having already been quizzed by Hayward as to whether he knew anything of these circumstances, and denying any knowledge of it, Mills obviously wished to be involved because he scrambled to cut a piece of the deep sea line, despite his colleagues frantic urgings not to. Down to Bligh's cabin he took his prize and presented it to Churchill, who wrapped it around Bligh's wrists and tightly bound them behind his back. So surly and abrupt was this manoeuvre that the nightshirt which stood between William's nakedness and the outside world was caught up in the cord, exposing his rear. It turned out to be the most violent act in the whole mutiny, the constrictive binding shed the only blood of the day. Bligh later said he wondered why Fryer had not come to his assistance, as he had a brace of pistols in his cabin, but did he mention it at the time, because Churchill then crossed the short expanse from one door to the other and relieved Fryer of his guns? They were worthless, however, not having any ammunition to go with them.

With John Fryer well guarded, Bligh was led up on to the quarter deck, by Fletcher Christian who kept a firm grasp on the end of the rope that trussed Bligh's wrists. The master watched his commander disappear out of sight at the hands of the rogues, and demanded to know what was going to happen to Mr Bligh. Shutting the door, his gaolers let him in on the whole plot. He was horrified on learning that four of his friends were to be cast adrift in the jolly boat (the small cutter), knowing it to be rotten. 'Damn his eyes, the boat is too good for him,' they replied, but agreed to ask permission for him to be allowed to go up and see Bligh.

Small wonder that his request was initially refused; there was a lot going on up there. As soon as Bligh arrived, foolish, reckless, seventeen year old Thomas Ellison, who was on his second voyage with both Bligh and Christian, having sailed on *Britannia*, became caught up in the instant excitement and giddy freedom. Throwing all caution to the wind and leaving his billet by the wheel, he rushed forward, declaring for all to hear, 'Damn him, I'll be a sentry over him!' And so he was. Quintal was sent to wake William Purcell, his loudly gabbled explanations of what was going on disturbing William Cole and sail-maker Lawrence Leboque. As they hurriedly dressed, the older man asked the boatswain's advice on what to do, but Cole rushed out, heading for the quarter deck. The reality of Quintal's words come home in the vivid scene before him – Bligh bound and held captive by his acting lieutenant, who brandished a cutlass held in his free hand before a congregation of gun totting, enthralled and attentive, hard faced men.

He turned round, and dashed down to James Morrison, John Millward and Thomas McIntosh, hoping to form a loyalist party to retake the ship. The news came as a total surprise to the three matelots, and Millward, jumping to the conclusion (as did Bligh) that the mutiny was pre-ordained, immediately proclaimed his innocence in the whole matter, following the fact that he had previously deserted at Tahiti. However he was sensible enough to realise he would be forced to join in and, sure enough, Charles Churchill was soon heard calling him to take up arms with them. Bowing to the inevitable, he obeyed.

All this time two young midshipmen (both with family connections tying them to William Bligh, both having deep rooted friendships with Fletcher Christian, both probably torn and severely miserable), Peter Heywood and George Stewart sat in their berth, gazing at the imposing figure of Matthew Thompson still standing guard over the arms chest just outside their door. On the opposite side, master's mate, William Elphinstone, stayed exactly the same.

Cole had had no chance to instigate his plan for a counter attack, and made his way back up into the air. He was press ganged into organising the hoisting out of the small cutter, but first of all approached Fletcher, asking for an explanation. Christian was behaving as a man of small words; he barked his orders and if anyone attempted to speak to him, he just passed them over with threats and warnings, including Cole. The jolly boat was hauled into the water, where she managed to float alongside, despite her bottom being almost eaten by worms. As soon as some men entered into her creaking hull, though, she began to slip further into the sea and frantic bailing was useless. The apathetic attitude at Tahiti had allowed the decaying state of her to go unnoticed too long.

Back down below again, John Fryer was not taking no for an answer, and carried on and on asking to be allowed on deck until Christian finally gave way. Up by the mizzen mast, flanked by Quintal and Sumner, he joined Bligh and Christian. The master managed to get more words out of Fletcher than anybody else of late when he implored of him, 'Mr Christian consider what you are about.' Mr Christian had done nothing else for the past few hours and replied, 'Hold your tongue Sir, I have been in hell for weeks past. You know Mr Fryer that Captain Bligh has brought this on himself.'

Now, a strange facet that keeps on cropping up is that everyone refers to Bligh as 'Captain', excepting James Morrison who pointedly calls him by the proper title of Lieutenant. Either Bligh constantly demanded to be regarded as their captain and it became second nature to them, or it was used as a misnomer, denoting the person in charge of the ship rather than actual rank.

Undaunted, Fryer tried again, telling Fletcher to put Bligh under arrest only, but that idea did not appeal to Christian, whose patience snapped. He told Fryer again, 'Hold your tongue, for I have been in hell for weeks and weeks past', adding the threat to send him back to his cabin. John Fryer had another try and asked him to give Bligh a better boat and therefore a better chance to reach land. The curt reply was that the small cutter was plenty good enough for him. The master then turned his attention to Bligh and whispered encouragement to him, explaining that he would try to stay on the ship and then come and pick him up. Bligh not only agreed with Fryer's plan to stay behind but let the whole crew know he approved. Already he had demonstrated how much he liked an audience to hear his voice, but it was surely inadvisable to speak so loudly with Christian listening right beside them.

Bligh went two blunders further, firstly telling Fryer that through intimation with their eyes, he had discovered Isaac Martin was on their side, and secondly he ordered him to knock Christian down. All this within the hearing of their intended victim and his faithful followers! Fryer decided to have a quiet word with Martin, so set off in his direction, thinking that Christian would not take any notice of him. The slightest step forward and the tip of a bayonet fixed to his chest, the newly risen sun glinting on the steel, as Fletcher Christian cautioned him – one more inch and the end would find its way past his ribs, through to his back. He was now sent down to his cabin, with the extra sentry of John Millward.

Fryer was not giving up though. He winked at Millward and indicated to attack Sumner, stationed beside him. Millward's gun rose to eye level, his thumb engaging it and there he stood, directing it straight at Fryer's head. The R's rolled as his deep throated West Country accent said, 'Don't wink or move any more Mr Fryer,' and the able seaman from the same area as Bligh stood to attention, ready to fire, for some considerable time. Fryer finally told him to 'uncock his piece,' before somebody got shot by accident and the Plymouthonian visibly relaxed.

Did Fletcher reflect upon the conversation between Bligh and Fryer? Until then the only thought in his head was to be rid of William Bligh, but suddenly it was brought to his notice that not everyone left on board would be with him in spirit. A second plan was formulated. The cutter was to be hoisted out for the same four men to be sent away in, plus John Fryer, John Smith, David Nelson and William Peckover. Maybe these added names were thought to be inclined to invoke a counter revolution. Exertions became greater as the cutter was prepared for launching. First of all she had to be cleared of all the yams and other accoutrements stowed away inside her and then fitted with thwarts, as she stood just as a shell then.

William Purcell was finally ready and brought on deck to help, and as he came up he noticed Peter Heywood standing on the booms, now dressed and desperately trying to take in the meaning of the unbelievable violation in front of him, his palm absent-mindedly resting against a cutlass one of the mutineers had placed there when assisting to launch the jolly boat. Purcell yelled across to him, asking what was he doing with it. Heywood came back into reality and discarded it immediately.

The activity was increasing. Cole was busy again, supervising the clearing of the cutter. He called upon many to help him, including Heywood, whose mind turned over the options available to him. He decided it would be best to stay with the ship, believing rumours that she was bound for Tahiti again, where he could later pick up a passing ship home, rather than trust his luck with the Tofuans, whom nobody knew anything about. When the shell was cleared, Purcell and his carpenters set about turning it back into a proper boat, running up and down the ladders to collect knees and other necessary equipment from the storeroom and fixing the thwarts (the planks that run width-ways across the boat for the passengers to sit on).

As they did this, Henry Hillbrant disappeared into the breadroom to fill a bag with supplies for those who were to be cast off, when he heard voices in the next cabin. Listening carefully, despite not being able to speak English very well, the German cooper could perfectly understand Fryer's conversation with Peckover and Nelson. Fryer had prevailed upon his guards to allow him to visit the cockpit and was rallying the other two with stories of daring do-or-die, as he recited the happenings of when he went up on deck and nearly single-handedly saved the entire ship. He told them that should they be ordered into the boat they were to refuse, and stay behind with him so as to retake her. William Peckover was terrified they would be called pirates, but Fryer told him he, 'would answer for that'. They got no further; Hillbrant had reported back to Christian, and Fryer was brusquely escorted back to his own cabin, where he remained 'building castles in the air'.

Fletcher Christian was becoming more lucid as he observed the progress made on the cutter. As she was hoisted over the side, the air ran blue as he constantly shouted at Cole to make sure nothing was carried away; jumbled threats followed muddled oaths, mixing together with perplexing orders as disorder and disarray abounded. Bligh joined in the mêlée, screaming abuse for all he was worth, despite the invariable warning of, 'Hold your tongue Sir, or you are dead this instant'. Impending death did nothing to dissuade him, he carried on until his usually robust vocal cords eventually gave up. Sympathetic Martin fed him with pieces of shaddock and he was soon back in business, exhorting everyone within hearing range to rally round to his cause and begging Christian to drop the matter. Christian replied, 'Hold your tongue and I'll not hurt you. It is too late to consider it now, I have been in hell for weeks past with you!' At some point during all this confusion a tiny bit of sanity and humanity prevailed, as able seaman Thomas Burkitt walked up to his ex-commander and pulled the tail of his nightshirt loose from the bindings round his wrists, thus allowing it to fall down and cover his derrière (and embarrassment).

The tackle was exerted to its final reach and the cutter bobbed down into the water. Peter Heywood was advised by George Stewart to change his plans and leave in the boat, and they both scrambled back to their berth to pack a few clothes. Boatswain Cole ordered blind Michael Byrne into the boat to keep her from hitting *Bounty*'s hull. Both Cole and William Purcell determind to leave with Bligh rather than spend the rest of their days wandering in the South Pacific; it would seem all thoughts of rescue were forgotten by then. Supplying mutual support they broached Fletcher together, asking for the larger launch. Three or four times they repeated their query, uncertain if they had been heard. Purcell tried a more emotive approach saying he wanted to see England again – the launch would give him the greater chance. Suddenly Christian realised what was being said to him, these men wanted by choice to leave with Bligh and, as unbelievable as it may have seemed to him, he certainly did not want to force anyone into staying against their will. He was probably bitterly disappointed, though, realising he did not have all his friends behind him.

Discussion ensued with his fellow conspirators. Charles Churchill was passionately against letting the largest of the ship's boats go, along with the most skilled and ablest of men. It looks like they came to some kind of compromise, because, as the launch was ordered out, the voice of the master-at-arms rang out once more; 'Keep them below!' Heywood and Stewart would have to unpack again.

Christian looked around. For well over two hours his men had stood constantly on guard holding guns and had twice gone through the motions of hauling boats out, a tough and exhausting job requiring at least ten people each time. Calling out to Bligh's servant, John Smith, Christian ordered him to serve a dram from William's own case to every man under arms and also to dress the lieutenant. Smith hurried about with a new purpose, firstly draping a jacket round Bligh's shoulders and helping him into a pair of 'trowsers', then touring the company with bottle and glasses. James Morrison was standing talking to William Cole at that moment, and Smith gave them both a tot whilst remarking, 'You may as well have a drop, though I am ordered to serve none but the sentries.' When all had finished, Smith disappeared below again to return the empty bottle to Bligh's cabin, and there stayed to pack more clothes in company with John Samuel, who was collecting William's papers. All the work from the past fifteen years was gathered in this one small space, the nature studies, the maps, the charts, the letters, the journal, everything that summed up the full exent of his magnificent talent as a highly gifted cartographer.

Also between decks, other activities were happening. Charles Churchill decided he wanted a servant of his own and chose young Robert Tinkler. The distraught boy rushed to the cabin of his brother-in-law, John Fryer, as soon as he heard of his impending fate and begged his sister's husband to save him. Fryer could offer the lad no more than a promise to do all he could for him. Elsewhere, William Purcell was putting all his belongings together, specifically including a mirror, which seems a strange priority under such circumstances; Thomas Hayward returned to his berth where Peter Heywood sat forlornly with his arms flung across his torso. Hayward told him to hurry up and get into the boat, but Peter just sat there. Hayward had not time to continue; having thrown some clothes into a bag he left again.

Morrison placed himself at the head of the main hatchway and heaved up all the chests that were appearing at the bottom of the ladder, as others joined in Purcell's train of thought and gathered all their worldly goods together. By now the launch was out and waiting for her tired and apprehensive occupants. Fletcher Christian ordered Thomas Hayward and John Hallet to climb over the edge and enter her first. Perhaps they had thought all along that, despite the frenzied preparations made, they would never really reach this stage and it was the realisation that they had to actually leave *Bounty* that made them burst into floods of tears, imploring Fletcher not to make them get in. Their pleas were to no avail and Tom Hayward was hurried in first.

Bodies and possessions followed as Churchill and Quintal prowled along by the rail, keeping a strict watch on all that was happening, often growling, 'Damn them, they have enough'. It was the carpenter's turn; he entered the boat and turned for his chests to be handed down, but Churchill demanded the one containing his tools be left out for their use. Again Christian stepped in with the wisdom of Solomon and decreed that some of the tools were to be removed, but Purcell could keep his chest. Furthermore he ordered the two other carpenters, Charles Norman and Thomas McIntosh, along with armourer Joseph Coleman, to remain on board. So much for the notion that those who wanted to leave, could do so.

With bag flung over his shoulder, the big, brash American, Isaac Martin, also stepped into the launch and settled down. In utter amazement at his audacity, Purcell inquired what he was up to and was told he intended to leave with them. Purcell stated in no uncertain terms that, should they ever get home again, he would personally make sure he swung. The fuss he was making alerted Churchill and Quintal, who hung over the side and demanded Martin's return, so the fellow from Philadelphia had no choice but to climb back in and be counted as a pirate. Robert Lamb had also stood under arms at the beginning, but nothing was said as he took his place in the launch; he was one of the originals who had muskets placed into their hands without knowing the reason why.

The boat was filling up and Bligh stood watching the slow procession vanish over the side. Peering down into the burdened launch he could see that she was already well down in the water, and besides himself there were still a lot more waiting. The desperation sounded as he pleaded for no one else to join the line; James Morrison detected the anguish in the cry and told William Cole he would stay and take his chances. Cole had all his possessions tied up Dick Whittington style in his bedding and was ready to go, so bid a friendly goodbye to his mate, promising to do him justice in England. True to his word, three and a half years and many adventures later, he did.

Those still below, John Fryer, William Elphinstone, William Peckover, Robert Tinkler, David Nelson, John Samuel and John Smith were brought up under guard and harried towards the quarter deck. The effects Samuel carried were checked over and all the precious charts and maps removed, plus compass and quadrant. Bligh's heart must have sunk seeing his beautiful collection removed from him; fifteen years wasted. His hands were hacked free of their bonds and Fletcher Christian surrendered his charge to the mercy of the sea giving Bligh his personal sextant by way of compensation. Bligh stood upon the gangway with Fryer beside him; first the master put what little time was left in Christian's company to good use, asking to be allowed to stay.

'No Sir, go into the boat directly,' came the quiet reply. Bligh still would not relinquish his command peacefully, countermanding Christian's words with, 'Aye Mr Fryer, stay'.

'NO, BY GOD, SIR,' Mr Christian erupted. 'Go into the boat or I will run you through,' enhancing the spoken menace by placing the tip of his bayonet on the appropriate spot. Fryer drew in a deep breath and spoke again, beseeching permission for Bob Tinkler to join him. Churchill instantly denied the request, but the question was repeated again and again until Fletcher gave the agreement desired and the teenager from Norfolk escaped. Christian turned his attention to William Bligh, telling him to go down into the encumbered boat, laying so deeply in the water that only seven inches of her gunwales remained above the surface. Bligh balked at the thought and any words that could remotely save his hopeless cause came tumbling forth.

'I'll pawn my honour, I'll give my bond, Mr Christian, never to think of this if you'll desist,' he begged. 'Consider my wife and family.'

'No, Captain Bligh,' came the firm response, 'if you had any honour things would not have come to this and if you had any regard for your wife and family, you should have thought of them before, and not behaved so much like a villain.' Christian knew from bitter experience the shallowness of his one time friend's promises and was not about to let him pass over any guilty feelings. Churchill judged the whinging had gone on long enough and chivvied Bligh over the side, as those staying behind leaned over the rails, shouting and jeering at the men huddled in the precarious long boat. Many times the old resentments over their rationing were resurrected with sneers of, 'Let the bugger see if he can live on three quarters of a pound of yams,' constantly flung at Bligh.

James Morrison hurled hunks of pork over to them, although

quartermaster John Norton allowed one piece to fall straight into the sea, instantly sinking before disbelieving, haunted eyes. This hefty sailor had earlier asked Richard Skinner to hand him his jacket. The only response was, 'You bugger, if I had my will I would blow your brains out,' and no coat! John Sumner told Cole to throw him his whistle saying he would have no need of it where he was going, and, asking to trade for something more useful, he duly passed it over, but nothing was returned. Thomas Burkitt turned into a little angel, noticing that William Peckover had only the clothes he was standing in, so hurried off and found some more which he threw to him.

As soon as John Smith was in the boat, William Cole suggested to Bligh they cast off immediately, worried that the continuing taunts of, 'Blow the buggers' brains out,' might turn into reality. They hacked away at the rope and veered astern, last minute messages frantically mingling in the wind. Michael Byrne was still in the cutter, sobbing and cursing the fact that his lack of sight rendered him useless, frightened he would be completely forgotten. Joseph Coleman stood crying as well, imploring everyone in the boat to recall he had no hand in this affair; was he eager for absolution because he had originally handed the keys of the arms chest into the hands of their abductors? He begged them to remember him to a Mr Green in Greenwich, which must have prompted James Morrison, standing next to him, to remark, 'If my friends ask after me, tell them I am somewhere in the South Seas.' Further along Charles Norman, the innocent man with an uncontrollable twitch of his head and eyes and smothered with smallpox scars, longed to go with them and wept for his wife and family.

Christian had planned to tow them to the shore but the calmness of the weather made that impossible and they made quicker progress using the oars, every dip as they rippled the surface pulling them further from the range of the menacing muskets. Bligh's last communication was to plead for arms to take with them, but Churchill declared they would have no need for them, 'Mr Bligh was very well acquainted with the people where he was going'. No doubt a good deal of laughter accompanied this base witticism, but Thomas Burkitt was to polish his halo and flap his wings again; he grabbed the nearest available weapons (four cutlasses) and threw them into the retreating launch. As she pulled even further away, whoops and delighted shouts of, 'Huzzar for Otaheite,' accompanied the sight of jubilant, dancing, cavorting men, celebrating their release from coercion.

It was eight a.m. The end of Christian's watch. In the space of four hours he had managed to irreversibly change the lives of forty-four sailors. If any of them ever resumed a normal existence they were to wait many years for the effects to finally wear away. Most were not so lucky.

This one over indulgence by a temperamental, dark, moody, strong, depressive Cumbrian has sent shivers ricocheting through two centuries, touching many individuals in many varied ways.

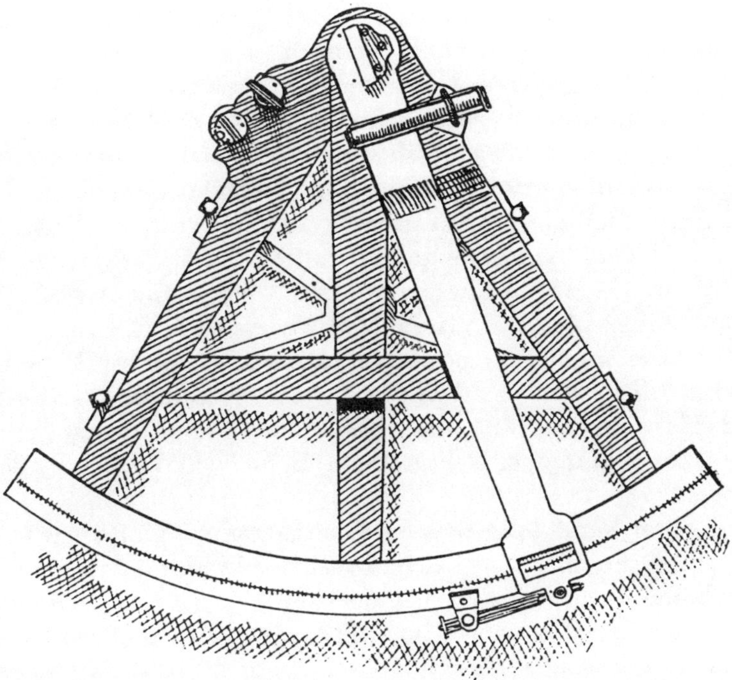

CHAPTER FOUR

'Want of Evacuation by Stool'

As William Bligh, William Cole, William Elphinstone, John Fryer, Thomas Hall, John Hallet, Thomas Hayward, Robert Lamb, Lawrence Leboque, Thomas Denman Ledward, Peter Linkletter, David Nelson, John Norton, William Peckover, William Purcell, John Samuel, George Simpson, John Smith and Robert Tinkler, rowed east south east, further and further away from the *Bounty,* two of them especially sat and pondered on what had brought them to such an unfortunate state of affairs. Bligh felt happy enough in the knowledge that all was well with the voyage until his rude awakening that very morning, and that he had done everything within his power to contribute towards the successful completion of their mission. He flattered himself with thoughts that the only reason behind the mutiny was those still aboard his ship wanted to return to the idyllic setting of Tahiti; never mind – he detected her sailing in a north westerly direction, this he considered a dupe to fool him into thinking they were heading away from the island. An artful idea was filtering through his mind; as he was innocent and would not have anyone at home think otherwise, the only thing to do was return to England and tell them of the dreadful calamity that had befallen him. If, in the meantime, he could save eighteen other lives along the way, what a feather in his cap that would be with the Admiralty. All he had to do was tell them his tale and his future was assured. He would join the annals alongside the seafaring greats such as Drake, Raleigh and, of course, Cook. Betsy would probably be glad to see him, too.

On the other hand John Fryer was sitting glaring at his commander, brooding over the injustice that had resulted in him having to watch his floating home disappear over the horizon. I do believe he wanted very much to be part of a swash-buckling adventure and was somewhat frustrated at not being able to play the hero of the day. Had he stayed on board as he so often asked, it seems doubtful if he would have actually tried to save Bligh; I have a suspicion he really wanted to be included in the 'glamorous' side, and was smarting at not even being given the choice. He decided the real reason for them being turned off the ship was they could no longer stand having Bligh around. James Morrison may have parted company from William Bligh but mercifully John Fryer was only too happy to pick up the pieces, writing a controversial narrative when he arrived back in England as an answer to Bligh's published account.

All was not to go smoothly for the nineteen men in the boat. They did not reach Tofua until after nightfall and had to wait until the following morning before finding a suitable place to land. Foraging parties were sent out to find more food but had dismal luck, so they hugged the coast searching for a more plentiful part of the island. Palms were spotted on a high precipice, and over the side went several of the younger members of this cobbled together crew, battling their way through choppy seas to gather in much wanted supplies, ending up with about twenty coconuts. How strange they were risking life and limb to harvest the straw that finally broke the camels back (so to speak). The boat came to rest in a cove and they feasted on the fruits of their labour.

For a few days they explored Tofua; not quite as easy as it sounds. The cove they had arrived in was surrounded by sheer cliffs, the only way in or out was by vines, Tarzan style. Bligh had a go at shinning up to have a look around but coming down proved to be an entirely different matter, and vertigo affected him so much he had to be rescued by David Nelson. Eventually he was lowered back to the sands, completely worn out by all the exertions. As the cove became more of a home to them, so the natives became more inquisitive, and William told them the ship had sunk and they were the only survivors. Using buttons torn from their jackets, trading began again and they managed to build up a decent supply of fresh fruit, which Robert Tinkler carried into the launch alone. From escaping being servant to Churchill, he was busily employed dodging playful natives while acting as man-servant to the whole boat load. Apart from worrisome mosquitoes and flys, their whole situation basically seemed comfortably under control.

Slowly the situation changed. Some of the island's chiefs visited, including a couple Bligh recognised as keeping captive when they were at Nomuka, though he regarded them as friends. He even believed their promise to accompany him to Amsterdam when the bad weather subsided; it looks as if they were playing for time. Dirty deeds were afoot to avenge the treatment of the Nomukans. The beach began filling up with devious natives who grabbed at the boat's line in an attempt to haul her onto the beach. William snatched up a cutlass and charged at the younger chief, Eefow, who immediately ordered his people away and the launch safely rode the slight surf in peace a while longer.

Yet more natives crowded onto the beach and Bligh's mind turned over and over the different courses of action open to him; he felt it best to wait until they could get away under cover of darkness, so made a show of going along with their request to stay longer. He stood, refusing to sit with them, realising if he joined in with their offered meal, he would be overpowered; the man was remarkably courageous, standing his ground as fires were lit, stones gathered and the ominous sound of them knocking together floated around the bay. Together with his men still on the land, Bligh served and ate a dinner of coconut and breadfruit.

After this fearful meal, all their belongings were gathered together and a cautious crocodile of marooned sailors wove a path into the sea, towards the launch, which John Fryer had edged as close as possible to the shore. When the local dignitaries spotted Bligh also making moves to leave they attempted to stop him, asking him to stay. With admirable presence of mind, he explained he never slept out of his boat, but come the morning he would be back with them. The reply was 'Mattee!' – they would kill him if he did not remain. The steady, repetitive, dull thud of knocking stones rose to a crescendo to reiterate the threat and Bligh acted to preserve his skin. Commandeering Negeetee (the Nomukan he had released from *Bounty*), he ran hand in hand with the unsuspecting fellow to the water's edge. The rock bashing fell silent. Commands criss-crossed. The natives were urged to attack; the white men ordered back into the boat, except William Purcell whom Bligh demanded stayed beside him.

There was just long enough for everyone else to scramble in before the native broke free of Bligh's hold and the rest surged forward to claim the prize. William had witnessed the same type of frenzied assault over a decade before at Hawaii when James Cook had drawn his last breath, and knew the severity of the predicament they were in. If they did not hurry and get away they would never move again. John Norton also realised the dangerous plight that had built up so quickly, but could not free the beach line, therefore, as Bligh clambered in, he jumped out in a desperate attempt to cast them loose. He took the full brunt of the charge, falling before the maniacal multitude who enthusiastically made full use of nature's armoury, methodically bludgeoning his brains out. Perhaps it would have been better if Richard Skinner had carried out his threat just a few days before, at least the quartermaster's death would have been quick and he would not have suffered so much. The jacket he pleaded for would only have fallen into the hands of the savages who stripped his lifeless body and paraded their winnings. His blood seeping into the sands was unnecessarily shed, for Bligh pulled out his pocket knife, hacked the rope in half and they made their get away accompanied by a shower of well propelled rocks and spears.

However the danger was not yet over as canoes hastily loaded with more stones launched in pursuit of the defenceless wooden boat, dragging Purcell along with her as he desperately clung to the stern before finally being hauled aboard. Fighting against the wind the oars pulled them away from the land but could not outstrip the fast moving local vessels, the accurate, painfully heavy bombardment continuing to assail them. Proving what excellent fielders they could have made, even against the might of W.G. Grace, Fryer and Bligh caught many of the stones destined for the oarsmen, but Freddie Trueman had nowt to fear as their efforts to reciprocate with the attackers' own ammunition fell dismally short. Brute force was not going to win this war, but Bligh's experience of the islands hereabouts was put to good use. He shouted to his companions to fling their jackets as far overboard as they could manage in a calculated ploy to outwit their foe.

The simple minded savages diverted their course to pounce upon the spoils and, with the timely help of the rapidly falling darkness, *Bounty*'s launch stole away. Churchill's last words were proven astonishingly prophetic; Bligh was only too well acquainted with the people, and they did not like him.

Their plight seemed hopeless; without arms to quell other over-enthusiastic friendly islanders they were stranded in the middle of an inhospitable ocean with scant provisions. Bligh suggested they head for Tongataboo, where he had also visited with *Resolution*, but Fryer had his doubts thinking it appeared that wherever Bligh had landed, retribution followed for them. His worst thoughts were confirmed when he learned that several of the Tongatabooans had been held captive for stealing, so he felt perhaps they should 'trust to providence'. Cole seconded this motion and the rest fell in with optimistic agreement, accepting they would have to exist on one ounce of bread and a gill of water each day. Peckover put forward the suggestion they make for Timor, 1200 leagues away. The idea appealed to Bligh, who henceforth took it over as his own, as there was the Dutch settlement of Coupang there, complete with a Governor. A quick look in an old book of longitude and latitude tables that John Hallet had managed to secrete about his person when leaving *Bounty*, showed they were heading for the northern side of the Endeavour Straits. With no charts and only an old compass, William Peckover's watch and Christian's own sextant, they relied heavily upon Bligh's exceptional navigational powers to see them through.

The nightmare was by no means over just because they had evaded the angry Tofuan's and decided upon their course. It only changed in horror. The overcast sky began to shed its load and they spent the first of many anguished, soggy nights exposed to the full impact of everything the weather could throw at them. The sea crashed over the sides and infiltrated what little space there was available. They bailed for all they were worth but made no headway against the intruder. Their belongings were in the way, making it impossible to get a good swoop at the water, and, more importantly, the bread (stored in flimsy bags) was submerging and being ruined by the salt water; they had to save it at all costs! Sacrifices had to be made and ropes, some sails and clothes were dumped, leaving each man with just a couple of suits. William Purcell's two chests were commandeered, one for storing the irreplaceable bread, the other (his tool chest all the commotion back at the ship had been about) was emptied (the impliments left to lay loose in the launch, probably going rusty), and, 'became a second convenience'. Does that mean what I think it means? If so, where was the first toilet? Nothing is said about his mirror; that no doubt ended up in Davy Jones' locker as well.

Leaving behind the Friendly Islands they passed on to the Fijian range, hitherto unknown. With the sea still flooding in, Bligh calmly sketched and charted as best he could all the islands they passed, cursing his luck at not being able to make proper and more accurate observations. They dared not land, wary of their latest tussle with savages, although plentiful fruit trees were easily spied. Perhaps the temptations to take their chances might have lessened had fish bitten the lines they constantly kept hanging into the sea, but only once did they catch anything, and that managed to dodge exuberant hands and abscond back to his natural habitat.

The morning of 8th May found them aching from another night spent cramped and at the mercy of the harsh elements, conditions that did not give them a moments peace. They welcomed the daylight and took to the oars again, when two large canoes were sighted making for them at an alarming rate of knots. As the sailing boats came in closer Bligh, in blind panic, urged his men to pull harder, scared they would be torn to shreds by more natives. Lawrence Leboque (termed an 'old man', being in his forties) turned a vicious tongue on his leader, saying, 'God damn my eyes Sir, you frighten us all out of our wits. Let the thieves come and be damned if they will, we will fight as long as we can.' He carried on baiting him, remarking it was, 'very pretty indeed, by God, that the Captain is the first man frightened'. John Fryer put an immediate stop to his impatience.

'You old scoundrel, if you speak another word I will come and heave you overboard,' he warned him. 'Pull away any other pieces of bravery.' Obviously the man did, and the race continued for three hours until the cannibals looked for their breakfast elsewhere; presumably having sailed close enough to witness the dreadful state of the small boat's contents, they realised the whole put together would not make a very appetizing stew at all!

Onwards they floated, managing to keep in the right direction. The allocation of food was abysmal, breakfast, dinner and supper consisted of one twenty-fourth of a pound (three quarters of an ounce) of bread, made somewhat more palatable by dunking it into the salty sea, and a gill (quarter of a pint) of water, sometimes with half an ounce of pork thrown in; even though it was swiftly deteriorating, Bligh kept a tight rein on the pig meat. The measurements were so accurate because he had constructed a pair of scales using coconut shells and pistol balls, each one weighing one twenty-fourth of a pound! Another indulgence was the teaspoon of rum he would dole out now and again to thaw them through. The water could be dispensed fairly liberally because new supplies were forever falling upon them and they were becoming experts at catching gallons of new stock in spread out canvas, plus quenching raging thirst to their hearts content as the rain poured straight down eager throats. There were of course two sides to this coin; being kept continually soaked, because even if the rain abated the sea was still rough and constantly swept waves over them, and, although the general idea was to be at two watches (half were awake and sitting while the others laid and slept), the discomfort was so great nobody managed to rest, especially during the nights which were perishing cold and unnervingly dark. They could not see each other's faces except for a split second when lightning darted through the obscurity.

Bligh was at his optimistic best, treating the foul weather as a fortuitous blessing, knowing that burning hot sunshine could quickly reduce them to insanity for want of fresh water, while on their way to certain death. Another advantage of having a boat full of the Pacific Ocean was the exercise gained from bailing it all out. He continued to perform prayers and give thanks for their survival.

As much as they desperately wanted to, there was no way they could dry their clothes, so Bligh recommended that they stripped, wrung the garments through the sea and put them back on again. By this method they at least gained some warmth and were suprisingly refreshed. It was something they carried on and on with until the clothes became too worn and threadbare to banish the biting chill. All this easement was unfortunately too fleeting and the hardships carried on plaguing them, their health and fortitude diminishing. Terrible pains creaking through their bones were now commonplace, some suffered for 'want of evacuation by stool', sleep would hardly ever come and their eyes refused to focus. On the 23rd May Bligh remarked, 'The misery of this day has exceeded the preceeding – the night was dreadful, the sea flew over us with great force and kept us bailing with horror and anxiety.' He began to fear that he would lose some of his men should the inclemency continue, and distributed two teaspoonsful of rum to help counteract such dismal possibilities.

For once Bligh started to doubt his own abilities, wondering if he would ever be able to find Coupang, and wanted to eke out their stocks even further in case they were obliged to continue onto Java. He cut out the allocation of food at supper, leaving them with just their gill of water to round off the day. Better things were thankfully around the corner; after fifteen days of constant pummelling, the sun shone on them. It made all the difference, lifting spirits and bringing a change to their diets. Out came the boobies, so called because they kept flying too close to ships and got caught in the sails, and noddies, both varieties inquisitively coming in close, enabling tired hands to pluck dinner out of thin air for several consecutive days.

Each bird was cut into eighteen pieces, the blood drunk by the weakest men (ugh! what a thought, though I suppose it contained plenty of iron) and shared out in the time honoured tradition of, 'Who shall have this?', whereby a section was held aloft and one of the men, with his back turned on the proceedings, nominated another of his colleagues. In this way the hapless birds, entrails, beak, feet and so on, were distributed and consumed. A couple of them had had the grace and forethought to dine before being caught, thereby carrying fish and squids in their digestive systems as extra treats for the famished sailors.

It was one o'clock on the morning of Thursday 28th May; Bligh was actually fast asleep and Fryer had taken over command of the watch only an hour before from Peckover, when through the stillness of the night came a familiar sound, the pounding, booming bellow of waves hitting rocks. The helmsman confirmed Fryer's hearing was not playing tricks and the master strained to peer into the night, making out the gloomy sight of rollers surfing over submerged rocks dead ahead. He put some of his men straight away to the oars, assisted taking in the sail and roused Bligh. Taking stock of the situation, Bligh hollered at the oarsmen, 'Pull my lads, we shall all be swamped!'; John Fryer neatly sums it up by cynically saying in his book, 'Very pretty encouragement for people in distress!' He tried to defuse the situation by simply saying, 'My lads pull, there is no danger,' and they moved away from the edge of the potential hazard.

As soon as daylight returned they started looking for an entrance through the Great Barrier Reef, where they could see inviting, calm and soothing waters, dotted with luscious and fertile islands. If they could just find a passage through, some were convinced the worst of their troubles would be over. It took a while, but what originally appeared as just a slight hole on closer examination turned out to be exactly what they were looking for, a break in the reef large enough for them to pass through. Bligh named it 'Providence Channel'.

The relief was beyond their wildest dreams, the calmness utter bliss to their tortured and battered bones. At the second attempt they landed on a seemingly deserted island and tumbled out of the launch for the first time in twenty five days, delirious and woozy, every ounce of strength sapped from them, and fell into crumpled heaps on the beach. Adequate energy was recovered to feast upon the new found delight of oysters, initially plucked from the nearest nooks and crevices, before giving themselves over to peaceful slumbers. Next morning the revitalised men got on with performing very necessary jobs. Bligh produced his pocket magnifying glass and soon had a fire burning, the rudder gudgeon (the socket which holds it in place against the side of the boat) had come away and needed replacing, provisions had to be collected, prepared and cooked. Cole, Fryer, Nelson and Peckover were part of a party that set out in search of more oysters and when they had prized enough away from the edges of the rocks for about five of them to carry, half of the group returned to base.

What a sight welcomed them back! Bligh was tired, worried and sounding his vexation off at everyone there, calling them every name under the sun and informing them had it not been for him they would not be where they were now. Leaving their spoils behind, the weary men returned to the oyster searchers, more than likely only too happy to escape again. The two Williams, Cole and Peckover, reported the scene they had witnessed to John Fryer and David Nelson, and the botanist, a man rarely heard cussing, immediately picked up on the irony of Bligh's words by remarking, 'Yes, damn his blood, it is his economy that brought us here.'

With all the oysters they could muster gathered in, Bligh concocted a superlative meal of shellfish mixed into a stew with some bread and pork, in a copper pot someone had had the aforethought to purloin back on *Bounty*. Fryer could not resist the chance and complained about the pint alloted to each of them, saying more could have been made by adding extra water. Bligh had deliberately not done so in order to avoid diluting all the goodness, which seems fair.

Other food stuffs were hunted out; birds were unobtainable due to the absence of guns to bring them down, but bushes covered in strange fruits beckoned those suffering the same torments as Tantalus, although these branches did not shrink from their grasp. On the contrary, this produce was so plentiful many thoughtless sailors thoroughly gorged themselves and only considered the possibilities afterwards, as their shrunken bellies rebelled against the forgotten succulence so violently they began to believe themselves poisoned. Blessedly, time proved them wrong.

The horrific rain they had endured so much earlier had not returned, which meant their water supplies, steadily going down, were not being replenished. Wire grass growing inland led them to discover water three feet below ground level and with little effort a well was excavated, providing all the liquid refreshment they needed.

'Restoration Island' was the apt name Bligh chose for this temporary abode because, apart from having landed on an island full of everything their needs required, they were there on 29th May, the anniversary of the day Charles II was restored to the English throne. They ate one last meal on shore, another of Bligh's oyster stews and this time he capitualted and served one and a half pints to each person. Fryer still was not satisfied though and, supported by Purcell, complained at Bligh withholding the bread; he, rather sensibly, wanting to reserve it for when they were back at sea. He also wanted to boost their sea store to the limit and ordered more oysters to be collected, but the gatherers pleaded tiredness and refused to go. Bligh, busy scribbling in his notebook, bringing this makeshift log up to date, obviously wanted to concentrate on what he felt a very important task, and could do without another bout of insubordination in the ranks. In no uncertain terms he damned and demeaned them, sending them away with verbal reprimands, while he turned his attention to finishing his journal and then rewriting the prayer book. When they returned to their voyage, different devotions were offered at the start and end of each day.

Twenty-four hours later they landed on another island, and piled out of the boat in an attempt to find yet more provisions. Fryer thought of an idea, having noted at the last island that not everyone had collected oysters with as much vigour as his party (could he have meant Bligh?); perhaps they should fend for themselves, apart from the desperately sick with whom he would willingly share. William Elphinstone decided he would rather go without than hunt for his own dinner, something Bligh would not tolerate. A compromise was agreed and they split into three groups, each party keeping what they found. There was one condition; what every man collected should be put into a communal pot and they would later take out the same amount. Wonderful in theory, but in practice. . .

The men scattered around the small island, tearing more oysters and clams from the rocks than had been available on Restoration Island. William Purcell gathered a large bag full and set back to the launch where Bligh, who had remained behind, demanded the overflowing bag from the carpenter. Purcell reminded him they were in different parties and refused; tediously Bligh went through the same old routine, raising his voice when denouncing the man as 'a damned scoundrel' and demanding obedience, raking over his past remarks again, ranting, 'I brought you here when, if I had not been with you, you would have all a perished.' Purcell was ready for the fight, echoing David Nelson's thoughts.

'Yes Sir, if it had not been for you we should not have been here.' Bligh must have caught an edge in the tone, for he demanded, 'What's that you say?'

'I say Sir, if it had not been for you we should not have been here!'

'You damn'd scoundrel, what do you mean?' To paraphrase the Bard, the Lieutenant doth protest too much, me thinks.

Purcell stood his ground, giving way to pent up resentments and settling past humiliations. 'I am not a scoundrel, Sir,' he said, 'I am as good a man as you in that respect.'

In a furious swift motion, Bligh swooped up a cutlass and challenged Purcell to pick another; the petty officer baulked at the sight of his frenzied commander brandishing a sword over his head and surrendered in amazement before these inane antics. The noise had alerted an interested audience, including John Fryer who stood back, laughing at the stupidity before him.

'No fighting here,' he told them, then recognizing his opportunity to be the hero had arrived at last, added, 'I put you both under arrest,' and called to William Cole to carry out his orders. Had the boatswain done so, Bligh would almost certainly have become the victim of yet another mutiny. Two attempts in the course of five weeks has surely got to be a world record.

The master's hated, jeering face infuriated Bligh even more and he turned on him, telling him not to interfere while he was in the middle of enforcing his leadership, explaining, 'That man told me that he was as good a man as I am.'

'When you called me a scoundrel I told you that I was not, but as good a man as you in that respect, and you said that you had brought us here I told you that had it not been for you we should not have been here,' toadied Purcell, no doubt beginning to realise the error of his ways and valiently trying to re-establish the status quo.

Bligh seized the opportunity to keep some honour and calmed down, saying, 'If you had not any meaning in what you [said] I ask your pardon.'

The crowd dispersed and carried on gathering oysters and he made another of his stews, this time adding beans and again serving one and a half pints to each person. There was no immediate fuss made, until they continued with their island hopping expedition and found themselves on another stretch of land further up the reef. Constipation continued to plague them, along with headaches and sickness, and the notion was soon put about that the latter discomfort was due to the beans in the last batch of stew. Bligh was happy to accept David Nelson's view that they were not poisonous and threw more into his latest culinary delight, which was consumed rather warily.

Only Nelson himself was taken seriously ill, while out foraging for yet more shellfish and had to be guided back by Messrs Fryer and Peckover, themselves half collapsing from lack of strength. What a sight the three must have made as they came home to the boat, but Bligh's concern was for Nelson only; he stripped him, laid him in the shade and fed him with bread soused in wine.

They had progressed on to this particular island in the hopes of catching turtles to boost their ever depleting reserve and Bligh disappeared to walk along the beach, ostensibly looking for signs of the marine reptiles but probably revelling in a little quiet solitude. He had left instructions with Peckover and Samuel to keep a fire burning under cover of a copse, and not allow any others to be lit, so the smoke would not give away their position to natives he had detected watching their progress from neighbouring shores. In the meantime John Fryer had fallen asleep, and on awaking, knowing nothing of Bligh's orders, hunted out dry kindling and made a fire of his own amongst some other trees. As the blaze caught, the parched wood spat glowing embers out amongst surrounding grass which instantaneously flared up and a brilliant bonfire filled the sky. Bligh's attention was instant and he screamed for them to quench the flames before the natives were alerted to their situation, causing an unnecessary commotion as John Fryer had already tugged up the surrounding grass and forced it to quickly burn itself out. All Bligh's anxieties returned and he refused to let himself sleep, worrying that savages would slaughter them before the tide turned and allowed them to sail on their way.

He hurried the sailors along, anxious to be packed and ready to leave at the first opportunity. Peckover and Samuel spent hours waiting for signs of turtles, but none appeared; all Fryer's fault according to Bligh, for had he not lit his fire it would not have got out of hand, and Bligh would not have needed to shout and frighten the creatures away. Hayward and Elphinstone kept watch, three more tried their hand at catching birds and the remainder rested. The three bird chasers were missing for four hours before returning with twelve noddies, a poor catch they conceded, two of them agreeing that had not their third, Robert Lamb, deserted and caused such a disturbance that most of the birds were frightened off, the haul could have ended up much larger. It was the final failure from an incompetent crew and Lamb was soundly beaten; though it was not realised at that point it was a punishment well deserved, because the culprit himself much later admitted he had devoured nine noddies while apart from his fellow huntsmen.

The non-appearance of head hunters immediately following the fire episode persuaded William to relax his intentions slightly, and he delayed their imminent departure to give the sick a badly needed respite, but the failure to sight, let alone catch, turtles (even after extra time) proved it was the right moment to carry on. One last islet was visited in the hopes of finding more provisions, but the effort was wasted and the frail craft wove its way back to the inhospitable expanse of the Pacific. The crucifying waves tore into them again and they were buffetted and thrown by the pitiless conditions once more. All too quickly they became cold, wretched and thoroughly saturated; exactly the same as before.

Whilst basking on their private islands, Bligh had prudently dried clams for this part of the journey yet now found several stolen, but try as he might to find out who had the audacity to take them, the thief evaded him. It did not matter too much, the ambrosial store contained plenty to see them through his estimated rationing. Happily he was even able to reinstigate the third allowance of supper every day. Dame fortune really did smile upon them on 9th June when she delivered a dolphin into their cache, providing two stupendous repasts; the flesh first, the stomach later. This second meal proved too oily for Bligh, who leaned over the edge and surrendered the contents of his tummy to the tossing waters. 'Prodigious,' he thought it.

For all this extra and continuing nourishment, the bulk of the men were sinking, frequently sleeping, their grasp on reality becoming vague and indistinct. The physical ravages were worse, expressionless, gaunt faces topped off emaciated bodies lodged on bloated legs. The surgeon, Thomas Denman Ledward, was useless to assist these needy patients; he and Lawrence Leboque (that 'old hardy seaman') were coping the worst, and Bligh had turned his remedy of warming wine (the rum finished and but a memory by then) exclusively to them. He offered one other form of comfort, they had left the coast of New Holland far behind and should sight Timor any day now.

True to his word, on Saturday 13th June, 1789, 'with an excess of joy', the island they had travelled 3,623 miles to visit was before them. Unfortunately Bligh steered them in the wrong direction, believing some out-lying islands to be Timor, and in horror the men watched their desired destination grow smaller. Nelson and Peckover broached the subject with Bligh, who called on John Fryer for a second opinion of where they were headed. When Fryer said he too thought the land they wanted was now behind, he was subjected to another outburst, questioned why he did not speak up before. The answer, quite simply, was because he had not been asked. They turned round, amid frantic irksome lectures spewing forth from their drained boss, and sailed along beside the welcoming shore, hunting for the European colony of Coupang. Although he could not be certain, Bligh thought it was on the south westerly side, so they went that way. Lots of smoke and neat huts alongside farmed land showed signs of life but none of the Dutch variety and they sailed on, the terrain changing to wild palms bearing no human existence.

A beautiful, cosy bay was spotted, with smoke curling from the valley beyond. Fryer and Purcell offered to wade ashore, presumably to find out if they had at last reached gold or, at least, ask directions, but Bligh formed the notion they wanted to desert him; he refused permission and kept going, almost landing right on top of an unseen reef. It must have shaken Bligh when the breakers nearly flooded them because, when a dog gambolling across silken sands in front of more huts heralded the next sign of habitation, he landed Cole and Peckover, telling them to find help. Eventually they returned with five Malay men, who were friendly and charming (not at all the savages Bligh still feared), and pointed them in the correct direction of Coupang – north-east. To make doubly sure of taking the right route, one of the men was hired as a pilot, and they embarked on the final stage of their awesome voyage.

Thirty minutes before dawn Sunday 14th June they anchored a little way off from the town of Coupang. During their time at sea, they had been occupied sewing a Union Jack from some signal flags found in the launch, and with all the pomp and ceremony they could invoke, it was hoisted upside down as a distress signal. The day was not very old when a soldier arrived to give Bligh permission to land, which he did, marching up the street as though he had only rowed 1200 yards, rather than leagues! Everyone else had to wait in the boat.

He was escorted to the house of Captain Spykerman, whom he was led to believe was the second in command in Coupang, for the Governor was far too ill to receive guests. He was therefore content to make an appointment to visit Governor Willem Adriaan Van Este later on at eleven o'clock. Meanwhile all his men were invited to join him by their host, giving him the chance to really dig the knife, and viciously turn it, in the back of his favourite bête noire, the man he constantly ran down in his log and called 'troublesomely ignorant', 'disruptive', 'turbulent' and even once threatened to kill; John Fryer was ordered to stay and look after the boat. Fryer was determined not to be deserted entirely and ordered John Smith to remain behind with him because, being Bligh's servant, he could take care of William's personal effects. These two desolate souls helplessly watched the rears of their colleagues stumble away to a table of plenty, while they remained forgotten.

Time dragged heavily by for these two until a soldier approached them with exquisitely welcome cakes and tea, which they rapidly devoured. Fryer remembered his manners and attempted to remember his Dutch in order to thank their kind hearted champion and was flabbergasted when the man spoke in perfect English; his father had been British.

Up at the house, Bligh played Lord Bountiful with Captain Spykerman's hospitality, feeding his men on tea, bread and butter. When they had finished someone wondered where Fryer and Smith were and informed one of the Dutch sailors they were two missing. He automatically told Spykerman, who lost no time in sending refreshments to them, but they had already filled their bellies and did not dare eat anymore.

Still they remained at the harbour, so used their enforced idleness to smarten themselves up; Fryer first shaved his beard off then spent half an hour smoothing and grooming Smith, who lacked both inclination and energy to do the job himself. 'All this time I might have gone to the devil for my good friend Captain Bligh,' later remarked Fryer. He was obviously very bitter at the way he was treated.

He was eventually approached by a man who asked him to visit Mr Timotheus Wanjon, second in command of the island. (Bligh was not to discover until his meeting with the Governor that he was fraternising with the wrong person entirely.) Wanjon must have wondered why: a boat full of skeletons had arrived in his port and they immediately went to Spykerman's home without anybody telling him who they were or what had happened to them. Fryer answered all his enquiries, through an interpreter, refused a glass of gin but gladly accepted the grog replacement, and returned to the docked boat, resolving not to leave it until given permission. Rather than fuel Bligh's fire, he was gathering coal for his own.

The long wait came to an end and he sat down to an early dinner with Ledward at Spykerman's, but instead of eating, all the exhausted man could do was sob his heart out and collapse on a couch. He slept until about five o'clock when an invitation arrived for him to go back to Wanjon's house, 'which I believe mortified Captain Bligh very much'.

Understandably he was in no fit state to make polite conversation and had to promise to join in the convivial pipe smoking and gin swigging with the menfolk another day. He took things a little easier, allowing the ladies to fuss over him and feed him 'sweet cakes' and more tea.

The appointed hour for Bligh's audience with Van Este was brought forward. The governor, having been informed of their plight, wanted to talk with him straight away, and despite being in a dreadful state of health himself, took immediate pity at the sight of the half dead man before him. He promised to issue orders to the effect that everything they needed would be granted and placed him in the capable hands of his son-in-law, Timotheus Wanjon. A house was purloined for their use and Bligh, true to self, organised and arranged everyone; a room for himself, a second shared by Fryer, Nelson, Ledward and Peckover. The rest of the officers were banished to the loft and the ordinary seamen were billetted in an outer apartment. Furniture was sent to them, a favour from the governor and positioned in the appropriate rooms; only two beds arrived, one placed in Bligh's room, the other put up for Fryer's use. Servants scurried around, making life as easy as possible for them, and one, 'a black man', took the master's arm and proudly showed him the cosy bedstead arranged for him.

Bligh, *naturellement*, interfered and told Nelson the bed he had ordered for *both* David and Fryer was ready in the other room. 'Sir, I beg your pardon but that bed is sent for me from the governor,' Fryer protested. Not that he objected to sharing with Nelson, it was just the bed was meant for him and was nothing to do with Bligh. The botanist agreed; he had heard all the arrangements and knew quite well it was John's, however they did end up sharing.

They were now at the beginning of a two month convalescence and suffered extensive medical attention from the local doctor. Their stomachs gripped and griped in harrowing attempts to be rid of constipation and sickness; intumescent legs and open sores scourged them. The doctor, Mr Max, advised bathing in the river before sun rise and soaking their legs in warm water every evening, plus taking some gentle exercise. All began to recover within the first week, apart from Bligh, who was running a high temperature and could not keep any food down.

On 21st June he at last felt well enough to leave the house and, being the Sabbath, headed straight for the local church, 'to return thanks to Almighty God for his late gracious protection and preservation of our lives.' The following day he explored Timor on a horse loaned by the governor. Every day saw him continue to grow stronger and his log again becomes full of minute descriptions detailing the local weather, people, trade, Malay customs, town and surrounding countryside, crops, fruits, markets, language, history. Nothing was too small an occurrence or geographical feature to escape William Bligh's notice. He attended a Chinese funeral, leaving us with an eternal, intimate record of all the rites and ordinances performed, viewed with the sympathetic though removed eye of an uninvolved stranger. It was merely a practice run, though, for he was to join another funeral cortège, stand at another graveside, and deeply grieve the death of David Nelson, the botanist whose life he had sustained and nurtured during their traumatic boat journey. With *terra firma* beneath his feet, nourishing food in his stomach, clean warm clothes on his back and regular medical attention, Nelson had quickly recovered his ailing health and taken to pursuing his first love – the discovery of excitingly new plants. Perhaps he treated his recently recaptured haleness too lightly, because he caught a chill, which turned to a fever and finally claimed him for the European cemetery behind Coupang chapel. Here he was laid to rest on Tuesday 21st July 1789, carried by twelve soldiers who were solemnly followed by Bligh and Mr Wanjon. Ten local Dutchmen and captains from visiting ships followed next, and finally, bringing up the rear, the other sixteen men with whom he had so cruelly been cast away not three months previous. The whole procession was led by Mr Temmisick, the Minister.

Bligh kept busy making preparations for their voyage to Batavia, from whence he planned to obtain a passage home to England. He soon found out no ships were sailing there directly, and was anxious to be away before the monsoon arrived, knowing the Dutch Fleet was due to sail in October. If he was not on it, he would have to waste precious months waiting for the winds and rain to pass. Although he had sent extensive despatches informing the Navy Board of his misfortune almost the minute he arrived (and also demanded 'In His Majesty's

Name' that Van Este send out letters containing his retribution list of the mutineers to all European outposts, so that if *Bounty* docked in any one of their ports the inhabitants would know to arrest her crew), personally reporting his mishap to his superiors and seeing the full force of English justice swing into action, was the only reason for living.

He began searching for a private vessel to hire, but the charges quoted were astronomically high, because each owner would have to stay at Batavia a full seven months and sit out the storms. There was nothing left but to buy his own (all of this 'buying' and 'hiring' he was indulging in apparently amounted to crediting everything to His Majesty's Navy and Victualling Board). He became the proud owner of the *Resource*, a 34 foot 7 inch long vessel. She needed extensive work carried out on her before being really seaworthy and his craftsmen were immediately put to work, along with some Chinese to help.

The Cape of Good Hope, Van Diemen's Land, Tahiti, and now Timor. Bligh went exploring again, making overtures of friendship to a native Emperor, as well as disturbing wretched Van Este with trivial requests, or socialising with Mr and Mrs Wanjon at their country estate. On his return he discovered the refitting on *Resource* was not up to his timetable or specification and loudly rebuked all concerned. The fact that four men, including Purcell, quickly became ill with fevers following their return to work, indicates they were still too weak to fashion new masts, rigging, sails, decks, anchors and cables, but Bligh carried on bemoaning the slowness of the unskilled Chinese who were obviously expected to carry on with apprenticed exactness.

He also had cause to reprimand John Fryer again, who had urged his brother-in-law Robert Tinkler to knife William Cole, following an admonition from the boatswain to the young boy for being impudent. The master suffered another lashing from Bligh's whipping tongue for his flagrant encouragement.

On Friday, 8th August the ship was finished and ready to sail; when Bligh wrote they could not leave due to Governor Van Este being so ill they expected him to die at any moment, I immediately thought how considerate and respectful of him. The delay was only because Van Este could not authorise provisions for them to take on board and until the unfortunate man was dead, nobody else could officially take his place. Eventually, Wanjon personally loaned William cash for the voyage.

The *Resource*, well stocked with food, water, specimen plants (including breadfruit) and an armoury of weapons on loan, sailed into the piratical waters of the Malay archipelago, pulling the launch behind her.

A short stop was made at Sourabya where Bligh was advised to wait until two other ships left for Batavia so they could form a convoy against attack; these outriders became useful in a completely different and unforeseen manner. Bligh dined with the Governor, while his crew, let off the hook for a few heady hours, invaded the local hostelries. Purcell's ill advised arrogance took on a new dimension as he told tales of woe to all around him, pouring on the agony of the disgraceful manner in which Bligh had treated him, and speculated on how his commander would more than likely be court martialed when they got home, suffering his deserved punishment either in the form of hanging or, magnificently dramatic wishful thinking by the carpenter, be shot live from the mouth of a cannon.

Trying hard to perpetuate a modicum of decorum, the report of Purcell's inebriated behaviour did not please Bligh, but worse was to follow. The Governor rowed him into the harbour in his own boat, from which Bligh should have gracefully boarded the waiting *Resource,* but when they reached the appointed spot, the ship did not arrive. With nowhere to go, he bobbed about in the craft, each strained moment with the polite governor stoking his temper. When he eventually got on board, backchat from John Fryer resulted in Bligh marching the master, and Purcell, at the point of a bayonet down into the hold and keeping them prisoner.

Fryer had thrown some nasty accusations at Bligh, who was determined to vindicate himself and, in doing so, sought the assistance of the Governor once more. John Fryer had to explain why he had accused Bligh of falsifying his records at Coupang and claimed that everyone aboard was weary of the disgusting misuse he meted out. Fryer surrendered unconditionally, begging Bligh to forgive him. William refused and furthermore, transferred the master and carpenter to the two accompanying ships.

Sourabya was last seen by the *Resource* on 17th September, and two weeks later she docked at Batavia, Java. Here Bligh automatically sold the ship and *Bounty's* launch and used the proceeds to secure a passage home for himself, clerk John Samuel and servant John Smith on the Dutch vessel *Vlydte*. The others had to fend for themselves. Some fared better than others; Batavia, a well-known breeding ground for malaria, committed four more foreign sailors to her hallowed earth – William Elphinstone, Peter Linkletter, Thomas Hall and Robert Lamb (who finally admitted eating the nine noddies just before his death) fatally succumbed to the mosquito carried malady that Bligh also caught and took away with him.

Fortunately for both him and everyone he came into contact with, his bout was not serious; he had certainly put it behind him by the 14th March 1790 when he disembarked off the *Vlydte* at the Isle of Wight.

* * *

On Wednesday 7th October 1987, BBC2 screened the very first programme in their series 'Wide World'. Two sea faring tales were coupled together; one a story of tragic disaster, the other an interesting saga of endurance and survival. This latter tale was entitled 'The Voyage of Bounty's Child'.

In 1985 the Australian great, great, great, great grandson of William Bligh, 60 year old Captain Ron Ware re-enacted his famous ancestors epic voyage, in his specially built, 23 foot long launch *'Bounty's Child'*, along with three other Australians, an Englishman, a Canadian, a New Zealander, a Tongian and an American cowboy who had never set out to sea before. The whole three and a half thousand mile trip was recorded and edited into a ninety minute film for the edification of the Australian viewing public, and it was while invading this country, scouting around for information for the BBC programme 'Australia', that Tim Slessor (editor for both BBC series) bought this sea film which he believes is, 'comparable with those earlier films made with Clare Francis from around the world.' Being a very keen sailor himself he was able to assess exactly how major an achievement the journey was.

The full ninety-minute programme was given to producer Richard Robinson who cut it down to the final twenty-five minutes the BBC broadcast, knowing that to the non-small boat specialist the waves that broke over them in leg five look exactly like the ones that crashed over them in leg three. He eventually chose the longest, most interesting single chunk that travelled 1500 miles from the New Hebridies, through the Great Barrier Reef, to Bligh's Restoration Isle, because it showed the tedium and squabbling that breaks out when people are very compressed together, and the muttering and cussing that arose over the food.

Having already completed over one thousand miles of their re-enactment, the BBC picked up the voyage as they left Venuatu (New Hebrides), where the charming and friendly islanders bid them a musical farewell; already we could see this journey was going to be a lot easier than the one endured by the original *Bounty* men. With only nine in the exact replica instead of eighteen, conditions were twice as comfortable, in addition to which Bligh had been unnerved by these natives' forefathers and totally ignored them. Rather than cannibalistic overtones coming their way, these latter-day castaways were sharing waves and smiles as they set off.

Ware was determined to recapture the feeling of the first voyage, and supplemented a somewhat meagre diet with whatever they could take from the sea. With their modern day fishing equipment they hauled in fresh fish with amazing ease – whereas Bligh's men had only managed one solitary dolphin which made him sick. Disputes arose over the quantities and selection of food, which mainly seemed to consist of dried fruit and dehydrated beans, as the sea remained more benign than anyone had thought possible. Boredom mingled with the fatigue of too many broken nights – only five of them could lay full length at any one given time and they were divided into watches of three men, changing every four hours.

Time was whiled away by a limited amount of exercise, singing and reading (they had a copy of Bligh's *A Voyage to the South Seas* on board), until just 200 hundred miles from the Great Barrier Reef the clement conditions altered into thrashing waves and whistling winds. The storms were welcomed as an exciting divergence as the adrenalin surged, and they sat about syphoning out the excess water with bright shiny pumps and raised the height of the boat's sides with canvas (just like Bligh). They were tossed, buffetted, drenched but exhilarated when they cautiously found a path through the threatening jagged coral of the Great Barrier and landed on Restoration Isle.

Here the BBC ended the story, but the nine men involved continued on to Timor and succeeded in achieving their aim – to match the record open boat voyage set by William Bligh and his erstwhile companions nearly 200 years previously.

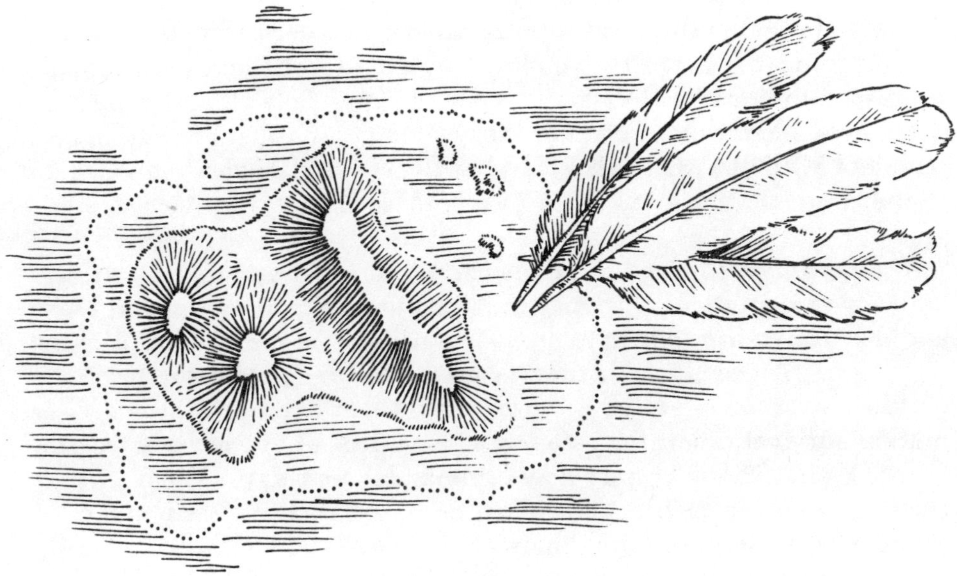

CHAPTER FIVE

Tubuai or not Tubuai, that was the question

Back on the quarter deck of the *Bounty* at 8 o'clock on the morning of 28th April, 1789, Fletcher Christian watched the launch moving further and further away and marvelled at the docile spirit in which her occupants had allowed themselves to be dismissed. Morrison writes, 'he said . . . that something more than fear had possessed them to suffer themselves to be sent away in such a manner without offering to make resistance.' Fletcher's wonderment did not last long, for he took immediate control, calling for the top gallents to be loosened. Thomas Ellison flew up the rigging to obey his current commander's bidding.

From now on *Bounty* was truly under new management. George Stewart and Peter Heywood were recalled up on deck from their cabin, just in time to dismally watch their exiled colleagues disappear, Morrison, the boatswain's mate promoted into Cole's hastily vacated shoes by a silent understanding, was called upon to haul in the cutter, complete with the still extremely bewildered and frightened Michael Byrne, and all the arms were gathered up and safely locked away again.

A slight breeze sprung up and they used this to take a north north west path. By the afternoon Christian had consulted Bligh's charts and books and decided upon a destination, but first had one crafty bluff to play; waiting until the initial euphoria generated by the majority of the mutineers ceased to excite, he encouraged them to concentrate on their mutual survival. Their first step was to confirm what everyone took for granted, that Fletcher was now commander and approached him as such, but much to their astonishment he repudiated this assumption. So confident was he in his standing with the men who had already totally endorsed him, he said, 'I have no right to command you and I will act in any station I am assigned to.' They instantly hailed him as their champion, enroled him as their Captain and handed over the ideal recourse to fall back upon should anyone later question his leadership.

He assigned straightforward roles to his depleted crew; following Bligh's example, who had promoted Stewart into his old rank of master's mate, Christian raised the Scotsman to second-in-command (much to the hardened rebel's chagrin), Morrison was confirmed boatswain, plus becoming store-keeper, Mills was the typical choice to fulfil the gunner's position, McIntosh naturally took over the carpenter's duties and Churchill stayed on as the trusty master-at-arms, taking full responsibility for the keys to the arms chests (there were two on board, though one was completely empty). Commander Christian divided his reduced company into two watches, one he personally oversaw while George Stewart harshly presided over the second.

Still playing a cautious hand Christian democratically asked where they wished to be taken, and they unanimously agreed to travel wherever he decided to go. He set a course for Tubuai, a remote island three hundred miles south of Tahiti, having read it was far off the beaten track and possessed but one bay that was treacherously difficult to navigate.

Within a couple of days the men who foolishly thought they had gained a victorious freedom, discovered they had only swapped one set of rules for another equally harsh regime. Being at two watches with desperately reduced manpower, made the tasks necessary for running the ship all the harder to perform, and although everyone was united in the common goal of continued existence, there was probably a certain amount of underlying resentment directed from the 'loyalists' to the mutineers. Christian had an answer to this animosity, ordering uniforms to be cut out of sails for each man and bound with braiding made from his own officers insignia, stating that a uniformity in dress would provide an outward sign of discipline to natives, giving them a head start in quelling the inhabitants of Tubuai. Also, any spare time they might possibly have spent brooding was usefully occupied. Another task he insisted upon was the clearing of the cabin, so the arabesque decorated windows were flung wide open and pot after pot of their thriving cargo were flung out, littering the peaceful sea with a pathful of instantly rendered useless breadfruit plants. Only a few were retained to cultivate after they had settled into their chosen hideaway. Christian moved into Bligh's cabin, the final proof that his tenuous hold on the ship was permanent.

It took almost a month to reach Tubuai, a volcanic island entirely encircled by a reef, with just one break in it to the north west. The whole hazardousness of it appealed to Christian and he sent George Stewart in the cutter to sound out the entrance, checking the channel beyond had water deep enough for *Bounty* to anchor in. The dangerous expedition in this tiny craft suddenly took on a horrifying element, as masses of huge canoes hurtled through the crusted waters and surrounded the cutter, frighteningly long spears waving and crashing amongst the mob that boarded the small vessel. Stewart was woefully inadequately armed to deal with such an onslaught, but ordered the two pistols they did have to be fired; one refused to work and the other misfired. Amid the general confusion, the stunned shriek of a native struck by the wayward shot pierced the air and his friends hastily retreated, taking but one solitary jacket for his pain. Stewart reported back to *Bounty* with a wounded seaman.

Christian was unperturbed, and insisted on forging ahead with his plans to build a settlement on this island, and the next day he carefully edged *Bounty* into the strait, ironically using all the skill and knowledge William Bligh had gladly passed on to him during their voyages on Duncan Campbell's *Britannia.* Again canoes were launched from the shore and sped out to meet them, accompanied by omnipresent, baleful conch shell laments. The natives were a sight quite unseen before, wearing sashes woven from the fibres of coconuts (finished off with tassels) over red matting bound round their middles, and stuffed into the folds of the material were flinty stones, because they were always ready for war. On their heads were strange looking caps, fashioned somewhat in the shape of a beehive, 'covered with white cloth, and on the top, a bunch of black feathers from the Man of War bird'; this headgear was so well designed and strong that it 'will resist a severe blow, and a cutlass will make no impression on them.' To complete the picture, 'pearl shells' hung around their necks and they carried either a spear or a club, which they were apt to make good use of.

The curious thing was the natives, all of them men, did not go on the ship or even stay, they just made their presence known and slid away again. Another twenty four hours passed before a large deputation arrived and formally boarded *Bounty*; an elderly statesman prying into all the new and wonderous items he could discover. The sight of the snuffling, mooching, caged animals sent him reeling in disbelief; the Englishmen were later to discover the only four legged creatures the Tubuaians had any knowledge of were rats. Christian managed to communicate perfectly, using the smattering of Tahitian he had perfected during his long, lazy days prior to the mutiny, and the language was near enough for the local inhabitants to understand. Presumably it would be like an Irishman conversing with someone from Scotland; both Celtic, both with a command of English but each with their own individual traits. Tahitian served very well, and Fletcher again used another lesson learned from the expert handler of Polynesians, William Bligh. He reiterated all this conversation with plenty of presents, as the grateful old man showed his appreciation by pointedly counting the opposition.

As soon as his guests left, Christian, maybe slightly disturbed by this visit and the parting promise to return, ordered the arms and ships guns out and ready for another, more deadly barrage. It came the following day. Firstly eighteen ladies, chaperoned by five men, pulled alongside and started to serenade the seamen, who lustily allowed them aboard. Christian for once let his reputation for women slip and saw through the trick distraction and was ready with loaded guns, men and primed cannons when the main bulk of the attack arrived. Announcing their arrival with the revolting conch shell dirge, Christian stood surveying the scene, possibly weighing up the abysmal odds, twenty five men against probably 1000, excepting the added advantage of the iron magic on the lesser numbered side. As his eyes intently toured the crowd before him, he caught sight of unwarranted movement further afield and watched as an attempt was made to part a bouy from the anchor it was marking.

He barked out his order and grapeshot flew over the crowded canoes in the direction of the offenders, some falling short into the war-minded, though as yet peaceful-actioned, throng in the waters below. The luckless occupants of the high ended, ornate vessels needed no further inducement and they fled again, taking their frightened women with them. Christian urged his men into the two surviving small boats and gave chase, shots ringing out in answer to a sharp volley of stones. The locals held the upper hand throughout and when Christian landed his men, not a soul was in sight, just the abandoned canoes, though it later transpired that eleven natives had been killed. Copying Bligh's example with the Nomukian chiefs Christian towed the empty canoes back to the ship and held them hostage, planning to bargain their safe return against being allowed to settle peacefully. During the night the weather whipped up a storm, snapping the ropes that held the canoes prisoner and activating their unhindered return to the beach.

White ensigns and Union Jacks were hoisted on 30th May 1789 in the ship's boats and a party of sailors, under the watchful eye of Mr Christian, left what rapidly became known as Bloody Bay to tour round and investigate the rest of the island. Again no one was seen whenever they set foot on the land, even though a thorough search was made at each landing and plenty of presents were left in eerily empty houses. They did not realise the natives had taken to the local swamp to hide from the destructive intruders and preferred to sleep in such unhealthy conditions until the danger passed rather than risk another fatal contretemp. They received proof almost immediately that their conclusions about the strangers were correct, going down with, 'colds, agues and sore eyes, running noses,' the only reliable source these usually robust people had that they were displeasing 'Eakooa' (or Deity). The swamp could not have helped much either.

Almost the same deserted emptiness abounded the next day when the foreigners took some sick animals ashore at Bloody Bay; as they pulled the oars through the lagoon, some brave souls could be seen hauling in the canoes, but by the time *Bounty's* cutter arrived, no one was around. The creatures were disembarked and set free to hunt for any available nourishment, while the men returned to *Bounty* as she lay ready to embark upon another long sea voyage.

Fletcher Christian had favourably assessed Tubuai as his last settling place. Unfortunatley, he had discovered during his excursion a few essentials were missing and now set off on a return trip to Tahiti to collect some necessities. He wanted more livestock; animals they could breed and eat, slave labour to help build his settlement and women to keep his fellow conspiritors happy – more than likely he did not trust the Tubuian women after the diversion they had attempted. A week later they arrived in Matavai Bay again, not in the joyful jubilant frame of mind you might imagine, because during the journey strict instructions had been laid down and were only ignored at a colossal cost. Christian realised too late he could not keep his word to release the men forced to remain on *Bounty* at the mutiny, because he not only needed them to work the ship and aid the construction of his wretched settlement, they also knew the exact details of his hideaway. If they stayed on Tahiti, the chances were they would eventually be picked up and taken home to England (as he once wished for them), but the strength of a promise, even if it were extracted from them, could not be regarded as strong enough to keep him safe. The only thing left was to make them stay firmly under surveillance.

He was mainly concerned on two accounts; no one should disclose the *real* name of the island, the slightest hint of it being absolutely taboo, and secondly, any man who attempted to run from them on Tahiti was doomed to instant failure and death. Again Christian was absolutely sure of his excellent reputation amongst the Tahitians and knew how they would all rally to his cause for the price of a few nails, as they had at the beginning of the year when Churchill, Millward and Muspratt deserted.

Although equality was supposed to be normal practice, with frequent meetings to bolster Christian's decisions, when the possessions of their abandoned colleagues were divided into lots and distributed amongst the remaining men, Fletcher was not above giving the best items to his supporters. Probably he was anxious to keep those he may need to rely heavily upon for his own protection and safety as supportive as possible, or he was just using the miscellaneous bits as rewards for the way they had thus far unquestionably reinforced his actions.

It was 6th June 1789, when they anchored again in Matavai to the customary enthusiastic welcome from the natives. Inquisitive as ever, they of course wanted to know why they were back so quickly.

'Where is Bry?' they asked, to which Christian, the charlatan who has always been portrayed as being so honest, at this point of the proceedings launched into his carefully prepared lies.

'He is gone to England.' The natives were not so stupid as to believe, from the descriptions given during their last stay, that Bligh could have made England so quickly. They pushed on, 'In what ship?' Fletcher, not being one to underestimate these people, was ready for such a reaction, and carried on deeper into his fabrication.

'In Toote's ship.' It was masterful; Toote was their accepted name for Captain Cook and due to Bligh's own insistance, none of the islanders knew of their idol's demise. William's cunning was completely twisted against him. The conversation took a natural turn when they next asked, 'How came you to meet with Toote and where is he?'

'We met him at Whytootacke, (the place the Europeans then called New Holland and we now know as Australia) where he is going to live and has sent me for all those who will come and live with him, the bull and cow and as many hogs as you will send him,' Christian answered, proving what a callous, selfish and despicable blackguard he was, being prepared to take all the people possible from their homes under the deception that they would be reunited with their revered 'Toote'.

Their inquisition was completed with, 'What is become of the breadfruit?' to which Christian answered, 'He has sent it home to England with Bligh,' presumably in the missing long boat.

The Tahitian's were content with his explanations and made the most of this added ten day's trading, gladly handing over the unwanted bull and cow, left by Cook in 1777, for a miserly few red feathers, plus 460 pigs, 50 goats, numerous birds and a few cats and dogs, purchased with the precious gift of iron the islanders set so much store by. Morrison, who along with Churchill, was in charge of the equipaging, confessed he thought they had all but stripped Tahiti of stores during the six months they stayed there before, but worked out that as soon as the islanders saw the ship arrive they had hidden a great quantity of their livestock, and kept it so during the friendly half year invasion. It would appear the lively, intimate welcome was not wholeheartedly entered into by all the natives, who used the riotous scene as a diversion while driving the animals out of harms way.

Christian slipped deeper and easier into Bligh's old lifestyle, making Coleman set up his forge ashore and indulge the locals every whim (although the demand was far too great for him to keep up with), while he took on the delightful job of entertaining the chiefs on board *Bounty,* serving them wine and arrack (a potent spirit distilled from coco-palm).

A couple of incidents, displaying either a newly festered arrogance or a guilty jumpiness, arose during their stay; on 10th June William McKoy was surrounded by a crowd of natives when he was on guard and, because they did not scatter as quickly as he felt they should, he did not hesitate to shoot at them. Miraculously, no one was hurt, and the desired effect took place. Just four days later, Churchill, while on night watch, noticed a canoe coming closer to the ship and called out to them. When no one answered, he lost no time in following his ship mate's lead, and discharged his piece in their direction, content to watch them scuttle away.

By the 16th, they were ready to leave, all the trading finished, the animals safely loaded and the human stock, nine men, eight boys, ten women and a young girl, were innocently embarking on a thrilling adventure. Three of the women were to figure more acutely in the future story; Mary, wife of Thomas McIntosh, Teehuteatuaonoa, who cohabited with Alexander Smith and Mauatua, consort to Fletcher Christian. It is my personal belief that she had been one of the ladies whom he had passed the time with during their original visit, and when she saw them return and realised they were looking for women companions, probably always being one with an eye for advancement, she grasped the opportunity to raise and better herself with all the intensity of a vixen protecting her tiny cubs. Not that she was so honourably minded, leaving behind a child (or maybe more) without a backward glance. Like so many a femme fatale both before and since, she used all her womanly charms and flirted her way back into his bed and affections, to the eventual cost of any opponents, including those of her own making. He may have offered her an ultimatum, 'me or your family'; he must have known of the existence of at least one baby from when they initially knew each other, but was he ruthless enough to demand no interfering children accompanied them? Subsequent events should hold this idea up, as no babies were born to any of the couples until they were firmly settled, over a year later; or if they were they were not allowed to survive.

Already we know what an achievement a liason with a white man was for the local girls, but a god who had left the realms of being an officer and gained the dizzy heights of sole command was a prize indeed. In fact, it was the once in a lifetime chance for Mauatua to move out of her rank as a *ra'atira* and step into the shoes of a queen. It was a classic case of dazzling social climbing, just like Anne Boleyn, Wallis Simpson or Madame Du Barry. Fletcher re-christened her with a British name, choosing the one of a lady who perhaps haunted his dreams, his old love from the Christian homestead he would never see again, Isabella. Mary's proper name we do not know, but Alex Smith's lady became Jenny.

They left Tahiti, with the promise they would send Captain Cook to visit again as soon as they had settled in at Wytootacke, and put out to sea, being obliged to cut one of the cables and leave behind an anchor that had become embroiled under the bay. As they sailed they did not know they had so many people aboard, but different faces kept appearing to reveal daring stowaways intent on seeing the great elusive Cook. Probably the young girl, along with her mother, was one of these. One was actually a friend of Bligh's, Chief Hitihiti, who was to be disappointed if he thought he was on his way to being reunited with his old acquaintance. It was too late for Christian to turn around and take them back and he stressed the point they would never see their home island again, which they accepted with a solid stoicism.

A stormy passage back to Tubuai resulted in the loss of the bull, who constantly missed his footing and took many serious tumbles, the last proving fatal. His hefty, listless carcass was dumped into the sea for want of something better to do with it, though surely the obvious answer was to eat it! The loss of this bull was particularly unfortunate as they could no longer breed from the cow. The added deaths of four pigs and a goat did not really hinder their replenishment, considering the large amount of stock they had brought from Tahiti.

Reinstated in Bloody Bay, a most unexpected, though pleasing, greeting welcomed them. Canoe after native laden canoe struck out from the shore to climb aboard *Bounty* in a quiet, orderly, friendly way. No spears, no clubs, no hostility, no awful conch shells rending the air, and as a reminder of the damage they could possibly sustain they had collected the bullets that had lodged in the trees after the battle of Bloody Bay and made them into necklaces. Fletcher Christian and his companions did not realise that the sojourn to the swamp, and more especially the ill effects on their health, had left them with a greater respect for the terrible consequences combat with these strangers could result in, for one of the highest held beliefs amongst the islanders was if 'they go to war in a wrong cause they think that any sickness which befalls them at the time is sent as a punishment'.

Fletcher used all good fortune to his advantage, putting the Tahitian's forward to stretch out the hand of fellowship and soon he was in deep discussions with Tummotoa, chief of the part of the island nearest to which they were docked, and incidentially the largest of Tubuai's three divisions. He took part in a special ceremony in which he was presented with plantin trees, as tokens of peace, yava roots, baskets full of fish and fruit and cloth, by everyone in the procession – the 'royal' family, all the landed gentry, their servants and women; there was somewhere in the region of one hundred people paying homage to him. When the ritual was over, the men took all Christian's newly acquired presents out to the ship, accompanied by Tummotoa, who stayed by Fletcher's bedside all night, on his knees in prayer. As he departed the next day he carried with him some return gifts, hatchets, matting, cloth from Tahiti and the most favourite of all, red feathers. Christian was invited to choose a spot to build his colonization. He could not find anywhere in Tummotoa's district suitable for his plans and boldly strode into the adjacent area, ruled over by Tummotoa's enemy, Taroatchoa.

Eager to steal his neighbour's ally away, he welcomed Fletcher with delighted munificence, much to Tummotoa's consuming envy, who frantically attempted to 'purswade' the white man to remain in his territory. Christian insisted he would stay friends with this upset chief, who, finding his pleas fell on to deaf ears, formed a formidable faction with the third member of the islands triumvirate, chief Tinnarow. They instantly banned trading between their people and the ship, thereby drastically reducing the provisions available to the sailors. On several occasions Christian attempted to redress the matter with Tummotoa, but as soon as he was spotted approaching, the chief promptly ran away. Christian quickly gave up, having more weighty matters to worry about than trying to placate a sulky sovereign; they could still manage well enough without his aid. He had decided upon the spot where he wanted a fortification built, on the eastward side of Tubuai. *Bounty* was still riding the waves just inside the only exisiting channel through the reef at Bloody Bay, slightly to the west of the middle of the islands north side, so she had to be moved nearer to the building site. A treacherous stretch of coral infested waters lay between them and their next anchorage, and the most delicate of care was needed to progress along the narrow strip of often shallow water nestling between the reef and shore. The ship was decidedly too heavy to pass at one point and they had to lighten her load, so some booms and spars were fixed to a grapnel, heaved overboard and left to float. They did not stay there but drifted away with the fresh winds; not that Christian was worried as he already had it in mind to entirely break up the ship.

Two days after the completed four mile peregrination of 8th July, Fletcher came back from visiting the site of his dream homestead to discover John Sumner and Matthew Quintal missing. Eventually they returned and were truly amazed when he chastised them for leaving without permission; they were convinced that as they had reached the end of their nomadic existence, they were finally their 'own masters'. Ever since the mutiny Christian had carried a loaded pistol with him and did not hesitate in whisking it out of his pocket and pressing the barrel at point-blank range on 'one of their heads'; Morrison irritatingly does not tell us which one, but I believe it was Sumner, solely because he parted company from Christian as quickly as possible after this episode, whereas Quintal stayed with Fletcher until the end of his miserably short life.

'I'll let you know who is Master,' Christian informed them and sent them below to be trussed in shackles. A night of pain and discomfort gave them the chance to think their positions through and as they were full of contrition in the morning, Fletcher allowed them to be released. It would appear he also spent the night contemplating the current state of affairs, because as a direct result of this he allowed two men each night the freedom to sleep on land, with none of the hands barred from shore leave on the Sabbath. To help relations along while whichever liberated couple were mixing with the locals, Christian handed out red feathers for them to barter with, from his cabin, but soon unhappily discovered he was being taken advantage of as a sizeable quantity disappeared. His immediate reaction was to place the blame squarely on young Tom Ellison, who had continued to be devoted to Christian and had fallen into the rank of his servant, thereby giving him means, opportunity and, (along with everyone else on the ship) motive. Christian might have dismissed Churchill's chances to procure a servant in the shape of Bob Tinkler, but was not above enjoying the services of one himself.

Ellison's shirt was stripped from his back and the young lad was tied ready for a flogging, his constant denials of the crime surely becoming more desperate as he came closer to the final punishment. His cries were heeded as all around confirmed they had not seen him with any feathers which could be construed as stolen, and he was cut down before the lash got to work. The fact that his saviour (whom he had sailed with on *Britannia* and must have idolised even then, seeing as he immediately followed him into the mutiny without any qualms or hesitation), was prepared to harm him so must have soured his hero worship, coming as an almighty shock to the teenager, who was another to part company with Christian as soon as the occasion arose.

It was now the middle of July 1789, and preparations were progressing for the construction of their longed for abode. Different duties were assigned to the men; William Brown, Nelson's ex-assistant, was sent with a Tahitian to clear a piece of land and set in motion the cultivation of yams, Henry Hillbrant was the chef, William McKoy helped Joseph Coleman at his forge and Thomas Ellison and Michael Byrne were put in charge of the boats and the Tahitian boys. All the rest worked at clearing the site for the fort agreed between Christian and chief Taroatchoa, each armed, though their weapons were placed under the watchful eye of a sentry as they toiled. 18th July brought great celebrations as the first turf was turned and a Union Jack run up, they toasted their futures with an extra measure of rum and formally named the place Fort George. Taroatchoa joined in the procedure by presenting, 'Mr Christian with two young plantain trees, and two roots of yava by way of a peace offering'. The cats from Tahiti were also usefully employed, shifting the rats that invaded this peculiar piece of the Empire.

As the practicalities of their predicament took shape, what went through their minds? The mutiny had been a success? They would never be found again (to the joy of some, and sorrow of others)? Everyone back home was determined on revenge? Or nobody knew what had happened? It is doubtful if any of them came remotely near the actual truth; that their attempt at Liberty, Equality and Fraternity was vastly overshadowed by the storming of the Bastille in Paris just four days previous, triggering off the biggest mutiny in Europe. Theirs became slightly insignificant by comparison.

Uncertainty gives a great boost and work forged ahead on a proper fort, surrounded with an 18 foot wide ditch, complete with a drawbridge on the northern side (facing the beach). The ships guns were strategically placed to cover all angles of possible attack, as through trial and error, no one having the slightest idea how to create a garrison, their endeavours took on a pleasing shape. James Morrison, who had no reason to thank Christian for the predicament in which he found himself, made a point of recording; 'Nor was Mr Christian an idle spectator for he alway took a part in the most laborious part of the work.'

For over a month the work progressed unhindered, until an ominous incident began an horrific chain of events. On 25th August the male members of the Tahitian party were out procurring coconuts, when they were waylaid by a gang of Tubuaians, who almost stoned one of the men to death. The boys rushed to Fort George and hurriedly informed Christian of what was happening, who instantly gathered arms and sailors and stormed off to the rescue. Finding the Tubuaians had the upper hand over his own Polynesians, he allowed two muskets to be fired (actually, he could have pulled the trigger himself) and the attackers ran off. The next day they received reports that one of them had been killed by the shots, but no corpse was ever in evidence. Once, when they were working peacefully at the fort, terrific screams and wailing had rent the air and they had rushed straight to their guns sending the Tahitians to discover what had caused such a commotion. They discovered there was a funeral in process and it was customary for the mourners to emit revolting cries as the body was placed in the ground, while cutting open their heads and chests with shells and wiping the blood all over themselves. Had anyone actually died during the shooting, surely they would have heard the funeral.

The islanders bided their time, but eventually some of the women from Tinnarow's area came to seek out the sailors sleeping on shore, their long dark hair, entwined with fragrant flowers, falling to their waists in ringlets proving too much temptation, and the men eagerly followed them, Alexander Smith blindly entering the home of Tinnarow. Having so willingly been enticed in he was held prisoner, another minor matter Christian had to deal with. Regaining his preposterous colleague was made surprisingly easy. As soon as he came into sight, Tinnarow ran off and Fletcher followed the young lady who had offered her sweet services to Smith, and now showed the way to where he was held, straight into the house and collected his man.

Unfortunately he discovered him wearing only his shirt, the rest of his clothes (which no doubt he had compliantly shed) stolen. Pleas for their return were ignored so Christian entered the still empty house once more, took out some intriging objects which he hoped were of sentimetal value, and burnt the house down. He was correct about the clubs, spears, carved images of gods and vast collection of red fathers, Tinnarow highly valued them and made overtures of friendliness to regain them. Christian demanded not only the return of Smith's clothes but peaceful relations with the men of his district. The chief agreed and proposed a drink to seal the bargain; Fletcher declined the offer, sending Tinnarow into a rage and he stormed off. Not that his mood was connected with being snubbed. He was not able to put into practice his plan to get them all drunk on yava juice and liquidate them.

For this purpose his servants had hidden weapons amongst the basket of food they were carrying to be offered as presents, but one of the boys had spotted them and warned Fletcher, who had sent him back to the ship with orders for Coleman to prepare the guns. Those at the fort were also primed, which Tinnarow spotted and used as an excuse to induce his self-righteous anger and swift departure. Sighting their arrival at the shore, Coleman discharged a four pounder, the shock and fear causing the natives to disperse. The shot itself carried on travelling, whistling through the rafters of a nearby home just as the owner was hanging a water container on one. The poor fellow, plus everyone else who witnessed this strange phenomenon, ran from the house and would never return, convinced some psychic happening had attacked them.

Christian still pushed ahead with his settlement plans; he who could do no wrong, the spoilt young man, the darling of the crew, was adamant he could brow beat the Tubuaians into passive acceptance of his rule. He was regally attended by the family of Taroatchoa, who fed and entertained him. He returned the compliment by organising shows for them, ordering the Tahitians to perform their traditional dances rather than ask Michael Byrne to strike up the fiddle and accompany displays of the English hornpipe. He did not seem to be of a mind to project European culture, even though the fort was flying the Union Jack and bore the name of his King.

With the fort three quarters completed, Fletcher next thought of forming a village, so they could dismantle the ship, using the wood for their new homes and permanently live on shore. This news boosted a thought amongst Peter Heywood, James Morrison and George Stewart to flee to Tahiti in the cutter once the masts were out of their slots. Morrison, as boatswain, knew he could prevent them from ever being replaced by damaging the pulley system used to hoist them in and out. Once the ship was disabled, they could never be pursued; there was just one obstacle which ruined their chance of escape – the cutter was badly in need of repair and Christian had given strict instructions it was not to be touched. They could not mend it without rousing his suspicions and eventually came to bless their misfortune. Morrison explained; 'tho the passage was short and it might perhaps be made with safety in 5 or 6 days, yet had we the Chance to Meet with bad weather our Crazey boat would certainly have made us a Coffin'; if ever they let the fates of the nineteen men who left *Bounty* cross their minds, it was probably with the same negativity.

The mutineers, rapidly becoming more and more discontent with their situation, were planning mutiny yet again, though against, rather than with, the original protagonist. Not everyone was enjoying the soft solace of a Tahitian lady, making do with the local women, who frequently slept onboard *Bounty* with them (the girl who had enticed Alexander Smith decided to live on the ship, finding many of her compatriots already there), but the natives were adamant that their females would not stay on *Bounty* any longer. To be allowed contact only on shore was a harrowing predicament in which to place these matelots and they demanded Fletcher force the issue with arms, wanting him to virtually kidnap the girls before they would do any more work toward making his treasured dream a completed reality. He refused, wanting to use dialogue instead of guns. For three days the arguments wrangled, the heated discussions quickly including an increase in their grog rations. Christian objected to this with the result of the lock on the door to the spirit room being forcibly rendered useless and its contents were immediately available to them all. Christian capitulated and countermanded this act of mindless thuggery by doubling the rations.

Still they were not content and on the 10th September 1789 he summoned everyone to a general meeting and allowed them to vote on their future direction. An overwhelming majority of sixteen to nine voted for a return to Tahiti, where they wanted to quit the ship and take their chances. Fletcher's constant, enveloping dream of settling on Tubuai was turning into an overwhelming nightmare and he was forced by his own democratic pratices to give it up. Once he had landed his fellow countrymen on Tahiti, he could never return to Tubuai, because as soon as they were picked up by a ship from their own navy, the first thing they would do would be to recite all the details of their aborted adventures. Perhaps he could have played a double bluff, going back while everyone else thought it would be the last place he would go, but events during the next week soon put a stop to any such thoughts.

Definite details were proposed and agreed upon; those going ashore would take guns and ammunition, plus a share of everything general on the ship, whereas Christian and the few who remained steadfastly loyal to him would be given absolute charge of a seaworthy *Bounty*, complete, 'with her sails tackle and furniture'. Preparations got underway to stock the ship with adequate supplies, a group of the men going ashore to find all the livestock, including the cow nobody had seen since she was landed. Their decision to move came none too soon, for rumours had reached the islanders that the moat around the fort was a mass grave, and they were the ones destined for it. No longer would they remain quiet and subserviant. They were not about to allow these foreigners to exterminate them and take over their homeland. They much preferred to turn the tables and use the handy ditch to bury the troublesome strangers. When the sailors landed on the shore, they were immediately pounced upon, given a thorough thrashing and sent back to the ship to warn Mr Christian the same would happen to him.

Christian ordered their return the following day not only to complete the job, but also to quell the fractious natives. 700 spear wielding, stone bashing, club brandishing residents greeted the armed party of twenty, who were aided and abetted by thirteen Tahitians, including one of the boys, who proudly stepped out carrying the Union Jack. The Tubuaians must have sensed, rather than had any actual knowledge, that they looked somewhat like an army battalion marching into an affray. The attack was quick, the fighting hard and unruly and the instigators finally retreated, leaving the presumably unharmed vindicators to gather in their stock.

Morrison turns master of the understatement when he says, '. . . we had some reason to think that they would be troublesome' – Christian agreed, because every white man, and the excellent marksman Hitihiti, was supplied with guns and plenty of ammunition. At the fort Taroatchoa was waiting for them with vital information; Tinnarow was claiming right to any of the animals which had wandered on to his land and was not inclined to release them, provocatively placing armed guards around the catalystic creatures. Christian issued his orders steadily and calmly; Taroatchoa's Tubuaians, who were friendly to his cause, were to surrender their clubs to his Tahitians and stay out of harms way in the fort, and one armed Polynesian was to walk between two armed sailors. He led the disciplined crocodile in silence through the wood, heading for Tinnarow's district, every bone and muscle taut and attentive, watching and listening for any signs of danger. It came all too soon.

Marching through a patch lined with bushes, Burkitt heard a movement in the undergrowth and went to investigate. A spear thrust through his left side, his Tahitian companion flattened the snipper with his club, grasping the offending spear, and the onslaught began. Hundreds upon hundreds of furious, tempestuous savages, howling and screaming, appeared from all directions in a full-scale attack. Christian rallied his men to face the barrage, each protecting a slightly different angle from his colleagues in an attempt to confront every possible line of invasion, as they shot into the ever increasing swarm of dusky skinned assailants. The front runners dropped, but still more kept coming forward, all the time baying like banshees, prolonging the attack.

Bounty's heroes broke ranks and made for an incline in the landscape behind them, the Tahitians providing covering fire for this retreat with spears captured from the enemy, before bringing up the rear. The furious warriors followed and suffered many more casualties, who brazenly rushed into the hail of shot flowing down the slight hillside where Christian's men had reassembled. Other native soldiers had taken stock of the situation and put their brothers foolishness to good use. While the sailors attention was duly diverted, they stole around the back and descended upon their foe under cover of a massive clump of bushes growing further up the side of the hillock. Another tactical retreat was called for, with the Tahitians suffering many wounds and Christian himself falling foul of his own bayonet, and a patch of taro ground only 200 yards away was picked upon as a desirable battle ground. In strict formation they covered each others tracks, one line tightly firing upon the enemy as their mates ran to a position to return the favour, and entrenched themselves behind the irrigation banks.

Although the persecutors appeared to be massed together as an unruly mob, it became more and more apparent that they were actually formed into companies of about 18 or 20 men under the leadership of their own individual major, who urged them on to greater glories. One of these was so enthusiastic, waving his hands and rallying his warriors to such a degree he made himself a standing target, and was summarily picked off. The volley of stones and spears continued to fly and sting, but natives filled with lead were becoming much more common, the bombardment subsided and those with breath left disappeared.

In the lull that followed, Burkitt, who had continued with his soldiering despite sustaining his battered ribs, grew faint and Skinner, who had accidentally immobilised his gun, took him back to the ship to recuperate. The rest waited quite some time before venturing out from the taro ground, but subsequently they crawled out to leisurely survey the gruesome sight of their mass annihilation. The Tahitians eagerly gathered as many of the spoils of war as they could carry, especially the spears and clubs, though one of the lads rather hoped he might be able to make a collection of jaw bones, cut from the corpses littering the countryside, which he planned to display around the ship. Permission was denied, but he was not inclined to leave behind such valuable prizes until his own life hung in the balance.

The whole party moved back to the fort (where Skinner rejoined them) and after reassuring their friends that all were well, they completed what they had originally set out to do, collect in their stock, as if the raging battle was just a minor tussle. It was more than that surely, leaving 66 Tubuaians dead and numerous more injured. The mission was a success, even the cow was relocated, only to be butchered and eaten next morning. That evening a young chief called Taroameiva arrived on *Bounty* with two of his companions and gave news of the previous day's excitement; Tinnarow's brother had been amongst the dead, slain by Fletcher. Any possible chance of playing his double bluff ended right there. The three Tubuaians were fearful of the reprisals Tinnarow might bring down upon them due to their friendship with the Europeans and asked to sail with them. Christian was delighted to welcome aboard three such willing hands.

During the next two days, water barrels were filled, provisions stored away, plenty of animals left (possibly as a vague form of compensation) and with more ease than when they moved in, they made their steady and light way back to the opening in the reef near Bloody Bay. Once out into the Pacific, they discovered *Bounty* was too flimsy to handle and poured sea water in to keep her buoyant, and sailed back to Tahiti.

Not Tubuai, that was the answer.

CHAPTER SIX

'Hope on, Hope ever'

Bounty left Tubuai with about 3000 inhabitants intact, and enough disease to ensure the population was reduced to 300 within forty years.

After three days at sea they pulled into the island of Mehetia and shared out all the previously agreed paraphernalia and stowed them in the great cabin, until anchoring in Matavia Bay once more a couple of days later. A long laborious haul followed as men and chattels were ferried to the shore in the one boat fit for sailing. A surf ran high, hindering progress, as Thomas Burkitt, Michael Byrne, Charles Churchill, Joseph Coleman, Thomas Ellison, Peter Heywood, Henry

Hillbrant, Thomas McIntosh, John Millward, William Muspratt, James Morrison, Charles Norman, Richard Skinner, George Stewart, John Sumner and Matthew Thompson made their relieved way ashore to start building new lives yet again. The natives bobbed around the ship in their canoes as usual and offered to help, but the white men preferred to travel in their unstable old cutter rather than in the impressive, expertly handled local crafts. It was not until all the general essentials, including a pig of iron, a grindstone, a copper kettle, and three gallons of wine each were safely landed that the truly useful items were allowed ashore; the arms and ammunition.

Fletcher Christian was torn assunder; he wanted to restock, especially the water barrels, but also wanted to get away just as quickly as he could. It was not until the best part of the day was over before everything was settled, with a little last minute haggling over some saws both parties wanted to claim; Christian solved the problem by keeping them himself but gave the group staying in Tahiti spyglasses and a compass to barter with. He also left sails and canvas and the precious icons stolen from Tinnarow's home prior to it being fired, as well as offering to leave the swivel guns, though this last donation was summarily refused.

He went ashore in the twilight, well aware that the true story of the events leading up to this third visit was now circulating, and he was fearful of the consequences piqued chiefs might try to render upon him. As soon as they had arrived news reached them of the visit of another ship, the *Mercury,* whose captain had dispelled the myth of Cook still being alive (presenting them with a copy of Zoffany's famous painting depicting all the gory details of his death). Puzzlement and confusion then abounded over the second arrival of the *Bounty* under the command of 'Titreano'; this pronunciation was the closest the islanders could get to 'Christian', but how was Captain Cox to equate the two, when no-one even knew of Fletcher's promotion to second-in-command? The realization that the Whytootackee colony did not exist must have given rise to many fears for the safety of the Tahitians who sailed away with *Bounty*, plus bitter disappointment that they would never see Cook again and all Titreano's promises were nonsense!

Christian solicited one last favour from his deserting crew. He required help with filling the water barrels, so he and his followers could leave within the next few days to search out an uninhabited island on which to set up another home. They were happy to oblige and Fletcher returned to Bounty, after a brief conversation with Peter Heywood and George Stewart. In this, his last communication with them, he confirmed their innocence and urgently told them to surrender themselves to the first British ship to arrive at Tahiti, thereby taking the full burden of the blame for their predicament on his strong shoulders. He passed on as much experience and advice as he had, before, finally, leading his fellow Manxman aside and left Peter with a message he only ever repeated to the Christian family.

An ideal situation presented itself back at *Bounty.* She was overrun with cheerful and loving natives Fletcher could certainly use in his adventure ahead, so, with the help of Ned Young, he cut the cable of yet another anchor (to avoid the activity and noise necessary to raise it) and quietly allowed *Bounty* to slip out to sea. Nobody either on land or water expected this course of action and by the following morning when the landed crew members arrived back at the beach, although still visible, she was fast becoming a mere speck on the horizon and had completely disappeared by noon.

Perhaps Heywood and Stewart were not as surprised as the rest to find they were no longer needed to assist with the watering duties, and probably with a philosophical shrug of the shoulders they turned from the waters edge and set about creating a temporary lifestyle for themselves. The others followed suit; Morrison and Millward re-establishing an old acquaintance with Matavai's chief, Poeno, whose invitation to stay was readily accepted. The rest of the men scattered throughout the districts of Matavai and Oparre, doing exactly the same, looking up old friends and settling with them.

News reached them of another English sailor who had settled on the island and Morrison, who became the accepted 'leader' of those who sought guidance, sent Churchill and Millward to Tyarrabboo, a district in the south he was visiting, to find out more about him. They also called on Matte, the local chief, with presents, where they told the full story of the mutiny to Matte's brother, Wyetooa, who was once Thomas Hayward's *tyo,* who had severed the cable at Oparre and determined to save his degraded friend. His one reaction to the story was he, 'cursed Mr Christian for not killing Lieut Bligh which he said he would do himself if ever he came to Taheite'. Bligh did, and left again in complete safety.

The mysterious white man was called John Brown (the third Brown to appear in the story; apart from William Brown the botanist's mutineering assistant, another William Brown was also mentioned in the muster list, although this twenty-three year old volunteer was transferred to the *Ariel* – before *Bounty* left Portsmouth). This latest Brown, who had arrived with the *Mercury,* was a constantly drunken troublemaker, so much so that all his ship mates were heartily tired of him, including Captain Cox who welcomed a letter asking permission for him to remain behind when they sailed. Eagerly he answered in the affirmative, believing in the change of heart that left this alcoholic wanting to live on a dry island with his bible, and readily supplied him with a few articles he requested. A month later the purged sinner found himself sought out by two men who were just as recalcitrant as he, plus they had an almost inexhaustible supply of liquor, and his grand designs fell by the wayside.

In Oparre, Morrison took all the men to pay their compliments to the young chief, Tu. Going through the ceremony of bearing their heads and shoulders that Bligh had refused to give credence to, they presented him with the images stolen from the Tubuaians, cloth, iron work and the highly valued red feathers. In return they each received from the local priest a plantin tree, a pig or fowl and a long, long speech of welcome.

All the formalities over and due respect made, they settled down into their enforced though enchanted existence in their own peculiar way. Peter Heywood busied himself with compiling a dictionary of the Tahitian language, Millward enjoyed the delightful company of one of his host's wives and most of them set about establishing a direct line of descendants. Churchill and Thompson went even further searching out higher and greater glories. Bored with the over abundant pleasures of the flesh and palate, Thompson took to raping a very unwilling, very young girl in the woods. He was given a thorough beating from her brother, who left him unconscious. Coming round he returned to his hut, only to find it surrounded by natives. Sore and angry, he fired his musket into the crowd, the indiscriminate bullet killing both a child and the father who cradled it in his arms.

Thompson and a small gang of brother renegades, Charles Churchill, William Muspratt, Thomas Burkitt, John Sumner and John Brown, decided it might be expedient to move on and they packed up their belongings from Point Venus and headed down south for Tyarraboo. What a welcome boon they were with their guns and potent ammunition and Churchill found a content *tyo* in the chief (presumably Matte). When his friend died, Churchill was hailed as his successor; perhaps Wyetooa had already passed on, explaining why he did not carry out his threat to kill William Bligh, though judging by his extreme devotion to Europeans he could just as easily have been the first to proclaim Churchill the new King. That does not, however, explain away the looking over of any other family members, especially if Matte had sons, so perhaps the persuasive muskets were applied by an overtly ambitious Master-at-Arms.

Whether subdued by force or charm, the people of Tyarrabboo peacefully accepted their latest chief's rule until the day Tom Burkitt heard a gun shot from Churchill's home. He raced to find out what had happened and found Matthew Thompson standing in the doorway reloading a smouldering musket and Churchill's corpse slumped inside the house, a bullet having exploded through him from back to front.

'I have done him,' explained Thompson. His gun had been stolen on Churchill's orders, which was the worse thing any of these fractious men could lose, and he had gone to retrieve his property. Did blind rage, cold vengeance or undesigned accident cause the fatal shot to rip into its victim? The reason was immaterial for it had to be vindicated; the crowd that had gathered lulled Thompson into a false sense of security by acclaiming him chief, but as with every lull a storm was about to break. Thompson was rugby tackled to the ground by the heftiest man there while others threw a plank across his prone body, forcibly immobilizing him as his attacker methodically hammered his brains out with a stone. Never again would he rape a young and defenceless, terrified girl.

During this time, on the northern coast, Morrison had become frustrated at the thought of having to sit back and wait for a presumed rescuer, and decided on a plan of action. Taking carpenter Tom McIntosh into his confidence he detailed his idea of building a ship to take them back to England, wanting to give the impression of having escaped the mutineers clutches and fled back in all innocence to safety. Morrison felt secure enough to adopt this attitude, having noticed as Bligh left the ship that he was not included in a verbal list of names, who were all threatened with retribution. However, it is amazing that Ellison, Hillbrant, Skinner and Millward, who must have been less confident in receiving a warm welcome home, also joined in with the boat building.

The word was spread amongst the natives that this ship was to be used solely for fishing and exploring Tahiti's coastline; this fabrication was to allay any fears the Tahitian's may have harboured about losing the recently returned weapons, and potential mercenaries. If they had even the smallest suspicion they were planning to disappear again, at best Morrison and his team could expect unimaginable hindrance; thinking of the worst would recall memories of nightmarish scenes from Tubuai.

Work began in November 1789, and they became as busy as when they were building Fort George. Trees were felled and sawn into timber, Coleman set up a forge to supply as much metal work as possible and everyone involved fell into a neat routine of long and arduous toil. It took months of dedication and improvisation (she was caulked with breadfruit plant gum) but finally a thirty foot, two masted schooner was launched with cider and solemnly christened *Resolution.* A clever, if paradoxical, touch, showing respect for Cook, whom the natives were mourning, while commemorating the ship that first took William Bligh to Tahiti.

The biggest problem for Morrison was finding suitable sails, and he had to conduct several experiments before deciding to use locally woven matting. They must have put the spare sails Fletcher Christian left with them to some other use. This last challenge overcome, *Resolution* was tried, tested and not found at all wanting – she handled beautifully.

In September 1790 she saw active service, becoming involved in conflicts breaking out between the different districts. Oparre's Tu (and father Tynah) enlisted the aid of *Resolution* and her crew, who indulged them by assisting with troop movements. Tynah's tactics of attacking both by land and sea, never before tried on Tahiti, triumphed and Tu was accompanied on a royal progression of victory around the island by armed Englishmen.

Six months after the outbreak of hostilities a celebration banquet was interrupted by ominous news. A large ship had docked in Matavai Bay.

It must surely be the greatest of ironies that the ship sent, 'to recover the . . . armed vessel and to bring in confinement to England . . . Fletcher Christian and his Associates, or as many of them as had survived and he (the Captain) might be able to apprehend, in order that they might be brought to codign Punishment,' was called *Pandora*.

The Ancient Greeks would have us believe that the first woman placed here on Earth was a beautiful creation by Zeus; a gorgeous lady fashioned out of clay at his bidding by Hephaestus, bestowed with gifts by all the other Gods and Goddesses and named Pandora. She was sent to ensnare Epimetheus, the brother of Prometheus, as part of Zeus's plan to revenge himself on the whole human race, because Prometheus had supposedly created mankind out of clay and stolen fire from the heavens for them to use. This displeased Zeus so much that he had chained Prometheus to a rock and allowed vultures to feed from his liver, but fortunately for him, it was restored again by night. As this despicable deed had failed, Zeus decided to use subtler methods and hence Pandora was created. She married Epimetheus and they could have lived happily together, except for a box Zeus had given her. He expressly ordered her not to open it, but the temptation became too great for this lovely lady to bear and one fateful day she swung aside the lid. All the ills and misfortunes that afflict us to this very day flew out, forever beyond her reach and, although she valiantly fought to restore them, as she closed the cover, all that remained was hope.

* * *

On page two of '*The Times*', Friday 19th March, 1790 we are informed that, 'A frigate of 24 guns is ordered got ready immediately at Portfmouth [sic], to go to the South Seas, on account of the late advices from that quarter'. The Admiralty were naturally anxious to regain their property and inflict justice upon the evil mutineers as quickly as they could, so *Pandora* was 'got ready' and sailed late in October, 1790. She was Commanded by the forty-eight-year-old Captain Edward Edwards, who had already remorselessly quelled a mutiny of his own during his career afloat, and therefore surely had the experience to deal with William Bligh's rebels. He was accompanied by a detachment of marines and a newly promoted 3rd Lieutenant, Thomas Hayward, Midshipman from the late *Bounty,* who was plainly an excellent choice to identify his ex-messmates and other sundry sailors.

What was eventually to become a very fateful journey, began long and inconsequential indeed; having rounded Cape Horn without any problems, they began the wearisome task of calling in at island after island for signs of their prey. They even sailed close to Pitcairn Island but discounted it as a deserted, barren piece of rock, until finally they came within the deep, seductive waters of Matavai Bay, Tahiti and dropped anchor on 17th March, 1791. During their long voyage the armourers were, 'busily employed in making knives and iron work to trade with the savages' in return for information about their ultimate quest, but suddenly they were no longer required; men from *Bounty* quietly offered themselves up into the hands of their captors. Little did these exiled British sailors realise when sighting the man-o'-war from Tahiti's luscious landscape that, rather than containing rescuers she carried gaolers, and they rushed into the warm surf in a madcap race to be the first to reach her.

This dubious honour was awared to Joseph Coleman, who had plunged into the water and started swimming long before *Pandora's* anchor had made contact with Matavai's coral. Peter Heywood arrived soon after him via a native canoe, and was as stunned as Coleman to receive a cold and inhospitable welcome. Another canoe brought George Stewart and he joined his friends under armed guard as soon as he stepped aboard *Pandora's* timbers. Bewilderment must have flooded through these three's sensations after the initial euphoria of spotting a British ship on the horizon, as they were marched down to Edwards' cabin. Knowing themselves to be innocent, hope probably rallied for a moment when they heard of Hayward's presence, but he bewilderingly pleaded ignorance of his one time ship mates circumstances and worsened the situation with his 'contemptuous look', stirring Peter Heywood into bitterness; he remarked how he hoped Hayward would, 'be able to vindicate his conduct,' as Edwards ordered the three itinerant *Bounty* men to be clasped in irons below.

The news of another English ship having arrived at the island flew around Tahiti to the ears of those whose desire to return home was not quite so acute as those poor unfortunates who were even then languishing in chains in *Pandora's* hold. Most of them fled to the mountains, leaving James Morrison, Thomas Ellison and Charles Norman to rush aboard *Resolution* and make for the high seas, as two boats from *Pandora,* one led by Hayward, arrived to arrest their progress. A full scale chase was on!

For all of one crazy March day they rowed, tacked and sailed the ship's pinnace and launch, carefully picking a path through the reef until darting along a channel between two homicidal looking pieces of ragged coral and blessedly hitting the open sea, in the futile hope of gaining ground on a schooner of about 16 tons, until darkness fell and forced Hayward to take his crew back to land, where they rested overnight before returning the following morning to the ship. Here he discovered more manacles had been brought into employ; Richard Skinner and Michael Byrne had also arrived voluntarily.

Poor unfortunate Michael Byrne, the near sightless fiddle player, had just the previous night finally received the news from local natives that he had been longing to hear since being put ashore by the *Bounty's* newly appointed commander; a British man-o'-war had mercifully arrived to take him home. Immediately he had set out on a long and hazardous journey that took him roughly half way across the island during the dark hours, while Hayward slept. Patently it did not make any odds to him what time of day it was as he always had to contend with his twilight vision, and probably explains why he had arrived in the early hours of the morning. Richard Skinner had clambered aboard of his own free will a little sooner, though presumably wished he had not when he personally learned of the greeting afforded to *Bounty's* crew by his fellow countrymen.

It was also during this visit that Hayward learnt of the existence of the elusive John Brown, who had boarded *Pandora* as well, though he was the only white man to escape the irons in the hold. His business aboard was to report the latest grains of knowledge concerning the whereabouts and progress of the schooner and her compliment, and thus ingratiate himself with the masters of those who were running amock on land with muskets and cutlasses.

The information Brown so willingly imparted to the punitive Edwards was that the *Resolution* had landed some eighteen miles away at Paparra Bay during the night. This was perfectly true, as Morrison and his companions had no wish to evade the recently arrived visitors; in actual fact they had been trying to sail out to *Pandora* when Hayward had begun his fruitless pursuit the day before. Their sole intention was to avoid interception and arrive of their own accord rather than under compulsion. From Paparra they moved inland and began a long trek across the island until they chanced upon 2nd Lieutenant Robert Corner and companions fast asleep in their launch. Edwards had dispatched these men from *Pandora* to search out the *Resolution,* but, as it was two o'clock in the morning and they were worn out, Corner allowed them to rest, as it looked as if they were in for a very busy day. Little did they expect their quarry to wake them up and peacefully surrender themselves, but this is exactly what Morrison, Ellison and Norman did.

Leaving them well bound and in the care of the master's mate, Corner set off with his marines towards the mountains in search of the last remaining few mutineers who were in hiding, when the ever spiteful Hayward arrived along with supersleuth Brown. The three reluctant fugitives protested their innocence and expounded on their desire to gain a passage home, but Hayward treated them exactly the same as he had the others, with starchy contempt.

I have wondered whether Brown felt any guilt in his actions, having worked, eaten, laughed, slept alongside these men for the past eighteen months, and would like to conclude he did, but his next actions disappointingly dispel all doubt. Along with Tom Hayward (who ordered the prisoners to be despatched back to the *Pandora*) and his marines, Brown delved into the thick density of the island undergrowth in hopes of catching up with Corner. A long hard slog followed as they advanced through the stiffling heat, beating their way through the solid forests as they continued onwards and upwards; all but Brown must have melted in their heavy uniforms. The natives ultimately came to their rescue and directed them to the mutineers' sanctuary, where the darkness revealed the dim outlines of sleeping men. Not completely knowing whether they had reached their rainbow's end or not, Brown performed his last Judas kiss; gently creeping forward he felt their toes, knowing that those of the natives were more widely spread than those on the feet of men used to wearing shoes. Confirming that these people were indeed those they sought, he passed the onus over to Hayward, who left them alone a little while longer, before attacking the next morning. Again, no resistance was forthcoming and the rest of the surviving mutineers who had opted to reside on Tahiti were apprehended. Thus Thomas Burkitt, Henry Hillbrant, John Millward, William Muspratt, Thomas McIntosh and John Sumner joined their old colleagues on board *Pandora*.

Captain Edward Edwards was not convinced about the security of his prisoners and sought to inflict a greater discomfort upon them. He instructed his carpenters to construct a wooden cell, a roundish structure on the quarter-deck measuring approximately eleven feet in length by eighteen feet wide, into which the prisoners were forced to enter by a scuttle of eighteen to twenty inches square cut into the roof, that was immediately bolted and secured after them. Two nine inch scuttles were also incorporated in the architect's design to allow some kind of ventilation, but even this primitive type of air conditioning did not stop the maggots filling the filthy water that ran through this hell hole to the scuppers. Any form of communication, in either English or Tahitian, was forbidden, even with the sailors, including the compassionate surgeon George Hamilton, who tried so hard to tend to the sickness caused by their inhumane treatment, but who was basically ineffectual due to the orders of his commander.

Another disappointment to Edwards was his failure to find the arch criminal Fletcher Christian; he questioned local chiefs almost to the point of interrogation to discover where *Bounty* had sailed to, but could only gather that she had left Tahiti a year and a half previously and nobody knew where she was bound; even Fletcher himself did not at that time know. One small piece of fortune did come his way however, when he found an anchor Christian had been forced to leave behind; here at least was some part of the ship he was instructed to find and so important to him, that it was hauled aboard and very firmly secured to the deck.

Pandora remained in Matavai Bay some weeks longer with her precious human cargo firmly installed in their new abode, while fresh provisions were collected for the voyage home and final checks were made around the island to ensure that no mutineer had escaped the dragnet, and it was during this hiatus that a very romantic, though sad, episode in this whole affair was played out.

Non-mutineer Midshipman George Stewart, the Scotsman whose family had afforded a great deal of hospitality to William Bligh during his stay in the Orkneys, had hopelessly and exquisitely fallen in love with a local girl, whom he called Peggy as her own name was totally unpronounceable. They had lived together in total bliss as man and wife and out of their love had produced a darling little girl, Charlotte, who was still just a babe-in-arms when the *Pandora* arrived at Matavai. During the men's incarceration in the cell on deck (which they lost no time in nicknaming '*Pandora's* Box') the wives, girlfriends and children were allowed to converse with their beloved ones through the vents, but this was such a traumatic experience for Peggy, she, in true Tahitian fashion, wailed and mutilated herself, and a very distraught George had to beg his captors to take her from the ship; a request that had to be forcibly executed as she struggled to stay as close to her white man as she possibly could. He was surely trying to prevent her from having any further cause to inflict such atrocities upon herself, but I do not actually believe she did cease, as she would have been just as miserable and disconsolate at not being near him. At least his suffering was no longer added too by having to listen to her desolation without being able to reach out and comfort her.

On 8th May, 1791 *Pandora* weighed anchor and gracefully slipped away from Tahiti, with fifteen extra men; John Brown had decided to accompany them home. Peggy must have felt so totally bereft as she watched the British ship slowly disappear over the horizon, taking her only reason for living further and further out of her reach. Even their baby could not console her and just two short months later, wretched and despondent, she died of a broken heart.

The heat became more and more unbearable in '*Pandora's* Box', vermin from unusable hammocks added to the discomfort of the men already prevailed upon by maggots and the stench from 'the two necessary tubs', not forgetting the manacles which had accompanied them from the hold were fixed so tightly that the skin was torn from their wrists. *Pandora's* voyage continued to peruse the South Sea islands, therefore remaining in the hotter hemisphere much longer than necessary, but Edwards was a man possessed and he anxiously searched for the missing mutineers for as long as was feasible.

Eventually, he had to admit defeat and finally charted a course for more familiar waters. They had roamed the Pacific for three months since leaving Tahiti and had to deliver their prisoners, so, being north of the Fijian islands, headed towards the Endeavour Straits. To reach these straits, the Great Barrier Reef has to first be crossed.

Sitting in the comfort of our own living rooms watching television, this stretch of water may look beautiful with its delightful marine life and pretty pink coral, but in reality it was a dangerous and hazardous part of the world with nasty undercurrents fighting for the same space below the surface, pulling and tugging one against the other. Even today with all our modern and sophisticated technology, it is still desirable to treat this reef with delicate caution, but back in 1791 a situation almost uncomprehensible existed when very few people had heard of the Great Barrier much less visited and found a way through it. It did not come by its name lightly!

Pandora found herself pinned against this notorious reef near what is now known as Cape York, Northern Queensland, on the evening of 28th August, 1791 with no apparent way forward. Edwards ordered the boats out to search for a through passage, while he stood off. The launches remarkably found what they were after; a channel to open water, quickly reporting back to the Captain, who decided to wait until the following morning, as nightfall was rapidly descending upon them. He now had to stop and haul the long boats back on board. This was a very tricky and perilous manoeuvre requiring many hands, even in broad daylight, when suddenly, during all the heaving and panting and pulling, a squall unexpectedly sprang up to surprise them.

They did not stand a chance. With no sail up, she was driven straight onto the jagged, brittle coral, her side torn to pieces, her rudder ripped right out from its setting. One of the cannons lurched free from where it was lashed in place and shattered the life out of one of the sailors as it hurtled across the deck, while a spar fell from the rigging and killed another of the ratings. Chaos and quickwits ensued, as the pumps were brought into use and all through the night the men fought to save themselves from a one-way journey to Davy Jones's locker. As the fight became more desperate, Coleman, McIntosh and Norman (all three named by Bligh as having been, 'detained against their inclinations' on board *Bounty*) were freed from their chains and brought out to help work the pumps. The frantic race against the elements continued well into the early hours of 29th August, until one of the pumps could no longer stand the strain and gave up on them; the beginning of the end had dawned and eleven hours after first striking the reef, *Pandora* was allowed to rest her weary bones on the seabed.

During this time, the inhabitants of the Box were confused and frightened, not knowing at first what was happening. As soon as the situation became clear to them, they summoned up some deeply hidden form of strength and loosened their chains, but Edwards ordered them to be replaced tighter than before, coupled with orders to the sentries to shoot if any more movements were detected. Their position seemed helpless and the hope that was left in the original Pandora's Box nearly flew straight out of the scuttles, especially when, in answer to their desperate pleas not to be forgotten, the Master-at-Arms cheerfully snarled at them, 'Never fear my boys, we'll all go the hell together!'

Because so many boats were in the water at the time of the wreck, most of the ship's compliment were saved, but *Pandora* managed to take thirty-five companions with her. Surgeon George Hamilton later recalled, 'The crew had just time to leap overboard, accompanying it with a most dreadful yell. The cries of the men drowning in the water was at first awful in the extreme; but as they sank, and became faint, it died away by degrees.' What an horrendous memory to carry through life and haunt your dreams with.

An answer to the prayers of the almost forgotten prisoners was suddenly, miraculously forthcoming; at the last possible moment the keys to their shackles fell between the uneven planks, and most of them were able to once again free their aching limbs from the metal instruments of torture. The beaten timbers hurried further towards their final resting place, when the boatswain's mate heeded the frenzied cries of the still trapped men and paused long enough to shoot back the bolt and remove the gratings. This enabled thirteen to scramble out; German Henry Hillbrant stayed to meet his maker. Having seen Edwards swimming out to the pinnace they knew some kind of survival might be open to them so jumped into the greedy waters, some unhappily remaining firmly handcuffed and shackled in leg irons. James Morrison recorded he was in the water for an hour and a half before being hauled aboard a boat and transported to the cay about three miles from the wreck, where all the other survivors had gathered. He was one of ten prisoners to escape a watery grave; Richard Skinner and John Sumner drowned, allowing them to witness George Stewart's reunion with his treasured Peggy.

Ninety-nine shattered men sat under the relentless sun; eighty-nine were permitted to errect makeshift tents out of rescued spare sails while the remaining ten were treated with indifference and scorn. They were, of course, the prisoners. Peter Heywood later explained their predicament in a letter to his mother, saying; 'The only shelter we had was to bury ourselves up to the neck in the burning sand, which scorched the skin entirely off our bodies, for we were quite naked, and we appeared as if dipped in large tubs of boiling water.' Matters were worsened by their skin having lost its weatherbeaten immunity to the sun due to spending five solid months under the cover of *Pandora's* Box, from which they emerged pasty, pale, wan and terribly white.

Booby birds and turtles were the only offerings in the provisions line and, beside, they manifestly could not stay there indefinitely, so eventually a flotilla of four boats containing all ninety-nine men retraced the path of William Bligh's launch and made their way to Coupang. For the second time in two years Thomas Hayward pulled into the Dutch settlement on Timor in an open boat, half starved and thoroughly bedraggled and dishevelled, having twice lost his original passage only part way through their designated voyages. He could well have been considered as an unlucky omen by the superstitious Navy men of the eighteenth century considering he finally ended his days at the bottom of the China Sea, having drowned during a typhoon.

So we leave our villains and heroes, languishing on the island of Timor until finding a passage back to England. As for *Pandora,* she lay one hundred and ten feet under the sea, easing herself comfortably into the soft and cosy, sandy bed and snuggled down slightly on her side to a long and peaceful sleep. One hundred and sixty-eight years passed before her Prince Charming came to wake her, not with a kiss but an Orion Anti-Submarine Aircraft.

Diver and film-maker Ben Cropp and naturalist Steve Domm prevailed upon the Royal Australian Air Force to assist them with their search for *Pandora,* and they obliged with their Orion which contained a magnetomoter, a piece of equipment akin to a metal detector. The RAAF discovered *Pandora* in 1977, she was immediately declared an historical site and left alone for a further eighteen months.

The proof that this soggy mass of derelict timber really was *Pandora,* required by the Australian government before they would give their blessing to an expedition, was finally forthcoming. Cropp discovered a pintle (a bolt used to secure the rudder) bearing the number 24 punched into the metal, the name 'Forbes' and a row of arrows, all details which could only be pertinent to *Pandora*! The 24 referred to the amount of guns she carried, Forbes was the supplier of fittings and the arrows donated property of the British government. Under the guidance and auspices of Ron Coleman, Curator of Marine Archaeology at Queensland Museum, a foraging pilgrimage to dredge and plunder *Pandora* swung into action. The best find initially was George Hamilton's watch, lying just four inches below the seabed with the glass completely unscathed. Even the mechanics were all intact and this example of one of the earliest time-pieces to include a second hand and stop-watch control, is now in near perfect working order.

A bigger expedition was called for and on 7th October 1986 a team of forty enthusiastic divers arrived for a six week stay with the *Sir Walter Raleigh,* flagship of Operation Raleigh, who readily agreed to help with the amazing search for artefacts and willingly donated time, manpower and equipment, including a desperately needed decompression chamber to combat the terrible effects of 'the bends'. Intrepid explorer extraordinaire and perfect gentleman, Colonel John Blashford-Snell, leader of Operation Raleigh and almost a latter-day Indiana Jones (minus hat and whip alas), to whom I am greatly indebted for all my information, kindly explained in rich, resonant, authoritative tones (coupled at times with a barely concealed chuckle and definite twinkle in his eye) details of his time with the *Pandora* project.

The accoutrements required to ensure the safety and success of their endeavours were astronomical. Apart from the decompression chamber, they had a huge diving platform (called the *David Gestetner*), which was an inflatable, landing craft that came from Liverpool, the *Prince Harry* and the *Prince William,* plus many other Avon boats, a small sea plane helping them and their brigantine *Zebu* taking out stores and supplies from the shore. There were over a hundred people actually involved in it, plus a land base, so this was an extremely big undertaking. All of these precautions were extremely necessary mainly due to three overriding factors; the depth at which the ship lay, (one hundred and ten feet is very near the maximum to which normal divers go), the strong currents that contributed towards *Pandora's* original downfall were still very much in evidence and there were lots and lots of sharks interested in what was going on.

Colonel Blashford-Snell took great delight in recounting the time an enormous dorsal fin was spotted just as they were preparing to dive. Everyone stood and gasped – at two feet out of the water it looked exactly like the opening scene in the film *Jaws*. The fin's owner, an inquisitive shark, came right along side the ship and cheerfully bumped the inflatable boat with her nose as the onlookers watched in wide eyed amazement, when suddenly one of the girls in the party recognised it as a whale shark, a completely harmless, toothless variety of the species. Having realised that all was well, this fearless young lady, Jasmina Hilton (ex-actress and excellent diver), leapt overboard straight onto the huge fish's back and joyfully went for a ride. Forty-two foot long Nellie, as they named the shark, became a pet and often visited them, sometimes bringing a friend with her.

Others, like bonswhalers and tiger sharks, were less welcome, though the really dangerous great whites that constantly visit the coast of Australia were mercifully missing, while other creatures of the deep gathered around to join in the merriment. Australian Army sausages were fed to delightfully tame potato cod, who took the meat straight from the crew's hands with a disgusting schlurp as the morsal disappeared from sight, rather like going down a drain. Another connoisseur of the sausage was a giant Moray eel who, at over seven feet long, would plant a kiss on the nose of anyone trusting enough to allow him! He now stands guard over the galley stove, a murky square object perched upon the foredeck where once the old salt's nourishment was prepared and water was distilled for the surgeon's useage.

Such pleasantries could turn into some very frightening situations with a devastating turn of speed, as clement weather whipped up into terrifying storms. In one week alone three days diving were frustratingly lost as winds of twenty-five knots whipped the seas into waves of three meters in height, yet the most terrible of tragedies happened during a peaceful, calm night; young Neil Carmichael disappeared without trace while on watch. This hazardous, adventurous undertaking was the chance of a life time for so many of the young Operation Raleigh members, but involved a great deal of dedication and self-motivation. The divers were prevailed upon to work long and arduous hours whilst activity on board the *Sir Walter Raleigh* was at its peak; everyone had their own specific job and was working with a ferocious intensity.

Way down below the ship's hull more energetic deeds were taking place. A giant vacuum cleaner type of contraption was sucking the sand clear from *Pandora's* well preserved ribs, to reveal many fascinating eighteenth century articles. No one is quite sure whether she was carrying chemicals aboard, but some sort of force field seems to have set up around the wreck, which means there was very little coral growth on the objects that were found with the help of the ship's plans, acquired from the Admiralty in London. These plans enabled them to determine exactly what part they were in, and they deliberately made straight for the Captain's and other officers cabins thinking those would contain the most interesting pieces. How right they were. In

Captain Edward Edwards' quarters were found dozens of inkwells, Colonel Blashford-Snell presumed, 'he must have been an intrepid writer', hour glasses with which he used to measure the speed of the ship, handles from his sea chest, pieces of sextants, wine glasses, bottles of port (some with the port still in), beautiful stained glass windows and his pistol, one of the few objects actually heavily encrusted with coral. Next door, in George Hamilton's cabin was the skeleton of one of the men who were killed immediately *Pandora* hit the reef, probably the one run over by the cannon; his shipmates would have carried his lifeless body down below to the surgeon's room and there he remained, his assassin now his tomb. Other human bones were also uncovered, including two matching femurs, part of a pelvis and a lower leg bone, but none in irons!

The archaeologists were absolutely delighted with this unexpected 'bonanza', as they happily described them. Peter Geisner, the senior archaeologist explained why: 'We can get all sorts of information from studies of bones. We will be able to discover how old the man was, whether he was healthy and whether he was well nourished. The seamen were away from home for a long time and most of them would not have come from the more affluent side of society so would not have been fed very well. From these discoveries we can get to know something about the sailors not only of their physical state but of the conditions under which they lived for long periods while at sea. This is the archaeological significance of doing the *Pandora* excavation, these are the sorts of questions we need to answer – what living conditions were like and how the men worked.' It is fascinating what they can discover from an old bone that has laid under water for almost two hundred years.

The broken pump that heralded *Pandora's* descent was also found, along with many other things usually found on board ships in the late 1700s that are helping historians piece together details of life in those far off days. Special note is being made, however, of all the ethnographic pieces that laid buried in the sand; as *Pandora* made her way from island to South Pacific island the men eagerly bought up souvenirs from the natives to take home with them, either as personal mementos or as presents for family and loved ones. Wooden clubs, stone implements, cowrie shells, carved fishing lures, axe heads, headrests and other carvings (all collected in 1791) joined the lovingly handled and revered artefacts that made their way gently to the surface in airlift bags, from which they were quickly transferred into special solutions for preservation. Conservationists were always busy, chipping at and preparing the final tally of over 800 pieces, which have found new resting places in Brisbane Museum, under the enthusiastic eye of Ron Coleman. A telex sent to Operation Raleigh's headquarters in London excitedly detailed the preservation of a spirit bottle found with its cork still in place. Initially it was, 'placed in salt water, then fresh water until the salt dissolves. Then it will be treated with resin in order to consolidate it. Without such treatment it would disintegrate.' One final find that could not be removed was the anchor from the *Bounty* that Edwards had so jubilantly hauled aboard at Tahiti; still firmly lashed to the deck where it was placed all those years ago.

Frantic activity was not confined to watery parts only; the land party was just as absorbingly occupied, studying the local wildlife on near-by Raine Island in temperatures that soared way past 100 degrees Farenheit in the shade! Such was the scientific team's dedication to their tasks, they checked tags on three thousand unwilling booby birds, who showed their annoyance at being disturbed with their sharp and painful beaks. The biologists also logged the amount of green turtles to shuffle their s-l-o-w way ashore during the night to lay their eggs. Despite the sharks waiting just off shore to attack the unsound and exhausted, and the squealing resentment of the boobies, over ten thousand of these 400 pound visitors arrived.

The whole expedition was deemed a success, yet there is still plenty of work to be done there. The ulitmate chore would be to raise *Pandora* from her aquatic setting, in the same manner as the famous flagship of Henry VIII's fleet, the *Mary Rose,* but impediments of a large magnitude here abound. *Pandora* is lying a lot further down in much more problematic seas, in addition to which the cost has been estimated at about twenty-five million Australian dollars. With difficult decompression problems to overcome initially, due to her keel being another twenty or thirty feet down, she might best be left alone to continue resting in peace.

Built in 1779, she was the first of nine ships to be named *Pandora*, her ultimate ruin setting the example for her last successor which, as a submarine, deliberately dived under the ocean's waves.

This final *Pandora*, concluding a collection of ships which included a sloop, cruiser and depot ship, was originally named *Python*, built by Vickers Armstrong, Barrow-in-Furness in 1929. In keeping with the folklore attributed to her namesake, she bore the motto 'Hope On Hope Ever', but was bombed by Italian aircraft while serving in Malta on 31 March 1942. Unlike her predecessor though she was salvaged and scrapped in 1955.

CHAPTER SEVEN

'They have the right to choose their own way of life'

Desolate panic and paranoia struck at the hearts of the partying Tahitians on board *Bounty*, when they discovered they were under sail during the night of 22nd/23rd September 1789. Christian calmed their initial fears by explaining he was only sailing round to Oparre, but it soon became obvious he was doing no such thing and was actually heading further out to sea. One brave young lady took immediate action, jumping over the rails and swimming for the reef through which they had already navigated a passage, but no one else was inclined to follow her example.

Fletcher surveyed his kidnap victims; out of eighteen women just a handful were content to travel with him, and six were positively, hideously unwanted – being 'rather ancient' was the cruel description used by Jenny – and when a canoe appeared as they passed the island of Moorea, these six elderly ladies were turned off. Two Tubuaian men remained loyal (chief Taromeiva was discovering distant kinsman on Tahiti) and were joined by four Tahitians to form a male Polynesian contingent, used and abused by the nine original *Bounty* men, who quickly forgot what it was like to be firmly under a brutish thumb and gloried in treating them as slaves. Finally there was one last passenger aboard, the infant daughter of William McKoy's lady. Twenty-eight people left from an initial thirty-five.

They soon paired off, though it was an uneven affair with twelve women shared out amongst fifteen men. Mauata, renamed Isabella, of course kept her hold on Fletcher, but Jenny, with 'A.S. 1789' forever tatooed on her arm after Alex Smith staked his claim on her, had moved into the secure and faithful arms of Isaac Martin. John Mills took up with Vahineatua, William McKoy with Teio (who shared her affections between him and her Tahitian daughter, Sarah), William Brown partnered Teatuahitea, Edward Young was with Teraura, Alex Smith found solace in Obuarei, John Williams' companion was Faahotu and Matt Quintal bonded a union with Tevarua. The Europeans happily catered for, the three remaining girls were distributed amongst the six Polynesians; Tahitian Tararo claimed Toofaiti for his own, leaving his three fellow countrymen to gratify themselves with the same girl, Mareva, while the two Tubuaians shared Tinafornea.

The search was on in absolute earnest to find a suitable island which they could cultivate and colonize. Christian had learnt enough from the months spent on Tubuai to desire an uninhabited home, but his other requirements were still the same, uneasy access, fertile ground and situated way off the main shipping lines. With thousands of miles of Pacific Ocean and as many islands to search through, given a fair wind, time and plenty of luck, they should find something corresponding exactly to their requirements. *Bounty* was given a free rein to 'run before the wind', and she took them to the Cook group of islands and a brief stop at Rarotonga; no one was to know for many years they were the first to discover this magnificently alluring isle. During their cruise amongst these islands a canoe came alongside them, offering coconuts and pigs for sale. The traders boarded with their goods, one of them taking a particular liking to Christian's jacket, encrusted with pearl buttons. Fletcher immediately presented his coat to the man, who strutted and swaggered as he paraded his acquisition before his friends, only to hit the water seconds later as a bullet instantly rendered him lifeless and swooped his body over the rails. One of the ship's renegades had caught sight of this bragging native and instantly fired at him, having jumped to the conclusion that he had stolen the jacket. The canoeists gathered their departed brother from the sea and hurriedly escaped. *Bounty* carried on.

Island after island was discounted; some may have looked promising but curling smoke, noisy drum rhythms, gaily coloured canoes or threatening figures would soon dispel any hopes of having discovered their private paradise. After six weeks roaming cheerless seas they arrived at the island of Tongataboo (where Bligh had wanted to take the launch), and they spent two days replenishing desperately depleted supplies. After six weeks, fraught with short tempers, frustrated hopes and bitter disappointments, Fletcher Christian finally decided on a course that gave renewed vigour to his companion's actions and polarized their thoughts. They were making for Pitcairn's Island (by some mutually forgotten consent of time the plural was later dropped), discovered during a voyage of Carteret's in 1767 (by young midshipman Pitcairn who was perched up the mast at the right moment). He had described it as, 'a great rock rising out of the sea'. It was reported to be uninhabited and, though amply wooded, unapproachable due to the constantly pounding surf against sheer cliffs that would not give way at any point to a decent beach. Fletcher could not have written a better synopsis of his requirements.

Another two months were spent hunting for the trade winds to carry them to their desired destination, two months of perishing cold as *Bounty* travelled deeper south, two months of hardship that resulted in some of the voyagers despondently begging to be taken back to the warmer, friendlier and more familiar surroundings of Tahiti. Their wishes disregarded the journey carried on, turning north into hotter climes, giving a slight respite to the unhappy, until Christian steered them to the very spot where Pitcairn's Island should have risen before them. She wasn't there. The grumblings and murmurings must have increased, but Christian was delighted, if she was incorrectly charted there was even less chance of being discovered. With a final burst of determination he wove a path along the line of latitude and was rewarded on 15th January 1790 with his first glimpse of his new home.

For forty-eight hours a storm refused to let them land and explore, but all to the good, as they quietly observed a complete stillness before them. No canoes, no fires, no huts, no signs of life at all. When the conditions allowed, they eventually guided *Bounty* as close as they dared, then Christian, Brown, McKoy and Williams took the cutter for a cautious recce.

The only landing place was inhospitable, great boulders smothered in crashing surf, yet they scrambled ashore and hauled their way inland. Strange sights greeted them, stone work, carvings, old foundations, proving they were not violating virgin soil, but the masters of the artefacts were long gone, and each encouraging step into the sweltering undergrowth proved the suitability of Christian's choice. Abundant trees teeming with vegetation, useful not only for sustaining life but for aiding manufacturing as well – wood to translate into timber for building, leaves to thatch roofs and from which to make cloth, and fruit with which to dye.

Action was instantly instigated. *Bounty* was brought as near to the island as possible and she was thoroughly dismantled, right down to the planks of her hull, over the next week. The time came when she was no longer viable as a ship and her skeleton was burnt, although if Jenny is to be believed, Christian, who was so much in favour of destroying *Bounty* at Tubuai, was now totally against firing her. Quintal insisted she be set alight, and the flames lit the sky on 23rd January 1790, though how much was left to incinerate is debatable, as some of her was already floating around in the region of Tubuai, and practically all the rest was on shore.

Makeshift huts turned into permanent dwellings as the time drifted past. Allocations of land were divided amongst the white men only, thereby thrusting the Polynesians into an existence dependant upon the benevolence of basically untrustworthy turncoats. Life settled down well though, the animals from *Bounty* supplied meat, a climb to the top of their mountain of an isle resulted in eggs and birds for dinner, fish were prolific and easily available, and Ned Young discovered a formula for turning the tea root into spirits.

Then one Friday in October 1790, Isabella gave birth to Fletcher's first child, a son he named Thursday October Christian – he had forgotten to allow for crossing the date line and Pitcairn timing was to remain one day adrift until the arrival of outsiders twenty years later, who corrected them. (Thursday even changed his name to Friday). A baby boom was on the way, though perhaps it was somewhat fitting that the first arrival should belong to Fletcher. During the next three years most of the wives proved fruitful; although no pure Polynesian babies were born, the little colony steadily increased as many half caste children joined them in their flourishing hideaway.

Within three years Fletcher Christian had arrived at his self-acknowledged station in life; a land owner wealthy in the love and respect of his fellow countrymen, with a successfully spawning wife who had already provided him with two sons and was carrying a third child. He also benefited from something else – something he might possibly have seen around the Christian homestead of Ewanrig, had most definitely witnessed during his trips with Bligh to the West Indies, and probably came to regard as a gentleman's right – black slaves. Their faithful Polynesian friends were never to be treated as equals, as all the ex-*Bounty* men copied their leader's ways and effortlessly slipped into the role of depraved and cruel rakes. And why indeed should they consider the feelings of these fellow human beings after unquestioningly accepting that the whole purpose of *Bounty's* voyage was to procure cheap sustenance for enforced coloured labour?

It was later reported by Alex Smith that Fletcher was both happy and morose; seemingly a contradiction in terms, but surely that is exactly how he had lived his whole life. On Pitcairn he drifted back into the island existence he had known and loved whilst living on the Isle of Man, but the heavy responsibilities laid on his broad back placed him into the very position from which he had ousted Bligh, and he suddenly discoved how tawdy and withered the grass on the other side really could be. During his most depressive moments he retreated to an inhospitable and remote cave, which could only be reached by vines, and set up a veritable hideaway complete with a little house hidden by the undergrowth and an ample stock of supplies. Here he would sit brooding, no doubt wondering about the fate of the men set adrift, no doubt wondering about his family back in Cumbria, no doubt wondering if a ship would one day find them and take him back to face a court martial. Those final few years of his life must have been spent constantly looking over his shoulder.

The contented moments when he was left alone to tend his garden and cater to the needs of his family were few and far between as trouble was brewing. The death of John William's wife sparked the flame, as he demanded one of the three 'left-over' girls be given to him, much to the dismay of the Polynesian men who were sharing them. Despite objections from Fletcher, lots were cast and Toofaiti, consort of Tararo alone was chosen, much to his dismay and her delight. Learning a lesson from Fletcher's past behaviour, Tararo disappeared into the hills, seething at the injustice. For three days he plotted revenge, having the mutiny before him as the greatest example of how to deal with this kind of situation. He returned to the fold, recaptured Toofaiti and planned to slaughter all the white men. He enlisted the rest of his compatriots and told them his idea, with the result that the faithful women devised new words to their songs, and as they went about their daily chores, merrily sang, 'Why does black man sharpen axe? To kill white man'. Fletcher understood and acted immediately, storming to the commune house of the conspirators and fired his musket, loaded only with deterring powder, at the first man he came upon. The man fled to Tararo and Toofaiti. The rest surrendered and begged forgiveness; it was given in return for the lives of Tararo and Oher, the other Polynesian. They were duly delivered.

Toofaiti was free to enrapture Jack Williams, who named her Nancy, and life carried on unhindered. Quintal and McKoy devised their own personal stills (McKoy once worked in a whisky distillery and obviously remembered some of the tricks of his old trade), and the pair of them promptly became more insolent and despicable in their treatment of the Polynesian men; old wounds were re-opened leading to the resurgence of old plans. One fateful day at the beginning of October 1793 the situation exploded.

As in all good mutinous attempts, the first stage was to secure arms, which the coloured gentlemen did by pretending they were going hunting for pigs for dinner. The women, apart from the heavily pregnant Isabella, left to climb up the mountain for birds eggs, leaving the white men toiling the soil in the spring air; Fletcher Christian was detached from the community spirit at his wife's request and was tending his own plot of land outside their home. Quickly the blood bath began with Williams the first victim (on hearing the crack of the shot, Martin rejoiced at the thought of the delicious meal they would all enjoy that evening). The murderers forged on, looking for their next target and discovered Fletcher bent towards the ground, waging war on some weeds. They shot him in the back then smashed his head with an axe. His painful moans reached the ears of Bill McKoy who was instantly wary, but accepted the theory of his companion Mills that he had only heard Isabella hailing her sons.

Too late for John Mills, they soon found out differently. The merciless men appeared and talked them into separating, then fired at the fervently hated McKoy. He escaped, calling a warning to Mills, and ran to the hills, collecting Matt Quintal on the way. Mills, however, believed himself well liked by the Polynesians and placed great faith in these thoughts; he was either arrogant or treated them with more kindness than his compatriots, but the bullet flew, and he hit the ground with a resounding thud. The American, Isaac Martin, who had been so undecided over the mutiny and, had he had his own way, would not even have been on Pitcairn, he who had taken Jenny from Alex Smith and was to be eternally remembered by her as 'Madden', was next. Wounded by a shot, he hauled his aching limbs to Brown's house, only to be shot again and finished off in the time honoured Tahitian method of having his brains smashed out with a hammer. Brown was then blugeoned by stones until he too lay still, but he was only faking death, a ruse which could have worked had he not moved before they left; the report of the gun and whistle of the pellet heralded his end.

The women were back and busy intervening; Quintal's lady Tevarua warned Smith of his impending doom and bid him hide, but his timing was out and, stealing from his cover too soon, he was spied and shot at, receiving a gaping wound in his shoulder, the surprise and pain of which floored him. His adversary fell on him for the kill, pounding his head with the handle of the musket. Smith successfully fought off these hefty blows (adding two broken fingers to his misery) and Lady Luck benignly smiled upon him when two point blank attempts were made to shoot him in the side, and both failed. It gave him the edge he needed and he eclipsed the ineffective attack with an assault of his own.

A bargain was struck between Smith and the rampaging liquidators, who escorted him to Christian's home where the women eagerly cosseted him, all except Isabella who was otherwise occupied producing Fletcher's daughter, Mary Ann. Ned Young suspiciously did not come to any harm, also being safeguarded by his feminine devotees. The massacre was over, with numbers even; four black men and four white men, though two of the latter were quaking in their hillside hideaway. The widows were redistributed and the situation should in all reality have calmed down, but one of the natives, Manarii, drank too much of McKoy's beverages and ended up killing one of his comrades. Young's wife, who was an unwilling witness to his atrocity, wept for her slain friend and was comforted by another Polynesian gentleman, an act of kindness which incensed Manarii into striking out at him as well. The women had had enough violence and remedied it with a little of their own; Manarii was executed.

McKoy (and probably Quintal) apparently remained in hiding, as Niau, 'getting a view of McKoy, shot at him', but when a couple of the ladies went over to see him, he was still alive. Young killed Niau in cold blood, but gave the only remaining Tahitian, who was petrified, having witnessed the steady demise of his friends, a promise he would not be harmed. The women had other ideas and hacked him to death with an axe.

The two refugees returned, and the four men, twelve women plus their children, forged a fairly happy existence, going about their daily chores and just stepping over the rotting bodies of their late companions who were left exactly where they had fallen. The women were adamantly against burial, and Jenny actually took to carrying Jack Williams' head around with her. Ned Young was revolted by this and demanded its internment, along with the remains of his other mutinous friends, but the idea of hiding them in the ground was just as abhorrant to the girls. Their frustration grew into a demand for a boat to be built that could take them home to Tahiti. The men made a show of complying with their wishes but deliberately botched the job, so when the craft was finished it promptly keeled over, thus forcing the ladies to stay. A mass grave was dug and the dead men's bones were thrown in, six months after their violent ends.

Babies continued to join this exclusive throng, though the circumstances around the arrival of one are intriguing, if disjointed. A charming couple, Hedley and Olive Rundel, who are keen amateur genealogists, were trying to solve the mystery of their ancestor, Matthew Quintal's, last child, Edward. His other children had been given traditional Quintal names, Matthew, Arthur, Jenny, Sarah, but there was no precedent for Edward. The fact that this baby was born after Matt died and to a different mother than the others may shed some light upon the mystery. His wife, Tevarua, already minus an ear her husband had bitten off during a fight, had fallen over the edge of a cliff to her death (the spot on the south west coast is now know by her other name, Big Sully), and Quintal, even though there was an abundance of available ladies, set his cap at Teraura, Ned Young's wife. She became pregnant by him, and Young, aided by Alex Smith, killed Quintal.

However, the situation was nowhere near as clear cut as it may appear. Ned Young should have been the last one to become jealous, having fathered a son, Edward, by Fletcher's widow, Isabella in 1794 (again, she had not wasted any time worming her way into the affections of the new leading light). Matt was executed for making drunken threats to the lives of Fletcher Christian's children. In later years Teraura (named Sussanah by her white man) was to marry Thursday October Christian, possibly the fulfilment of years of affection for the Christian brood. This could have inflamed the green eyed monster in 'Old Matt' (who was in his mid 20s), though Thursday was only eight or nine years old at the time and, even though the Tahitians were notorious for allowing their children to grow up rather more quickly than would be considered seemly nowadays, she must have been far too busy to become embroiled with a young lad as well. Whatever the cause, Matt's threats were taken seriously enough to warrant him being killed before his son was born.

Mrs Rundle thinks the rest of the islanders chose to call the boy Edward, which looks perfectly feasible; either it was an attempt to pacify Young or honour him, as the women all adored him – look how he was protected by them during the massacre. Or it could have been the final triumph over a dead man, to implant the Young family name into the Quintal's could be construed as a sign of absolute power. Ned Young, it would appear, was the latest Lord and Master.

He died on Christmas Day the next year, 1800, from asthma, leaving Alex Smith as the sole survivor of the men, William McKoy having plunged to the bottom of a cliff in a drunken fit four years earlier; the site on the north side of the island just below Christian's cave, is also commemorated. It is 'McKoy's Drop'.

Smith had a slight smattering of reading and writing, mostly due to tutoring from Ned Young during the last few years, and he suddenly (it is said while in a drunken stupor) turned to a bible he found in Fletcher Christian's sea chest and devised a unique form of religion for his flock to follow. The women and children left in his care had to contend with some drastic changes in their lifestyles, not least was their saviour's repentant desire to resume his proper name, John Adams. Devotions of one form or another were practised five times on Sundays, there was fasting twice a week, dancing was forbidden and their morals made a miraculous U-turn; not that this new found piety stopped Isabella and Ned Young's son Edward marrying Thursday October and Sussanah's daughter, Polly – Isabella's grandaughter.

Eight more years of seclusion remained to them, until an American ship, the *Topaz* of Boston, Massachusetts, happened upon this small isle in the middle of nowhere in September 1808. Pitcairn was heaven sent as *Topaz* was desperately low on stores and needed to restock, so Captain Folger endeavoured to find a landing spot. Of course he found none, but his need was so great he had to keep on trying, having noticed signs of life. His patience was rewarded when a canoe rode the choppy waves out of Bounty Bay and came alongside them, containing, to his complete surprise, three English speaking young men. Folger was taken back onto Pitcairn and introduced to John Adams, who regaled him with the history of their settlement and in return Folger told all he could remember regarding the fates of Adam's ex-shipmates. At long last, the Pitcairners knew what had become of the boat load of pitiful victims.

Topaz left fully provided for, gratefully carrying on with her voyage and Folger carried with him an old compass and chronometer from *Bounty*. At Rio de Janeiro, word was sent to the Admiralty detailing what they had discovered, but Napoleon was keeping them too preoccupied for an event from twenty years ago to warrant any attention. So John Adams, alias Alexander Smith, deserter and mutineer, was promptly forgotton and metaphorically pardoned due to an overwhelming spirit of apathy toward anything not connected with the menacing French usurper.

Gradually more visitors called at Pitcairn and were treated to a potted history of the mutiny, and subsequent events, from Adams. The trouble was, none of them ever tallied with each other, especially where the death of Christian was concerned, which, combined with other sources, give us at least seven differerent versions of Fletcher's final demise. (The figure thirteen has been mentioned, but I've not been able to discover so many). He was slaughtered by the Polynesians and died, or he survived the attempt on his life and with a very sore head climbed to his inaccessible cave and finished his days out there, or he was shot trying to leave the island, or he actually did manage to get away and back to England, or he led the life of a pirate in South America, or he committed suicide by throwing himself off a cliff in a fit of remorse, or he died nine months after arriving at Pitcairn. Marvellous, fanciful ideas, but the general consensus amongst the saner, sober folk is the first version.

Passing ships provided an unexpected boon for another of the islanders. Jenny had never relinquished her hopes of returning to her beloved Tahiti, and seized the first opportunity to obtain a passage back home. In all, her journey took over six months, via Nugahiva, but she got her heart's desire, only to find missionaries had invaded her homeland, and it was to these she told the exciting details of her adventures with the *Bounty*. They wrote it all down and posted it to the

Sydney Gazette, who printed the story in their 17 July 1819 issue.

Adams also took advantage of a visit from one of these ships by asking Captain Beechey of the *Blossom* to marry him to his blind paramour, Mary, who was confined to her bed. Beechey could not quite see the need after so long, but agreed just to indulge them. When he left he carried a special message, asking the British Government to instigate a relocation scheme, as they were becoming overcrowded on Pitcairn.

In 1823 the arrival of John Buffett and John Evans from the British Whaler, *Cyrus*, heralded an influx of immigrants. Buffett was given permission by his captain to stay and help Adams, who was increasingly finding the responsibility of patriarch too heavy for him to bear, but Evans had deserted. They quickly instilled new blood into the community, Buffett marrying Dolly Young early in 1824 and Evans taking Rachel Adams as his wife later that year. Wasting no time, children followed in 1825. Buffett took a lot of the pressure off old Adams, starting as the school teacher and working his way into the position of pastor, the most influential post on the island. His concern for the welfare of their souls overflowed into an excess consideration for the well being of one of his pupils, and in October 1928, Thursday October's daughter Mary made Buffett a dad again.

John Adams died at the age of 62 on 5th March 1829 (Mary joined him in the grave only nine days later), just after another newcomer George Hunn Nobbs, moved onto the island. A man of dubious background but probably of infinite charm, he set himself up in opposition to Buffett. Both were conducting Sunday services at one point and dragging the Pitcairners asunder as they had to decide which one to attend. Nobbs ultimately won, and he went on to hold the islanders in the palm of his hand for an astonishing 55 years.

In England, Captain Beechey had passed on Adams' request for help in moving to somewhere larger, and the authorities came up with the novel solution of sending them to Tahiti. In March 1831 the 77 islanders were unwillingly shepherded on board the *Lucy Ann* and taken back to the land of their forebears. They hated it there. All the traditional loving welcomes left them cold and full of moral indignation, and when they began to die from the diseases that easily attacked their sterile persons (the first to succumb was Thursday October) they became desperate to return home. 65 finally stood on the familiar red soil of Pitcairn Island on 3rd September 1831, having bought a passage for $500 on an American whaler. The money had been raised by subscription from the susceptible Tahitians who easily sympathised with the homesick strangers; I wonder if Jenny helped them?

Their joy at being back soon disintegrated into dismay when they saw the predicament their island was in. The place had been ransacked by natives from Bora Bora who had paid a visit during their absence, and pigs were roaming free, devastating the crops. Worst of all, the illnesses that had claimed so many of their loved ones had accompanied them from Tahiti and Edward Young, along with four others, breathed their last.

Into this depressed community came Joshua Hill. Thoroughly unscrupulous, he totally intimidated these innocent people, alleging the British Government had sent him and should they oppose his rule all he had to do was to send word to the consul, and a detachment of soldiers would soon arrive to back him. He reigned as 'President of the "Commonwealth" of Pitcairn' for six years, quickly establishing a regime of dictatorship. The whistle of the lash returned, as Buffett was given three dozen of the best for having sired Mary Christian's baby, and Evans was treated to one dozen for audaciously wishing to see a copy of Hill's authority. These two men left for the Gambier Islands.

Nobbs compliantly watched, his fire-and-brimstone approach obviously having disappeared, then left for Tahiti. Hill threatened to execute twelve year old Charlotte Quintal who had stolen a few yams. When her father objected he found a sword firmly placed across his throat, with the demonic Hill demanding a full confession of his sins, until the rest of the islanders pulled him off Quintal. In desperation they wrote to Nobbs and begged him to return. He agreed and resettled with them, as did Evans. The end of this nightmarish existence came in 1837 when another ship called in. Hill, who had already proved himself to be a terrible name dropper (once claiming to have attended Napoleon's coronation), told the captain that the Duke of Bedford was a close relation of his. Extremely puzzled, the captain introduced himself as Lord Edward Russell, son and heir of the Duke of Bedford, and he had never met Hill before. At last this fraud was exposed and the Pitcairners promptly expelled him.

It made them think though, and they sat down and drew up a list of ten laws, covering all aspects of their behaviour and life, (the fifth law introduced the first ever case of compulsory education), and appointed Edward Quintal as their Magistrate, who presided with two councillors, one elected and one he personally chose. With subsequent elections on the 1st January each year, everyone over eighteen was allowed to vote, a practice which began in 1838; thus they were the first to introduce votes for women.

A period of peacefulness prevailed. The only upsets were of nature's making, with devastating storms and natural deaths. In 1841 a flu epidemic raged through the islanders after a visit from the British ship, *Curaçao,* claiming the life of Isabella Christian, who had turned into a harridan of a figure as time claimed any usefulness she may once have proffered. She was described in terms of horror by visitors, her 'corpse-like' appearance neatly fitting the fairy-tale vision of wicked witches and step-mothers. To the very end the reason for her nickname of Mainmast did not leave her, she never ran to the cuddly fat of her compatriots. Once she had died, only one of the original settlers remained, another of the Tahitian women.

Buffett had also returned and started a healthy and useful trend by teaching the young males carpentry, concentrating especially on carving souvenirs which were eagerly snapped up by the crews of visiting ships. It is a trend that continues to this day, with hand made mementoes from Pitcairn in constant demand, providing them with a thriving business which helps to augment their wages.

Through the goodwill of the passing vessels, Nobbs had struck up several correspondences and friendships with influential people in England and finally arranged a passage back, where he was officially ordained as a proper Pastor and met Queen Victoria. The impression he left with her must have been amicable, because when the island Council decided that nearly 200 people living on such a small rock was too crowded, their request for a new home was favourably received. Queen Victoria gave them Norfolk Island.

Run a line north west from Cape Reinga, the uppermost tip of New

Zealand, to Cape York, the highest point of Australia, and you should pass slightly to the right of Norfolk, an island which had witnessed many appalling and harrowing scenes since it was colonized in 1789, as a penitentiary to house the toughest convicts transported from Britain to Australia. Its cultivation began almost the same as Pitcairn, a ship carrying physically (instead of mentally) chained prisoners landing just a few months apart on hitherto unknown land. Mutiny and the lash had also prevailed on Norfolk, with some horrendous commandants that made Bligh look like a compassionate man, until 1854 when the convicts were removed to Tasmania. Two years later a new province was established.

On 3rd May 1856 the Adams, Buffetts, Christians, Evans, McKoys, Nobbs, Quintals and Youngs boarded the *Morayshire* and embarked upon a five week journey that took them 3700 miles across the Pacific Ocean to the site of their latest dwelling. The size of Norfolk may seem small being five miles by three, but it was enormous to the recently arrived Pitcairners; well over double the room they had been used to before. Also, the internees had left stone buildings, flourishing gardens full of new delights, and toilets! Evil relics from the previous inhabitants were swiftly disposed of as the gallows tumbled into the sea.

As a whole, they made a good job of settling down, but for some homesickness was too much to bear and after eighteen months, seventeen of the Young clan risked the long and perilous trip back to Pitcairn. After six years of unrest in their strange residence, another eleven Youngs returned to the 'great rock' with sixteen other friends, and Pitcairn was back in business.

Ben Young eventually built up a tenacious stronghold over the island, beginning on his departure from Norfolk when Rachel Evans (John Adams' daughter) gave her Pitcairn lands to his father, Simon Young. When Ben revisited Norfolk many years later, Edward Quintal passed over his land rights on Pitcairn to him, so, when his father Simon died, Ben became the biggest land owner on the island, holding not only the Young family plots, but also the Adams' and the Quintal's.

Gradually Pitcairn began to thrive again, though it was tough to begin with. Shipwrecks helped enormously, especially when extremely grateful survivors sent useful presents once they had returned from whence they came. Word of their honesty and kindness reached the ears of Queen Victoria, who sent them an organ to reward their 'domestic virtues'. They would have preferred a pastor as George Nobbs was happily ensconsed on her previous gift of Norfolk Island. When the American Seventh Day Adventist Church sent details of their beliefs, the islanders read with growing enthusiasm the messages within. Ten years later, in 1887, a missionary arrived from the same sect and easily converted the whole island over to his way of thinking. In 1890 a ship arrived with more missionaries who offically baptized the Pitcairners in a rock-pool.

The passing of another century has seen the island gradually ease into the modern way of living whilst managing to keep the unique isolation of Pitcairn intact. One of the biggest boosts was the installation of their 'ham' radio which gives them constant contact with the outside world especially, most importantly, any passing ships. Through this radio link they found themselves a very special friend, Jim Russell. He made contact with Tom Christian initally and discovered that orders for any goods they needed were being placed with a gentleman in Germany, who relayed the messages to a company in Liverpool. Jim realised this was causing a lot of unnecesary cost, so he took over, as a call from him to Liverpool was so much cheaper than from Germany. Over the next three or four years he became conversant with the needs of the islanders, and sent out some intriguing items ranging from screws to a generator. On one occasion he even sent himself; in 1976 a jetty had been built in Bounty Bay by the Royal Engineers and was so battered by the ocean swell, a repair operation swung into action and Jim offered to lend a hand, as there were only twelve able bodied men on the island.

The engineer in charge of the repair project welcomed Jim's offer of practical help and willingly agreed to his conditions in return. Jim wanted a passage with the Royal Engineers, not only for himself but for a shipment of supplies, weighing a total of six tons, which included a refrigerator, a deep freeze and the generator to supply the power to run them. Once there he spent eight glorious months, putting faces to familiar voices and acquainting himself with the entire population of the island. Life was calmer and slower for him, there were no newspapers or television to bring in worries from home (they can just about pick up the world service, although it is difficult to hear because of all the interference), and his generator only gave electricity for two hours in the morning and five hours each evening, which is sufficient to keep the freezer frozen. Videos are creeping into some of the homes, so when the power is switched on they can watch, for example, the latest Royal wedding, and telephones are also available for a few expensive hours each day.

To get a slight smattering of the atmosphere on Pitcairn, listen to the noise of your nearest motorway. Jim lives fairly close to the infamous London orbital, the M25, and when he first arrived at the island, thought he was home again; the sound of the surf pounding constantly against the rocks was uncannily reminiscent of the roar of cars on the motorway. Unfortunately the bracing sea air and beautifully mild climate cannot be recreated, but he says the landscape of North Wales is not unlike Pitcairn's mountainous terrain.

Jim witnessed at first hand how the number of inhabitants is shrinking. After the expansion that resulted in the mass emigration to Norfolk Island, they again reached 200 residents in 1936, but the fall has been steady, as more and more of the children leave at 15 or 16 to further their education at a Seventh Day Adventist college in New Zealand. Once away from home they find a new life beckoning them, and very few return as they take up jobs that simply cannot be done on Pitcairn; one of the girls trained as a registered nurse but the only position she could have on the island would have been assistant to the assistant to the nurse, which is unthinkable, considering they are one of the healthiest group of people imaginable.

They have had their ups and downs when it comes to health; some years ago one of the men was very ill and the islanders prevailed upon the doctor of a passing ship to stop off and look at him. The doctor diagnosed tetanus and asked if there were any horses around. They answered that yes, they had a few, which confirmed the doctor's worst fears – that was how this patient had contracted his illness. The poor chap died, and so did the horses! Without preamble, they were driven into the sea, and there has not been a horse on the island since.

Although the pastor's wife is a nurse, they do not have a resident doctor (ironic that when a doctor did visit for a couple of months, three people died during his stay) and they have to fight sickness as best they can with antibiotics from their well stocked dispensary. In April 1988 a crew ship arrived carrying a huge dose of Asian flu which flooded through the entire population, and proved too much for the frail constitution of 89 years old Andrew Young.

With this recent loss the total number of residents stands at 47, with every likelihood that it will continue to decrease as more leave and less arrive to settle. More immigrants have continued to infiltrate the community, one of the most persistent being Carrie Boyd from Norway. Since watching the film *"Mutiny On The Bounty"* at the age of twelve, she had set her heart on visiting Pitcairn. As she grew older, left school and started work, the fascination for the utopian story never left her, so she learnt several new languages, trained as a ship's radio officer and sailed the seven seas, often going straight past Pitcairn. Her resolve increased and she sought the necessary permission to land from the Governor in Auckland, and was refused. She made several applications, citing her lifelong dream as the reason for wanting to land, (had she wanted to study the ecology or something like that Jim feels permission would have been no problem at all) and eventually, because the islanders themselves had no qualms about letting her visit, she set foot on their magical isle.

After a couple of stays, her future was settled; she married Brian Young (the present magistrate), has easily adjusted to the ways of the island and has two delightful children. A ship calling in from the South Atlantic gave her the chance to take a holiday back in Norway, and after much persuasion from Brian she agreed to go, but soon regretted it. As lovely as it was to see family and friends again, the perishing cold and rain made it a miserable time for her, and she was very glad to return to Pitcairn.

Carrie is not the only person to move onto the island. One young man born on Pitcairn went to school in New Zealand and found himself in his mid-thirties in Auckland with a wife and child he could barely afford to support. His father entreated him to return to where he could build a decent, if not materialistic, life for his family, by joining in with the souvenir making business that is still going strong since the days of John Buffett. They gather wood from the uninhabited neighbouring island of Henderson for carving model fishes, turtles, birds and *Bounty* replicas in addition to making walking sticks and miniature wheelbarrows. These are the handiwork of the men, while the ladies weave baskets and paint specially prepared delicate leaves. All are stock piled until a ship comes along, then it is into the boats to tout their wares in true Polynesian style.

When Jim was staying on the island they caught an eight foot shark, which was proudly hauled into the harbour. The Pitcairners cut out its jaw, delighting in having another stock of teeth for their model sharks, then slit open its stomach to reveal an undigested shark with yet more teeth for them. They then proposed to dispose of the bodies by towing them out to sea and dumping them. Jim was astounded at this and asked why they did not eat the flesh, knowing it to be considered a great delicacy elsewhere, but the islanders were adamant they would not consume it, as their religious doctrine forbade it. Fair enough, said Jim, let the chickens have it. Again, they were not very happy with this idea, so he, being an enthusiastic gardener, suggested they chop it up and mulch it into the ground as a fertilizer. Not even that thought appealed – they towed it out to sea.

He has tried to regulate their haphazard approach to gardening, but his efforts were wasted because when it comes to agriculture they really are exceptionally blessed. If someone decides they want to create a new garden then they bring out the bulldozer and push aside whatever bushes are in the way of the proposed site. Tyres ruck up the soil ready for planting the seeds, which miraculously grow without any tending due to the marvellous climate they enjoy. Most of the crops do not reach a very high standard, though the melons never seem to miss, but everything they produce is of sufficient quality and quantity to sustain them should the need arise. The island is of course also endowed with a variety of prolific fruit trees, including coconuts, apples, grapefruits, limes, lemons and bananas; in fact the only one that has to be physically planted and tended is the pineapple.

Usually though they are well stocked with provisions ordered and sent over from England three times a year, but as the time approaches for the next shipment to arrive some things are naturally running low, and should the ships not arrive on time, they can then fall back on to what is already there. But fruit can become a monotonous diet and they rely on the imported foodstuff more and more now, such as flour and cooking oil. Also they have to wait for spare parts for all the mechical aid that is making life much easier for them – when they work. Sturdy motorbikes are a blessed relief, especially when it comes to hauling goods from harbour to Adamstown, via the aptly named 'Hill of Difficulty', or bouncing around the rough terrain from one part of the island to another, but when they break down as so frequently seems to happen, they either have to search for some kind of substitute that will suffice, or wait until the next ship brings the new part.

In September 1987 Jim and his wife Noreen were visited by two friends from Pitcairn, Ben and Irma Christian, who explained that whereas we write out shopping lists to last us on average a week, they have to plan four months in advance and should anything be forgotten, they again have to do without until it is time for their next order. Irma's eyes were a little misty as she mourned the lack of big shops, and more importantly the immediacy of them that we just take for granted. It must have been difficult for her, having lived in Australia for a while in order to complete her education (she was one of the few who returned afterwards), to adjust back to living such a remote existence, but she really seems to have coped extremely well.

It was hard to imagine exactly how very remote they actually are, until she described their position as 3300 miles east north east of Auckland, 1200 miles from Tahiti and even Mangorava, the nearest inhabited island, is 300 miles away. The isolation does not bother them; it is home to them and they are justifiably very proud of their beautiful, rugged isle with her formidable cliffs, and brown and reddish black rock strewn coastline. Irma fervently believes that living so close to the good, clean, non-polluted sea air, coupled together with all the exercise of which they unthinkingly partake, has a lot to do with the general healthiness of her fellow Pitcairners. In all her sixty years she has never known of an abnormal birth; no Caesarians needed, no breach births, every one, including three of her own, have gone perfectly.

Ben and Irma packed a lot of activity into their first stay in Europe; a trip to the Isle of Man, guests at a garden party at Buckingham Palace (they were sponsored by Jim, as Ben had recently been awarded a medal for his 26 years of service on Pitcairn's council as secretary) and visits to the Foreign Office, to discuss necessities for the island, and the Crown Agent where the commemorative stamps that make up a large part of their overall income are printed. Their finances are expertly handled by the Administrative Headquarters in Auckland, New Zealand, where their Governor is based, and all accounts are settled by book work. Cash stays on the island, which is used to pay the monthly salaries of the office and maintenance workers who cope with the immediate running of Pitcairn. These wages are not at all comparable to those of the outside world; another reason why so many who have left Pitcairn are not returning.

The council on which Ben served so faithfully meets once a month to discuss any impending island business, such as applications to leave or improvements to be made. Any decisions decided upon are relayed to the Governor who gives the final judgement, depending on whether their desires are affordably realistic or not.

They are the proud communal owners of two aluminium boats, which are proving so easy to handle because of their buoyancy tanks. Also, when they hit a rock, they do not burst into pieces like the old wooden ones tended to. Small improvements like these boats are gradually helping to project Pitcairn firmly into the twentieth century, but the physical isolation remains intact due to the terrible oceanic conditions still raging round them. As much as people would like to, they just cannot stop and call in. Jim Russell has proposed an ideal solution but, as always, it remains only an idea until financial backing can be summoned up. He feels a breakwater should be placed in Bounty Bay to make a safe harbour because, although they have the jetty that boats can pull alongside and unload against, craft have to be immediately hauled out of the water and taken up a slipway into the boat sheds, as any left out overnight would be thrown onto the rocks and smashed to pieces. He already knows from his contacts on the ham radio that the people who spend their lives cruising the Pacific in yachts would love to visit Pitcairn, but with no safe anchorage at present the mere thought is an impossibility. However with a certain amount of still water two or three yachts could gain a safe haven for a while during a storm, or if some repairs were needed.

Jim remembered how a middle-aged couple limped up to the island in a total wreck of a boat, with its mast gone, engine failed and steering completely lost. The Pitcairners welded together a few bits and helped out as best they could until the vessel was fit to travel on to Mangareva, but had they got their safe harbour it naturally follows that a repair system could be invoked. This would then create more jobs and bring in welcome extra currency, because not only the immediate problems would have to be catered for but the people themselves would need feeding and supplying. As long as the numbers were kept to a reasonable level, such an idea could work out very well for all concerned. Of course actively encouraging a tourist industry would bring in other problems which might be a little overwhelming for the part-time policeman. On the other hand, it seems as if something needs to be done to keep them operating as a viable community.

Glynn Christian, great, great, great, great grandson of Fletcher Christian and well-known cook on British television, believes they need at least 150 inhabitants to become viable again, in addition to a great deal more interest from the British Government, for Pitcairn is a colony with exactly the same status as Hong Kong, Falklands and Gibraltar. Yet, for example, it is taking months, if not years to get very expensive post through to the island. Playing devil's advocate, I enquired why it was necessary to preserve the island at all, in view of the fact that there are so few people there; why not just move them again? An undertone of anger at my audacity ran through Glynn Christian's words as he explained that not many are there because they have been overlooked – 25 years ago the population stood at his magical figure of 150. Neither is it our place to tell anyone where they should live, though should they, as a thriving community, decide to move that was a completely different question, and one he would wholeheartedly help with. He actually had my full agreement when he declared it is not for us to tell them where to live, it is actually our responsibility to make certain they remain there, as Britain has an obligation toward all its colonies, just as parents have to their children.

Glynn visited Pitcairn in 1980, following a stay in hospital due to a bout of food poisoning when he had enough spare time to contemplate his future, and he decided to research his famous ancestor's life. Expecting to find the island well looked after, profiting from all the people who were making money from the re-telling of its heritage and being looked after by the British Government, Glynn was surprised to discover it was falling to pieces, hence his biography of Fletcher Christian is called *"Fragile Paradise"*.

It seems with only 47 people on the island that, were they a colony of animals, they would long ago have been listed as an endangered species. It is obviously our responsibility to encourage them to maintain their birthright, continue to expand and become more and more involved with the twentieth century. As Prime Minister Margaret Thatcher said at the time of the Falklands crisis, 'They are few in number, but they have the right to live in peace, to choose their own way of life . . .' What applies to one distant, far-flung dependency must unquestionably apply to another, although it is not an invasion Pitcairn faces but indifference and ignorance.

CHAPTER EIGHT

A round-up of retribution and rebellion

William Bligh was left standing on the quay having left the *Vlydte* on 14th March 1790, and immediately informed the Admiralty of his plight. Within days his horrific story was reported in the newspapers and he gratifyingly found himself a minor hero; by the end of 1790 he had worked his way up to cult status, living on the story of how he single handedly saved his men from the clutches of *Bounty's* pirates. Even King George III invited him to the Palace and eagerly took in the details of Bligh's dauntless derring-do; he was mad enough to believe anything. The subsequent appearance of the rest of the survivors did nothing to dispel the mythical aura he had built around himself, he whined, wined and dined in all the best places solely on the strength of his extraordinary tale.

Two books poured forth from his dynamic pen, '*Narrative of the Mutiny on Board His Majesty's Ship Bounty and the Subsequent Voyage of Part of the Crew, in the Ship's boat*' and '*A Voyage to the South Sea, Undertaken by Command of His Majesty, for the Purpose of Conveying the Bread-fruit Tree to the West Indies.* Both became best sellers, the welcome income far outweighing any financial difficulties caused by the failure to complete his original task.

On 22 October 1790 he was court martialled for losing *Bounty*, but this was only a Naval formality. On board the *Royal William* at Spithead, he was exonerated. This left him free to pursue his vindictive quest against William Purcell, the man who stood by him in the face of death dealing natives on Tofua. On the same day as his own trial he saw his accusations against Purcell only partly proved and the defendant was merely reprimanded – surely a paltry outcome in Bligh's eyes. Following the procedure of clearing his name, three significant occurrences happened; *Pandora* left to search for the mutineers, in March 1791 Bligh was assigned to lead another expedition to Tahiti to collect more breadfruit, and he was promoted to the position of Captain. At long last it was quite right, proper and permissible to refer to him by this title; some just nicknamed him 'Breadfruit Bligh'.

Still with absolute faith in his abilities (he constantly stressed that the breadfruit on board *Bounty* were flourishing and healthy until matters were taken out of his hands), the Admiralty gave him *carte blanche* to fit out a second sojourn to the South Seas. He chose a West Indiaman, the *Providence,* along with a brig, the *Assistant*. The hard earned insight he had gained from his first command was not lost during the preparations for this voyage, as he insisted on taking marines on board and it was not until August 1791 that he was content to set sail. Nobody bothered him with delays; when *he* deemed he was ready, they left, with Lawrence Leboque and John Smith in his crew. Bligh left behind his rapidly expanding family, five girls and Betsy pregnant again. The baby was yet another daughter, Ann.

Full of wired boxes especially designed for the transportation of breadfruit trees (with moveable roofs to shelter the plant from the weather and glass panels to catch the best of the sun), *Providence* sailed with comparative ease for eight months to Tahiti, via the Cape of Good Hope and Van Dieman's Land. Not for Bligh this time the indignity of waging a losing battle against the clock and the elements at Cape Hope. Once back on the familiar and much loved ground of Tahiti, he discovered what had happened to *Bounty* once they parted company. Mary, consort of Tom McIntosh, cradled their eighteen month old daughter as she filled him in with details of how she had accompanied McIntosh to Tubuai, explaining how they had attempted and abandoned their plans to settle on that island. Bligh was obviously very flattered when she told him how Byrne, Coleman, Ellison, Hillbrant, Norman and her own McIntosh could not mention his name without crying; she therefore hoped that no harm would come to such compassionate men. Fancy Ellison and Hillbrant being included in her list; must say something about Christian's treatment of these two for them to lament the loss of their lieutenant. Bligh delved deeper, searching out as many of the misfortunes that had befallen his one-time crew as he could find and recorded a good, though sentimental and biased, account of the fates of the likes of Churchill and Thompson. One thing else he meticulously did was note the children born to *Bounty's* men; even if he no longer cared much for the fathers, he seems to have had a deep rooted love for youngsters.

Although the whole expedition was an unmitigated success in practical terms, he was still abusing and demeaning initiative and generally driving everyone to distraction. His first lieutentant (and step-nephew) Francis Godolphin Bond even went as far as to suggest Bligh was well and truly deranged; in his defence he was plagued with dizzy spells and splitting headaches, which even forced him into dictating his log – they could have been a legacy from his open boat voyage.

Nothing dogged *Providence's* physical progress and Bligh fittingly delivered thriving breadfruit plants to Jamaica (having re-visited the Fijian islands and comprehensively charted them in more comfort on the way), and reported to the Admiralty that their trust in him was admirably placed. They returned the compliment by not allowing him home; during his absence war had again broken out and he could not just sail independently across the Atlantic, but had to wait until he could fit in with a protective convoy. In the meantime, he was to cast about for any French ships that might stray his way. Eventually he arrived in England during August 1793, with an absolute, sanguine confidence in his achievements and expecting even more praise to be heaped upon his humble head. Both lofty achievement and expectations were to take an almighty tumble.

His enforced stay in the West Indies had at least given him the chance to see the breadfruit properly established, and he left firmly of the opinion that the long awaited cheap fodder for the slaves was finally there to stay. It was not to be – when the trees matured, the captive plantation workers refused to eat the food they provided.

In England, his efforts were offically recognised by the Royal Society of Arts, following a handsome purse of one thousand guineas by the thankful Jamaicans. However, that was as far as his glories went, the bubble of adoration he had left on had burst a year previously; on 19th June 1792, the survivors from *Pandora* were escorted into Portsmouth Harbour, with an entirely different story to tell.

The Dutch at Coupang were as willing to help *Pandora's* castaways as they had been those of the *Bounty,* but the ten prisoners were not to see any of their hospitality as Captain Edwards demanded their immediate confinement in the local gaol. There they stayed (in conditions which horrified the local doctor – wonder if it was still Mr Max? – when he managed to gain Edwards' permission to let him make a routine visit), until continuing the miserable journey back to justice. It was at Cape Town that Edwards finally relinquished his jurisdiction over the wretched men, when they were transferred to *HMS Gorgon,* where the meaning of the word charity was resurrected. Back in Portsmouth three months later they were housed on board *HMS Hector*.

Thirteen weeks of, in all likelihood, mental torture passed, though the ten men were spearheaded into an amazing bout of activity, James Morrison more so than the rest. He meticulously prepared his defence, assisted others with theirs, formulated his *"Memorandums"* and probably wrote the volume we now call *"The Journal of James Morrison"*. Although it purports to read as a contemporary diary, it was surely impossible for him to have transported it home on *Pandora.* No doubt an original did exist, but that must have disappeared quite a while before, maybe he just left it behind on Tahiti. Looks like Morrison was shaped in the Bligh mould when it came to writing, neither of them could bear to be without a pen in their hand for long.

Peter Heywood was also well occupied, compiling a sentimental defence, which focused on his lack of years and experience, and recorded on paper his extensive knowledge of the Tahitian language in the form of a dictionary; his original must have suffered the same fate as Morrison's journal.

On Wednesday, 12th September 1792 their trial began. The scene was set just two days before when Edwards was court martialed for the loss of *Pandora,* and honorably acquitted. Aboard *HMS Duke* The Right Honorable Lord Hood presided over twelve captains, who were to spend the next week listening to lengthy, extraordinary details of a mutiny which had taken place over three years before on the other side of the world. Each day *Duke's* gun would herald the start of another session of inflamed passion and contradictions, perjury and promises kept. Thomas Hayward conveniently forgot how he had fallen asleep whilst on watch, but was blithely content to paint Peter Heywood as a compliant participant. On the other hand, William Cole remembered the vow given to Morrison and clearly spoke up on his behalf.

The judges carefully sifted through the weighty evidence and came to the following conclusions on Tuesday, 18th September 1792: Michael Byrne, Joseph Coleman, Thomas McIntosh and Charles Norman were not surprisingly acquitted, in fact the remarkable thing was that they were brought to trial in the first place. Thomas Burkitt, Thomas Ellison, Peter Heywood, John Millward, James Morrison and William Muspratt were to hang, with Heywood and Morrison, 'recommended . . . to his Majesty's Royal Mercy'. Frantic appeals were instantly made against the committals, one coming from Nessy Heywood, Peter's sister. As soon as word of the court's decison reached the Heywood family on the Isle of Man, Nessy set out on a desperate journey to London, enduring many trials and tribulations, including terrible damage to her health, as she travelled by fishing boat and coach, by way of Liverpool.

Once in London she actually obtained an audience with Queen Charlotte and begged her to intervene on behalf of her brother, throwing herself at the German woman's feet to bolster her chances and highlight her sincerity. Whether Queen Charlotte helped is not definitely known, but Peter was pardoned by His Majesty King George III on 24th October, as was James Morrison. William Muspratt also escaped the hangman's noose, on a confusing technicality worked out by his counsel, Stephen Barney. He had wanted to call Michael Byrne and Charles Norman as witnesses for his client, but was refused permission to do so as they were still awaiting sentence themselves, so when Muspratt was convicted Barney claimed that the sailor's defence had been incomplete. The slight doubt that vital evidence was perhaps suppressed was enough to get Bill Muspratt a discharge.

For the other three there was no such fortune. On *HMS Brunswick* in Portsmouth Harbour the signal for execution was made at 25 minutes past 9 a.m., 30th October 1792 and on that autumnal morning, Thomas Burkitt 'was run up the starboard fore yard', becoming the angel he had convincingly acted during the mutiny; his humanitarianism towards the ejected men in the launch (and particularly to Bligh when releasing his caught up nightshirt) stood for nothing in the cold light of day. Millward and Ellison twitched side by side on the larboard yard arm; Millward, who had been called to arms by Churchill and only half-heartedly, though resignedly, obeyed. And young, foolish Ellison, whose wild offer to stand guard over Bligh instantly damned him; his commander was not able to inform the court that Mary had witnessed Ellison's gushing tears for him on Tahiti. Not that I suppose he would have done if he had returned in time – as if remorse and repentance had anything to do with the revenge courts doled out to inexperienced, impressionable first time offenders.

Peter Heywood rushed to the Isle of Man and his much relieved, welcoming family, but at some point stopped off to talk to Edward Christian, and passed on the verbal message Fletcher had given him on Matavai's brooding beach. Subsequently, Edward began to search out affidavits from as many of *Bounty's* men as possible, to try and ascertain the correct nature of the treatment and atmosphere during the fateful voyage of 1787-89. The resulting publication was a personal vilification of Bligh's character, especially as it was appendixed to Stephen Barney's minutes of the court martial. What could not come out at the trial for fear of associating the defendant (or witness) too closely with the ring leader, was now anonymously admitted (to have publicly sided with the mutineers even after the court martial could well have ruined a very promising career). Edward Christian's trained-in-the-law mind put forward a very convincing testimony; never denying his brother had broken the rules, he gathered several character witnesses such as the delightful sentiment that, 'every officer and seaman on board the ship would have gone through fire and water to have served him' – every officer except one, perhaps?

Christian ended his justification by playing to the gallery; in his opinion the traumas experienced in the boat voyage were but a drop in the ocean compared with the anguish Fletcher went through. However, Edward Christian concluded, from this misfortune was a lesson to be learnt – Navy beware, push a man too far and he will take your ship!

Enter stage left William Bligh. He came home from Jamaica to find the court martial over and his reputation ragged around the edges as a result. When *"The Minutes of the Proceedings of the Court-Martial"* by Stephen Barney were printed in 1794, with Edward Christian's very incriminating *"Appendix"* at the back, Bligh immediately provided a cross-examintion. It was not brilliantly argued, but it opened up the flood gates for a magnificent piece of work from the elegant, stylish pen of Edward Christian, who quickly retaliated with *"A Short Reply to Capt. William Bligh's Answer"*. Bligh could not match the intense style and vivacious mastery in the acid composition from this highly talented wordsmith, and must have blessed the chore of refitting *HMS Warley* which fell to him in April 1795. It was an awful job the Admiralty foisted on to him, but served the purpose of keeping him busily occupied – he no longer had the spare time to make another show of trying to keep up with this latest thorn-in-his-side Christian. That family was surely the bane of his life.

The abysmal ship *Warley* was handed back to the fleet at the end of 1795 in the guise of the immaculate *Calcutta,* and Bligh was rewarded for his efforts with command of the warship *Director* early in the new year. He took four days leave to spend with Betsy and girls (twin boys born to them in 1795 had sadly both died on the day of their birth), before sailing up to the Nore, off the coast of Sheerness, Kent (waters he was becoming more and more intimate with, having already taken *Calcutta* there), to begin patrolling the North Sea. For over a year he cruised in punctuated stages, back and forth to the Dutch coast with plenty of shore leave for his crew in between each trip, as was the case with all the ships of this fleet. Inactivity was leading to more serious instances of disobedience than were ever thought of on *Bounty* and hard punishments were following, even what has to be the worst fate of all was used – 'flogging-round-the-fleet'; self explanatory really; the man under sentence was towed around the fleet for a seperate dose of the lash at each ship.

Individually, all the captains were handing out their own punishments and Bligh was certainly no exception. By May 1797 the sailors were ready to riot. Bolstered by the news that a successful mass-mutiny was concluding at the Spithead, the men of the Nore, roused by a hothead called Richard Parker, followed suit. Bligh was turned off his ship yet again. For a month he was based in Sheerness, writing either letters or an account of all that was going on around him, until starvation tactics ended the mutiny of the Nore. On 17 June Bligh was back on *Director* and Parker, the self-styled president of the 'Floating Republic', was nearing the end of his life. Not long after, his mortal existence was succinctly snuffed out as he dangled from a rope attached to the yard-arm of the very ship he had briefly commanded. A few other sailors suffered the same fate, but apart from some floggings, every mutinous sailor connected with the Nore fleet was unconditionally pardoned.

Finally, the great day for which they had all been preparing arrived in October. Dutch vessels were venturing out and ready for a fight; Admiral Duncan was not one to disappoint them and led his ships into the fray. Off the coast of Holland, at Camperdown, Bligh was re-initiated into the harsh realities of water warfare after sixteen years absence; he had experienced one previous, solitary taste at Dogger Bank.

Duncan planned two simultaneous assaults and detailed *Director* to join the convoy headed by Vice-Admiral Onslow in the *Monarch;* each ship was to engage in one-to-one combat with the Dutch, but the reality of the situation proved this stratagem impossible. *Director* could not get near any prospective target and Bligh was getting weary just floating hopefully about. Suddenly he noticed the Dutch flagship *Vrijheid,* escaping advances made from Duncan's ship and instantly decided to assist. Breaking rank he wove *Director* through the line of fire, rammed *Vrijheid* at her bow and pummelled her full of shot, bringing down the masts and rigging. By the time Bligh had finished with her, she was no longer fit for sailing and her Dutch Admiral, de Winter, was forced to surrender. Bligh triumphantly sent his First Lieutenant aboard.

Once the noise and chaos of the battle subsided, Bligh was admonished for deserting his post and interferring with Duncan's prize, which he had well under control until *Director* pilfered it from him. The excitement over William's heroic attempts shot down in flames, he returned back to the Nore.

Another battle, another ship. 1st April 1801 saw Bligh fighting against the Danish forces under the rapidly rising Lord Horatio Nelson at Copenhagen, in *HMS Glatton.* During the night before the clash, tipping over into the small hours of the day itself, Nelson called upon every ounce of Bligh's navigational skills. They took the small boats and meticulously sounded out the deepest, most advantageous course to attempt in the forthcoming battle.

Nelson gathered his captains on board his ship *Elephant* and laid out his plan of action; *Glatton*was given *Dannebrog* to engage – the Danish flagship. This taste of conflict was more in keeping with the text book; Bligh stayed with the ship to which he was assigned, pulverised it, and witnessed its reduction to a blazing wreck. When the carnage had finished, Bligh was summoned back onto *Elephant* where Nelson gratefully thanked him for his loyal behaviour. William Bligh was a happy man once more.

On the 8th May he was paid off in Chatham, despite his election that same month to the Royal Society. The next years were spent surveying different parts of the British Isles; a keep-him-busy-and-out-of-mischief commission. He did a good job of course, (in the Town Dock's Museum, Hull, there is a selection of his Humberside charts on display; they are a joy to behold, bold, sensitive and so accurate there has never been found the need to revise them), but his life was now one long frustration. The Napoleonic war was continuing, Nelson was still fighting in foreign parts, but he never called upon Bligh's services again. The twisted bitter pressure built up in William's head, until the famous, never properly controlled temper viciously broke upon John Frazier, his Second Lieutenant, who injured his leg and begged to be relieved of his watch; Bligh could only see a malingerer before him and another court martial swung into action. Frazier was absolved from any guilt and promptly brought counter charges against his Captain. It was Bligh's turn to be admonished and the case was 'part proved' in February 1805. He was sentenced to watch his filthy turn of phrase.

Joseph Banks, always quietly supporting Bligh in the background, produced the solution for him, a stint abroad as Governor of New South Wales. The final phase of his eventful life was beginning. For twenty years Sydney and the surrounding area had been home to convicts, their gaolers and, more frequently with the passing of time, freed men. These released felons were allotted plots of land and slowly a community of small holdings had built up apart from the military and penal fraternity. However, those members of the New South Wales Corps who choose to stay on after a compulsory term of three years service were also granted land on which to settle. When a two year break, between Governors two and three, left the all be it temporary running of the State in the hands of the Corps commander, Major Francis Grose, a good deal of dishonesty came into play.

Grose dealt out masses of land rights to his men and individual settlers, allowing convict labour (who were government property) to be used on these private farms. The yoked men were paid in illegal rum. As in George Orwell's *"Animal Farm"*, a firm leader became established and when Governor King arrived he discovered an almost watertight monopoly in the hands of the largest landowning soldier, James Macarthur. King could make no headway in stopping the traffic in liquor or in redressing the balance of commerce and asked to leave. On 6th August 1806, William Bligh arrived in Sydney to try his hand, accompanied by his eldest daughter, Mary Putland and her husband.

He was not helped by the strengthening of Macarthur's position following a court martial King had sent him to face in London, due to a duel he fought with a fellow officer. Whilst in England, Macarthur had extolled the virtues of wool from a new breed of sheep he had introduced on his farm in New South Wales and came home acquitted, without a blemish on his character. He was also given a letter from the Colonial Secretary telling King to give him another five thousand acres. When William took up office, Macarthur was riding high.

Floods in the small holding area of Hawkesbury were adding to the distress of the little man in the street and Bligh neutralized this threat by handing out provisions and promising government custom for their next harvest. He gained gratitude and respect from the recipients of his kindness, which bolstered an arrogant attitude in his dealings with the crooked militia. Clashes of an almighty magnitude ensued, especially between Bligh and Macarthur, which resulted in the 'Rum Rebellion'.

Macarthur was brought to trial for helping a slave to escape on his ship, but the judges, officers from the New South Wales Corps, were his supporters, and they deemed there was no case to answer. Bligh simply threw him back in gaol. While he languished there George Johnston, a staunch advocate of Macarthur and by default, the major in charge of the Corps, marched his troops and an angry mob he had efficiently agitated, to Government House on 20th January 1808. There he arrested William in the firm belief that his imperiousness, which was bordering on dictatorship and tyranny, must now be halted.

When the soldiers first arrived and surrounded the house, Bligh ran upstairs to a small room and hid under the bed. His newly widowed daughter Mary turned tail in the opposite direction and rushed outside to face the *hoi polloi*, snarling at them, 'You have just walked over my husband's grave and now you come to murder my father!' Johnston ignored her and gave the excited gathering free reign to storm the house.

Eventually Bligh was unearthed and, jeered and jostled by the crowd, shepherded downstairs, where Johnston placed him under house arrest. There he stayed for a year, until he was asked to return to England; deviously he agreed, but once on board *HMS Porpoise* reneged on his word, citing it had been extracted under duress. Instead he claimed command of the vessel and sailed to Van Diemen's Land to entreat help from her Governor, Colonel Collins. An initial affinity with Bligh's plight degenerated into loathing as Collins refused to become involved, and William remained stranded on the *Porpoise* until his saviour, and replacement, arrived. Colonel Macquarie reached Sydney in December 1809. Bligh sailed to greet him in Janury 1810 and spent the next four months as a thorn in his side, until setting out for England in May. Mary stayed behind, married to Macquarie's aide, Maurice O'Connell.

At another court martial in England, Johnston was found guilty of mutiny. Macarthur was also transported, as a witness, and, with the threat of instant arrest if he ever returned to New South Wales, was never seen there again. In the most unorthodox of manners, William Bligh had rid the colony of the monopolies ring-leader, the very job he had been sent there to do. But at what personal cost?

His active career was over and he settled into domestic life at his London house in Durham Place, Lambeth. He was promoted to the rank of rear-admiral of the Blue, backdated to July 1810 and finished his life on 6th December, 1817 as a vice-admiral, having survived three mutinies (and one near miss).

Earlier that year John Fryer had also died, aged 64, on 26th May; he had continued as a master throughout his life at sea, though on a couple of store ships that made him the highest ranking man on board, and therefore commander. His last five years were spent in retirement on half pay, suffering from 'a disease of extreme nervous irritability'.

Of the remaining men from *Bounty;* Peter Heywood, who had such a harsh initiation into the delights of riding aqua waves, pushed on undaunted with his chosen profession and died in 1831 at the pinnacle of the naval ladder; he was an admiral. James Morrison was not hindered by his conviction for mutiny either, and served at the battle of Copenhagen as a gunner. He has laid in a watery grave off Madagascar since his ship, the *Blenheim,* foundered there in 1807. Thomas Hayward actually managed to obtain the title of captain before drowning in the China Sea and John Hallet met the same fate, as a Lieutenant, on *HMS Penelope.* Robert Tinkler became a post Captain. Thomas Denman Ledward started out from Batavia but disappeared without trace whilst at sea and William Purcell ended his days on 10th March, 1834 in the madhouse. As for the rest, William Cole, Joseph Coleman, Lawrence Leboque, Thomas McIntosh, William Muspratt, Charles Norman, William Peckover, John Samuel, George Simpson and John Smith, I have not been able to discover details of their individual departures from this existence; one thing is for sure though – they have all gone to a better land than this by now.

CHAPTER NINE

Money spinners

The Royalty Theatre, Well Street, London must have witnessed some frenzied activity as soon as news of the mutiny and Bligh's arrival back in England became common knowledge, because on Wednesday, 5th May 1790, only six weeks after the Admiralty was informed of *Bounty's* fate, they opened their doors on a three part presentation, concluding with *THE PIRATES;* or, *THE CALAMITIES OF CAPTAIN BLIGH.* From the comfort of a box costing the princely sum of 3s. 6d (17½p) or a place in the Upper Gallery for 1s (5p) the audience could watch *Bounty's* departure from England, her arrival and successful trading at Tahiti, native women dancing for, and fawning over, the sailors and their unbounded disappointment as they left them. 'An exact Representation of the SEIZURE of Captain BLIGH, in the Cabin of the *BOUNTY*, by the Pirates' came next, the excitement increasing as he and his 'faithful followers' were forced overboard. All the desperation in the long boat followed, finally ending in England. It is surprising though to find from the over indulgent publicity notice that this piece of theatrical 'fact' was brought together under the guidance of one of *Bounty's* own men, as one part of the action showed the long boat's 'miraculous arrival' at the Cape of Good Hope.

The nineteenth century ignored the story as far as I can determine with regards to any theatrical re-enactments (though morbid curiosity surfaced when the discovery of Pitcairn Island brought forth printed information on what had happened to the ship, although it was only treated like the last piece of a jigsaw puzzle – once slotted neatly into place the whole picture was thrown back into its box), but the 1900s had one advantage over times past, the development of motion pictures.

Australia took up the call first, realising in 1916 what a tremendously exciting film could be taken from the pages of British history; action combined with costumes were ideal factors in those silent days and brought forth *"The Mutiny Of The Bounty"*.

In March 1929 Australian producer Charles Chauvel returned from a busman's holiday in Hollywood where he had gathered lots of new ideas he was determined to put into practice. Three years later he formed Expeditionary Films, especially 'to film stories off the beaten track'. His first project was *"In The Wake Of The Bounty"*, a documentary intended to highlight life on Pitcairn Island, interspersed with dramatic elements retelling the inhabitants' famous ancestors' struggle to found an unnoticeable colony there. Chauvel and his wife Elsa accompanied cameraman Tasman Higgins on trips to Pitcairn (making them the first people ever to film on the island) and Tahiti, where they completed the documentary side of the project and returned to Australia. They nearly did not get the film into the country, as customs officers objected to the reams of film containing Tahitian ladies dancing topless. Eventually they reached a compromise.

At Cinesound's Bondi studio, Chauvel busied himself getting the interior scenes ready for his still non-existent cast, when his assistant director, John Warwick, drew his attention to a photograph published in a newspaper of the commander of a schooner in New Guinea. This young adventurer had been persuaded in 1930 to appear with his ship in a documentary film about headhunters, shot in the Sepik River – complete with crocodiles. Chauvel agreed with Warwick's suggestion that they had possibly found their Fletcher Christian here and contacted the man in the picture, tested and hired him for three weeks at £10.00 per week. Errol Flynn was about to make his first, properly scripted film. Years later he confessed he was, 'without the least idea of what I was doing'.

The work was completed, along with four other members of the cast playing Bligh, Young, Isabella and 'The Blind Fiddler', on a tale of reminiscence, beginning with an old tar in 1810 remembering in flashbacks the voyage of the *Bounty*. False interiors, filled with acting as wooden as the walls, intermingled with uncensored shots of dancing natives and general Tahitian scenes, until all mingled away to life on Pitcairn in the 1930s, finishing with a passing ship failing to respond to a desperate radio call, supposedly to highlight the remoteness of the island.

The finished, seventy minutes of *"In The Wake Of The Bounty"* was released and shown around Australia only, until the all powerful studio of Metro Goldwyn Mayer in Hollywood bought it. They had the idea of transforming Charles Nordhoff and James Norman Hall's 1932 liberty-taking trilogy, *"Mutiny On The Bounty"*, *"Men Against The Sea"* and *"Pitcairn's Island"*, into a movie, and butchered Chauvel's offering, using only the documentary elements to make two tiny nine minute clips entitled *"Primitive Pitcairn"* and *"Pitcairn Island Today"*, which were used to promote their 1935 blockbuster, *"Mutiny On The Bounty"*.

Irving Thalberg produced what was to become a classic film; highly entertaining with some wonderfully reconstructed 18th century British Navy scenes. It was totally removed from actual historical facts, but what did big movie moguls with huge dollar signs dangling in front of their eyes care about that? The opening scenes followed Clark Gable, as Fletcher Christian, down narrow Portsmouth streets to the local tavern, where he press ganged some of the inhabitants into His Majesty's Service; one of these was Tom Ellison who heart-wrenchingly left his young wife and baby behind. The mysterious narrator of the Nordhoff and Hall book is next revealed, Midshipman Roger Byam (played rather delectably by Franchot Tone) who agrees to compile a Tahitian dictionary for Sir Joseph Banks; this Byam character can be none other than Peter Heywood. The film makers' decision to rename one of the Heywood/Hayward's is just about understandable, but Messrs Nordhoff and Hall's intentions are less clear. These two adopted sons of Tahiti based their book around the anecdotes of a non existent sailor.

Even before *Bounty* sailed, Charles Laughton's sadistic Bligh insisted a dead man receive his prescribed twenty lashes, an act of brutality for which the audiences of the mid-thirties were apparently completely unprepared, considering the commotion it caused in the newspaper reviews. Another scene, considered unbelievably real, was the keel hauling of a seaman raving mad with thirst, his body crunching against the stern cleverly represented in a fairly convincing underwater scene. Other unrecognizables appeared on *Bounty's* deck; a Mr Morgan was introduced as the botanist and Mr Maggs provided some great comic moments as the land-lubber cook, while Morrison was promoted to the rank of boatswain.

They fought their way though terrible weather, going from one extreme to the other. One of the best storm sequences ever witnessed at the pictures was followed by the small boats pulling *Bounty* out of the doldrums. During this outward voyage, Bligh definitely discouraged music (thereby making fiddler Byrne redundant). Also they included the authentic mark of a British sailor (at least in the eyes of the American storytellers), a tattooed arm. It was beautiful, intricate and much too modern for the primitive, jet black and very rare designs filtering out of the South Pacific islands. It's like wearing a digital watch in *"The Rivals"*.

Tahiti was a riot of monochromatic beauty with tastes of native life ('simple, kind, Royal people', cooed Byam), including cooking in pits under leaves and the always necessary dancing scenes, looking a touch Hawaiian to my untutored eye. In next to no time they sailed away (with the surgeon still very much alive: they were saving him for harsh treatment at the hands of gruesome Bligh later) when, amidst plenty of sea sick photography, the most boring mutiny, incited by McKoy, occurred. Men tamely fought with each other while a few obediently fell from the rigging to their deaths in front of the camera, and Laughton was sent over the side, though he never uttered what are probably thought to be the most famous words in his entire career: *'I'LL SEE YOU HANG FOR THIS, MR CHRISTIAN!'* That honour was, I think I am correct in saying, left to Tony Hancock, who used to impersonate Charles Laughton's Bligh in his stage act.

Over a year after taking *Bounty,* Clark Gable and Franchot Tone celebrated Christmas on the island, comfortably ensconsed in thatched roofed love nests with their doxies; Gable's Christian the adoring father of a baby girl. Suddenly their idyllic felicity was interrupted by the appearance of the *Pandora* on the horizon and Gable beat a hasty retreat with a handful of companions and his family, pulling away from the opposite side of Tahiti as the *Pandora* pulled in, captained by a really vengeful Bligh (who had survived a terrific storm in the open boat). Byam opted to stay behind and was cruelly parted from his pretty girlfriend, Tehani, played by Mexican actress Movita, and chained in the ship's hold. An incessant search for Nemesis made Bligh lose all his good judgement and accidentally run *Pandora* on the rocks, resulting in an excellent ship wreck, when he personally conducted Byam into the lifeboat. After two hours and ten minutes of unadulterated indulgence, *"Mutiny On The Bounty"* finished with Bligh being called as a witness at the mutineers' trial, while on the other side of the world *Bounty* ran aground on the rocks of Pitcairn.

David Niven had left Britain to try his luck in Hollywood, but had only gained work as an extra, when he spotted *HMS Norfolk*, a County Class cruiser touring the coasts of Mexico and America. He knew her from mutual times spent in Bermuda and Mexico and lost no time in renewing old acquaintances, and refilling old glasses, on board her. The next morning his wobbly mind focused on an amazing sight just outside his porthole, a fully rigged 18th century ship, completely manned by pigtailed sailors was publicising the up and coming film *"Mutiny On The Bounty"*. Niven wanted to discover more and found his old friend Robert Montgomery, a man with a passion for sea vessels, on her, and together they drove one hundred miles inland to the MGM studios. Here they met director, Frank Lloyd, and Niven tried to persuade him to give him some part in the film but Lloyd was too busy to be bothered; his constant pacing and ferocious expression while worrying about Laughton's seasickness giving the star the inspiration needed for his characterization of Bligh. Niven commented, 'the only thing he wanted was Frank's eyebrows'.

Rumours that producer Thalberg was interested in signing Niven for his film flew around Tinsel Town, which caused an awful lot of studios to suddenly request interviews with him; Sam Goldwyn reacted by inviting Niven to his office and promptly offered him a seven year contract. His glittering career was underway, though he was not used in *"Mutiny On The Bounty"*!

Irving Thalberg's initial problem was to persuade Clark Gable to accept his offer to play Fletcher Christian; after a shaky start in the movies, taking on a definite conglomeration of roles, Gable was finally finding his niche as a rough diamond, a charmer who could get away with the occasional slap around the face of his leading lady, and was uncertain if Fletcher would perpetuate the image he wanted to nourish. Thalberg obviously won the day, but Gable still had his misgivings, explaining, 'I talk like an Ohio miner, I'm not going to talk like a British seaman of 200 years ago.' The producer's headaches did not stop there; constant personality clashes between his two major stars broke out, with Gable refusing to carry on at one point after accusing Laughton of deliberately shielding him from the camera. Negotiations and persuasions took all day before work got underway again.

Filming went ahead off Santa Catalina island on the coast of California, using the same specially constructed ship David Niven had spotted, when on 18th June 1935 Reuter flashed the headline around the world – 'CHARLES LAUGHTON'S NARROW ESCAPE FROM DROWNING'. The sea had become particularly choppy and Laughton had toppled over and fallen through a gap in the railings that had deliberately been cut away, doubtless to stop it interfering with camera angles, landing on a wooden platform especially built for the cameramen to work from. He was caught by a technician and suffered only a few bruises, but what a lot of fuss the newspapers made. Surely even if he had tumbled into the sea someone would have pulled him out long before any danger could have befallen him.

More drastic and serious was when, a month later, the ship sank in Cuyler's Harbour, thirty five miles from Santa Barbara, California, with three engineers on board. One of them, cameraman Glen Strong, was swept away and sadly reported missing. The newspaper reports assured their readers that no filming was in progress at the time of the accident.

"Mutiny On The Bounty" opened in England at the Empire Theatre, Leicester Square, London on Boxing Day, 1935, a Christmas present to the people of Britain from the Americans, showing exactly how our history *should* have happened. The following February the film was nominated at the 8th annual Academy Awards ceremony, in the categories: Best Picture; Best Director; Best Actor (Charles Laughton, Clark Gable and Franchot Tone) Best Script and Best Musical Score. It won only the Best Picture Award.

The world had to be content with Gable's super masculine, dynamic Christian and Laughton's barbarous, uncivilised Bligh for nearly thirty years, until Nordhoff and Hall's tome was turned into another film by MGM in 1962. The idea was put forward as early as 1959 when a script was presented by writer Eric Ambler, but it was unacceptable; they had to come up with something as far removed from the first cinema offering as possible. By the middle of 1960 a team of professionals was gathering to make *"Mutiny On The Bounty"* (mark II). Aaron Rosenberg was producer, Sir Carol Reed the director, Trevor Howard agreed to portray Bligh and Marlon Brando, husband of Movita, the Mexican actress who played Byam's love Tehani in the origial version, was cast as Fletcher Christian.

Brando was attracted by the prospect of enforcing a rebellious attitude against authority, delving further into the Pitcairn settlement by adhering much more to the third part of the trilogy and working with Carol Reed, whom he liked enormously. It wasn't to be. The story was already too long so the Pitcairn saga was sacrificed to time schedules and budgets, much to Brando's disgust, and Sir Carol was replaced half way through the shooting. In November 1960 Reed had led a friendly invasion of Papeete, Tahiti, letting loose technically minded men who re-routed a river, uprooted and repositioned trees, built huge canoes, set up a development laboratory and landed masses of equipment while the assembled cast, containing British actors Richard Harris, Percy Herbert and Gordon Jackson, imbibed the local traditions. Another person there was Charles Higham, author of many highly acclaimed biographies including *"Brando, The Unauthorized Biography"*, who kindly told me details of when he had travelled with Keith Monroe the *Saturday Evening Post* correspondent to Morea, the location used for many of the film's breathtaking scenes.

His first introduction to the exotic world of *Bounty* was to witness the whole cast and crew lined up on the beach to film a fishing sequence, in which the native men in their out-riggers were beating the water with stones tied on to ropes in order to drive the fish into the nets of waiting ladies, who had spread themselves across an inlet entrance. With thousands of people helping to land 1200lbs of fish, his welcome could surely not have been more exciting or exhilarating. Tragedy struck though during the three weeks he was there, when a spectacular canoe chase went unforgiveably wrong. Looking somewhat like a cops-and-robbers' car pursuit on water, Christian hurried after three deserting members of his crew but, as the cameras rolled, the leading vessel collided with a reef, ripping the canoe apart and spilling her contents in a bloody mass across the coral. The corpse of an extremely good looking, eighteen year old son of a native chief was carried ashore, and solemnly flown back to an unprecedented uproar which resulted in the closure of all work on the film for over a week, as diplomatic and sensitive discussions took place. The whole incident was an unfortunate accident but it took a great deal of expensive persuasion before the grieving islanders would allow shooting to start again.

Charles Higham mixed easily with all the members of the team, joining in with the swimming and barbecues on the beach during a wonderful, happy time. He found the Brando everyone described as a sullen, temperamental, selfish bore was really a compassionate, good natured and sensitive human being, eager to learn of the plight of Australia's aborigines, and Brando found in Charles the ideal person to inform him, living as he then did in Sydney. Horrified by what he learnt about their conditions, Brando later fulfilled a promise to visit them. Charles was impressed with the great deal of thought he put into portraying Fletcher. Brando bothered to think around him as well as inside, perfecting an Oxford accent and cleverly introducing the audience to a fop, a slightly effeminate weak man, uncomfortable with life on a vessel at sea. He summed up the essence of an eighteenth century dandy and in doing so gave himself a leeway to transform Christian into an individual; there is no excitement in a character who is the same from beginning to end (as sadly Clark Gable gave us), the thrill is in witnessing a drastic change. When Bligh stepped too far, the stunning moment came (which Higham admires as one of the great moments in Brando's career). He strikes out at Trevor Howard in an act of defiant mutiny. It was a magnificent moment because the worm turned and suddenly this pathetic creature became a man.

Reed's vision was to promote Bligh as the hero up against the villainous Christian, and Howard proved to be the perfect foil for his plans. Trevor had the knack of making you believe he had spent his entire life on a quarterdeck and was running the ship by exact Royal Navy laws. This was the key to his performance, he was not a despot, he was someone who had a rule book and stayed with it.

The ship used was precariously top heavy, over laden with cameras, booms and other paraphernalia perched high in the rigging, complete with their necessary operators. This constituted a dangerous situation as she listed back and forth, under the guidance of woefully inadequate merchant seamen. Although respected in their skill at handling comtemporary ships, they were inexperienced in working an exact replica of a ship that had been extinct for well over 150 years. Two seperate visits were made to Tahiti during the making of this film, firstly under the guidance of Carol Reed. Niggling problems, such as erratic weather and lighting conditions, constant re-writes to the script by both Ambler and Brando, the star's sudden (never allowed to be serious) decision to swop his role for that of John Adams, and Reed becoming ill with gallstone and heat troubles, resulted in the director being unable to agree to MGM's demands that he complete in 100 days. He was promptly replaced by the white Russian, Lewis 'Milly' Milestone, seventy years old and tougher than the whole cast and crew put together. He took them all back to Tahiti and began again in the summer of 1961, when Brando, who had got on exceptionally well with Reed, lived up to his reputation for being unprofessional and difficult. He arrived later and later on the set and once there he constantly interrupted the proceedings by mulling over the meaning of his lines, and often changing them, consistent with the 'method' actors' approach. Reed had always accommodated this peculiarity, but Milestone was less compliant and clashed terribly with his inherited star.

Nearly everyone fell foul of sea sickness and/or dysentry, life was becoming more and more miserable. When back in America Milestone decided against continuing with the project, everything stopped for a good six months. Eventually a decision had to be made and an unknown director, George Seaton, was ordered to finish this plagued version of *"Mutiny On The Bounty"*. He oversaw the death scene of Fletcher Christian, and for this Brando decided he needed 200lbs of ice. Stripped to his underwear, he lay in it until frozen and shaking; it was an old trick of his, used to assist him in faking 'death tremors'. Properly in the mood for dying he spread himself on the studio floor doubling for Pitcairn's volcanic rocks, the clapperboard snapped, the camera whirled and, Brando forgot his lines. With them written on his leading lady's forehead, he finally managed to expire and promptly took to his bed with a cold. Work stopped again.

Twenty million dollars were spent on a film panned by all the critics; one of the reasons given was that Brando's accent was too incomprehensible for American audiences. It was the last movie Lewis Milestone ever made.

Viewing it twenty-five years later with all the furore well and truly buried, if the true story is put aside, it really is not as bad as was made out. It is quite an entertaining piece of nonsense, though a few 'old salts' are in evidence and there is something distasteful, if not downright sordid, in the sight of them cavorting with the voluptuous Tahitian maidens; don't forget *Bounty* was crewed by young men with an average age of 23.

MGM finally released 177 minutes of film in glorious Ultra Panavision 70, starting their tale with the arrival of Mr Brown the botanist from Kew. Obviously he was no seaman as he was immediately taken to task for calling *Bounty* a boat, and so the scene was set for lots of trite nautical observations, such as orders to loosen topsails and calls for all hands on deck. The acting of the lesser cast members as they worked their way through over-indulged melodrama left a lot to be desired, but it has to be said, Brando definitely saved the day by injecting some enigmatic, charming nuances which he carried off to perfection, despite being hampered by such an awful storyline. His initiation into the world of Tahitian embraces with chief Hiti-Hiti's daughter Miamiti is a beautiful, romantic, even sensual moment carried to a delightful ending, as Bligh interrupts their passion in the bushes and demands Fletcher does not meddle with the King's daughter. With a very British stiff upper lip in evidence, he obeys and leaves her with a captivating, 'Sorry old girl'. Fate takes a hand and Hiti-Hiti refuses the breadfruit he had previously promised to Bligh because his Miamiti was so cruelly deserted. Bligh has no option but to order Christian to resume his wooing of her; Brando's ironic sarcasm is wonderful as he agrees to try his best.

He certainly did do his best, both on and off screen; part time local waitress Tarita, who was plucked from obscurity to play this lead female part, carried her devotions over into real life and was soon living with Brando. Thus came about the strange factual feat that Marlon Brando fathered children by actresses involved with both of MGM's versions of the story of *"Mutiny On The Bounty"*! His second wife, Movita, produced a second son for him, Miki, during their very short-lived and bizarre marriage, after which Tarita became the mother of two other children and, despite the absence of a gold band on the third finger of her left hand, he has remained devoted to her ever since. Coincidentally, his son from his first marriage is called Christian.

The alure of Tahiti was too great for Brando who, having finished *"Mutiny On The Bounty"*, moved on to newer and more exciting projects, yet still found himself pulled back toward the South Seas. More than likely, Tarita had a great deal to do with his feelings for her homeland, and, in 1963 he bought his own piece of paradise, an atoll made up of thirteen tiny islets, twenty-five miles from Tahiti. On this dangerous, coral ringed Utopia he could forget his cares and worries and escape from the modern world. Curiously though, he built an hotel there.

In the film, Howard's Bligh had taken on board double the amount of plants orginally catered for to appease the Admiralty, but to avoid losing any through lack of water the men's allowances were rationed to one ladle full, which first had to be retrieved from the highest yard arm. A sailor too ill to climb the rigging became raving mad with thirst and had been drinking sea water. He desperately needed to flush it out with fresh. Christian obliged, Bligh kicked the ladle from his hands and precipitated the punch from Brando so admired by Charles Higham. Within a few minutes Fletcher Christian had taken command of the ship and Trevor Howard, with a launch full of extras, was cast away. He was quickly transported through the magic of film to his court martial where he was acquitted, though admonished for his excess of zeal.

Meanwhile, Pitcairn had been spotted by accident, a boat full of stars landed on sumptuous sandy beaches and built their colony. Charles Lederer, who had replaced Eric Ambler as writer, devised a nail biting sequence on which to finish the story. Brando suggested to his fellow mutineers that they accompany him home to put their side of the saga. Richard Harris, being the lead supporting actor and therefore given the most lines and greatest amount of floggings, asked for the night to think it over, during which time they set the ship alight to prevent Christian from leaving. He noticed, fought hard to save *Bounty,* was horribly burned in the process and lingeringly died. To the very end, the picture only allowed infinitesimal, tantalizing glimpses of the real story, and how are the uninformed to sift the wheat from the chaff?

At the next Academy Awards *"Mutiny On The Bounty"* was nominated for Best Picture, Robert Surtees for his direction of the photography, and for one evocative song, 'Follow Me'. Even those who hated the film usually admitted loving Bronislau Kaper's music, though it is a shame his gloriously stirring music accompanying *Bounty's* departure from Portsmouth degenerated into strains of 'Rule Britannia'. Not one of the Oscar nominations won.

The subject of the *Bounty* was dropped for a further twenty years when suddenly, quite independently of each other, two separate projects took shape; a fifth film went into production in 1983, while the stage musical *"Mutiny!"* was moulded into the proper production that opened in London's West End on 18 July 1985. The latest attempt to thrill the cinema audiences was certainly different from the other four; as the promotional posters proclaimed, 'After two hundred years, the truth behind the legend', *"The Bounty"* was almost one hundred per cent correct. It still contained an element of poetic licence, but at least the overburdening influence of Nordhoff and Hall was refreshingly absent, the mutiny itself built from hesitant beginnings to a thrilling crescendo and the actors were believably young.

In the drawing-room of Anthony Hopkins' home, complete with grand Steinway piano tucked away in the corner, I sank next to him into welcoming cushions on his comfortable sofa and, watched over by the elegant portrait of his wife, talked to him about his role of William Bligh in *"The Bounty"*. In a memorable hour of entertaining conversation he explained his personal understanding of the character, how some of the most important scenes were technically put together and of how he initially became involved with the film.

It all began in 1978, when he was living in California and one day, right out of the blue, he received a telephone call from Katherine Hepburn (whom he knew from having worked with in the film *"Lion In Winter"* some years before). He was puzzled by this call, until she told him a friend of hers, the very eminent director David Lean, wanted to meet him; Tony actually said he couldn't believe it! Naturally, he asked why and she explained that Lean was casting a film, and then to my absolute delight he lapsed into a wonderfully accurate imitation of Hepburn's famous grating, drawn accent and continued, 'about the remaking of the mutiny on the *Bounty* and he wants you to play a part, I guess, so would you phone him? He's staying at Bel Air Hotel'. He had great fun impersonating her, so much so that all the pleasantries which passed between them were also conveyed to lengthen the brilliant imitation.

Upon telephoning the Bel Air, Tony and his wife, Jeni, were invited to dinner by David Lean, where he was handed an extraordinary two-volume script, written by Robert Bolt (the gifted playwright who has given the world the legacy of *"A Man For All Seasons"* and *"Vivat*

Vivat Regina"), and was asked to play the part of William Bligh, a man he only knew through the portrayals of Charles Laughton and Trevor Howard. Hopkins was full of praise for the marvellous performance Laughton had put into his rendition of the role, but through reading Bolt's version, he came to realise that Bligh was not the unscrupulous, unjust monster that Laughton had created; Bolt showed him that although Bligh was historically a tough taskmaster, he was still one of the best navigators the British Navy had produced – in fact many young seamen had wanted to learn skills in this department under him.

The scripts interested Tony Hopkins enough for him to accept. Lean got the preparations underway in Tahiti and commissioned the building of an exact replica of *Bounty,* when without warning, Dino De Laurentiis, the producer, pulled out the money and the film was virtually cancelled. Unperturbed, Tony went on to different projects, including his highly acclaimed performance of Sir Frederick Treves opposite John Hurt's marvellous Joseph Merrick in the 1980 movie *"The Elephant Man",* and in the following year followed in Laughton's footsteps again by playing Quasimodo in *"The Hunchback Of Notre Dame",* while on BBC2 he showed exactly how *Othello* should be played.

Four and half years after the cancellation of the film he answered another mysterious telephone call; this time he found himself speaking to Bernie Williams, a British producer, who asked if he was still interested in being Bligh. Laurentiis was still involved, but other drastic changes had in the meantime occurred; Lean was no longer director, so Roger Donaldson stepped into his shoes, and the script had been drastically cut. It was nowhere near as good as the original because so much had been taken out, but Tony agreed to pick up the pieces, and in March 1983 they set about recreating the voyage of the *Bounty.*

The research started in earnest and about a week before filming began he went out to dinner with Stephen Walters, a self confessed expert on the *Bounty* saga, a very nice fellow, though a little eccentric like all dedicated experts. As the meal progressed everyone in the restaurant became aware of their plans, because Walters had such a loud voice, and as somebody walked out they wished them good luck with the film! During their conversation, he disclosed that Bligh was a Cornishman, and asked if Tony would try an authentic accent. Hopkins' extensive experience and training instantly came to the fore and his common sense told him it would be a bit baffling to do that, but a few days later he was reading through his lines when the thought crossed his mind to try it in a kind of theatrical West Country accent, and it fitted perfectly; it sounded just right. He gave a graphic demonstration, the R's rolling like thunder as he growled, 'Mr Christian, Sir', and, 'Mr Fryer'.

Immediately he gained a sense of the character; he had found a craftsman, someone they would have termed in those days as being from the merchant class (as his father was a customs man) and that is how Tony approached him, as a man who was four square, a man dedicated to duty, dedicated to the book of navigation, with an important feeling of great naval discipline. He knew Bligh never keel hauled anyone. Although it went on in the eighteenth century, it was illegal and he was a stickler for the law, so the thorough villain Laughton created in his wonderful performance was sadly inaccurate. He did not enjoy flogging his men, in fact he petitioned the Admiralty to abolish the cat-o'-nine-tails because he knew in his heart of hearts that it was useless, it just destroyed a man if you whipped him. Many men actually died under the lash, but if they physically survived having their backs literally ripped open, they were useless afterwards, the demoralization involved in being flogged broke their spirits.

Hopkins gained an enormous insight into the commander of *Bounty*, realising what a hard man he was, making the men dance every morning on deck because he believed in physical fitness, making them drink a concoction of vinegar and oil, and cabbage water (which Tony ventured was pretty unappetizing) because he was so scared of scurvy and that was the best method they knew to eradicate it in those days. His actions were a manifestation of a sense of duty. Tony understood Bligh had many failings simply because he was a human being and realised his main problem was that he was a very aloof man who did not readily mix with people, and also that he had a foul tongue. Tony believes Captain Cook wrote in his diary, 'Mr Bligh has a salty tongue, he's a pugnacious man – but what a navigator', followed by exclamation marks (they were drawn in the air for me). He appeared to Tony to be a hard man to please as well and an authoritarian, yet strangely enough was very sensitive, a paradoxical character who was a good sketch artist and cartographer, a botanist, who used to draw plants, a naturalist and a devoutly religious Protestant. He used to make them all say prayers, in the morning and at night before they bedded down on their incredible voyage. Hopkins believes it was a remarkable man who saved those men in that open boat and was full of admiration at how, when they were being chased between the Fijian Islands by the cannibals, he was sketching for the Admiralty, charting the islands! The actor conceded, 'I do like the guy, he was an extraordinary man'.

During the making of *"The Bounty"* he came to understand how life on Tahiti wove a remarkable effect on people; they stayed there for nine weeks and strangely for a paradise it had a perplexing, depressing impression. He was talking to an American doctor there with them, who explained that if you are a European and stay out in the sun all day, experiencing what the American's call (his mid-Atlantic diction came in beautifully at this point) 'Vi-tamin D toxicity', when mad dogs and Englishmen go out in the midday sun there is an overdose of vitamin D that has a very depressing effect. He personally could remember how many of his colleagues did become very lethargic, not only with the heat but very very bad tempered and depressed, just like a great melancholia had descended upon them.

Matters degenerated when the film crew left the land and shooting began on the water. The beautiful replica of *Bounty,* built exactly to scale in New Zealand in 1979 for David Lean, from the original plans, yet with a few luxury items such as an engine incorporated, was a disaster. Marvellous for artistic authenticity, she was a headache to work on because she was much too small to accommodate all the technical staff and their equipment, quite apart from the actors. Two toilets served approximately fifty people, some of whom suffered sea-sickness. Conditions, although comfortably modern below the eighteenth century façade, were cramped with everyone getting in each other's way. Being constantly so close gave rise to a great deal of irascibility, especially on the technical side; the actors, when not needed in a scene, could bask on the sun deck or go downstairs and lie on a bunk in an air conditioned cabin (though that was turned off during the actual moments of filming because of the noise), but the camera-men had to contend with the sun suddenly disappearing behind a huge sail or cloud. Just as everything was turning they would lose the sun and have to stop and start again. That then caused nightmares in the continuity department, because the motorized ship would have to be brought round in a two mile sweep before they could carry on with the same piece of background. Tempers frayed very quickly, with a lot of screaming and shouting going on, and the best insight ever into how the actual mutiny happened.

The day they filmed the seizure of *Bounty* was scary and serves as an excellent illustration of the general atmosphere. By then the magic of Tahiti had well and truly taken its toll on everyone, some members of the cast were getting upset with each other, Mel Gibson as Fletcher Christian was behaving badly and complaining about the way things were going, when a thought like a thunderbolt struck Tony Hopkins; it would prove pretty dangerous to have people (especially in their frame of mind) running around with swords and such things, and he insisted on rehearsing first. His fellow actors shrugged aside the idea, claiming they could just improvise but he held his ground knowing that when you have scenes which are raucous and riotous, inviting everyone to go mad, they must be properly rehearsed and choreographed, otherwise, if they do not know exactly what they are doing, someone could end up losing an eye, or being seriously injured in a different form. The finished section is the best representation of the mutiny ever presented to the public, and part of the credit for this has to fall very firmly into Tony's lap.

On Tahiti, he found the local inhabitants were taking the excitement of having a film company around a little too literally, some of them coming to believe he really was Bligh. He felt aloof from them, they would not talk to him very much, whenever he bid them a cheery good morning he would receive the reply, 'Ah Captain Bry, you bad man'. His workmates started to fall under the same spell, dining and socializing with him at their hotel, but once they stepped on board *Bounty* he would feel alienated from them. Although stressing he is not a methodite – he does not become so involved with his part that he no longer knows who he is – he did confess to perceiving a *slight* change of identity.

Unhappily he found himself in a position to observe that the people of Tahiti today are nowhere near the friendly image manifested by their ancestors of two hundred years ago. They are now French Polynesian, no longer the gregarious, friendly people they used to be because of Western influences (started by the white 'gods' of the *Bounty).* Drug taking and alcoholism seem to have replaced their lost traditions, and they are now downtrodden and poverty stricken; it is not the peaceful, beautiful paradise it obviously was at one time.

Tony would joke about the exotic locations he visited to make *"The Bounty";* when anyone asked where they filmed he very nonchalantly, yet truthfully, with his soft blue eyes all a crinkle, replied, 'Oh Tahiti, New Zealand . . . and Wembley!' It was in fact at the Lee International Studios in Wembley that the interior sets for one of the most visually effective and stunning parts of the movie were constructed – the sequence when *Bounty* fought to round Cape Horn. A lot of work and detail were put into that set, platforms built on great springs which the whole film crew plus many extra workers would rock to recreate the violence of the storm. The fire brigade helped by pouring thousands of gallons of water onto the proceedings, having first meticulously set up a drainage and sluice system. Amid chaos and pandemonium, the actors bounced around on these dangerous platforms for two days, always the possibility they could be swept off their feet a predominant danger if they were not careful. Indeed, they were all warned to brace themselves against the enormous pressure from the water once the sluices were opened, and plenty of ropes and a net were provided for their safety; of course, what looked more natural on a sailing ship than masses of lines everywhere?

Out in Gisborne harbour, New Zealand, they produced the soggy, exterior moments to accompany the work done in Wembley. The ship was moored alongside the harbour where four massive chutes had been erected, complete with huge tanks on top containing about five tons of salt water. Hopkins' immediate impression was to wonder how they were going to manage to film without catching all the cranes and modern buildings in the background, but two barges bobbing beside them contained the answer. They were specially there to smother the whole proceedings with big smoke screens which would eventually be taken as representing fog. On the command of 'action', *Bounty* remained upright and moored to the side, while the cameras tilted, the smoke swirled, high velocity hoses shot water into great big fans which transformed it into a massive spray and redirected it onto the actors, giving them a sense of a gale, and the worst form of torture was let forth. The tanks at the top of the chutes individually released massive waterfalls (at one point Mel Gibson was washed right off his feet) and they were attacked by bits of jelly fish which stung them on the face, having been dredged up from the harbour with the sea water. The dangers were minimised by the ever present, life saving ropes, which actors gladly made good use of, if they felt the deck disappear from under them.

A third manoeuvre completed the storm sequence, this time not requiring any actors, just the magnificent skill of a special effects team. A third size model of the ship was used in a huge frothed up tank of water, and they overcranked the film, that is sent it through the aperture many frames faster than normal, which gives a slow motion effect and makes the waves look bigger and more fearsome than they really were. Aided by this trick photography, the Wembley interiors and New Zealand exteriors were blended together to make an impressive, powerfully realistic storm at Cape Horn. Incidentally, the model used was finally burnt to simulate the firing of *Bounty* which ended the film.

Anthony Hopkins summed up his involvement in *"The Bounty"*, and with Bligh in particular, by recalling what he felt was either an extraordinary piece of synchronisity or a magical coincidence. He was staying in London just before the film started at a time when there was a lot of messing around with changes to the script, when one morning he was sent a particularly awful version to peruse. His temper, which had been on a very fine thread, finally snapped over the abysmal script in front of him, and he determined to give Bernie Williams a dressing-down, but was unable to get hold of him. Tony worked himself up into so tight a state that he could not sleep that night, and when he found himself pacing the floor early the next morning he decided to walk his bad humours off, and take time just to sort things out in his own mind. As he spoke, it was obvious he was reliving the lovely sunny morning and retracing his steps from Piccadilly, down St James', along Trafalgar Square, towards Waterloo Bridge, down Lambeth, past Lambeth Palace, across the road until, still fuming about his problem, he stopped to rest beside a Church. Leaning against the wall he glanced over and there was a tomb, bearing the inscription *'William Bligh'* Immediately he thought he was on Candid Camera, but no, he had stumbled across (or been led to) the very place in which Bligh was finally laid to rest, reunited with his darling Betsy and their day old twin sons. He entered the churchyard as far as possible although the grave itself is fenced off by the Tradescant Trust, looked at it and, thinking how silly, how funny the situation had become, he started laughing.

Also however he took full advantage of what providence had dealt him, and addressed the ornate, crest adorned sarcophagus, saying, 'Well, William, if you're down there, if you can hear me, I've got a bit of a problem with the re-write. I don't know, maybe you can help me, if you're around – can you hear me?' He chuckled again, and censured himself, thinking it was really ridiculous, then wove a philosophical way home, a peaceful calmness telling him it was all so unimportant, the man was dead and gone and everything boiled down to it being only a film. Back in the apartment after just five minutes, Bernie Williams telephoned with heartening news. 'Look,' he said, 'you know that re-write we sent you? Well forget it, it's awful.' With the greatest relief Tony agreed, thanked him, hung up and gave credit where it really was due. He recalled, 'I thought, "Well thank you William Bligh, wherever you are." I think he had a word in there somewhere; I believe all that.' The man might be dead and gone but he still carries some clout. Hopkins succinctly summed up Bligh's character by describing him as flawed, human but heroic.

This fifth film, *"The Bounty"*, failed to grasp the critic's and the public's imagination, and became reduced to the sorry state of sitting on the half price rental shelf in the local video hire shop, although it was very well received when BBC1 gave it pride of place in their schedules for New Year's Day, 1988. With an excellent cast, including cameos from Sir Laurence Olivier and Edward Fox, it should have gained higher glories, but even its other major star, sex symbol Mel Gibson (he of *Mad Max* fame) could attract little attention.

Gibson fell a lot under the disruptive influence of Tahiti that Tony Hopkins spoke about; Mel admits to being a brawler by nature, and would never dream of turning his back on a fight. In Tahiti he instantly dived into an altercation which exploded between the film crew and some extremely big locals, ending up very much the worse for wear. It was not a sensible thing for anyone to become involved in, let alone the star of a movie beset by other problems, and he caused a great deal of unnecessary consternation by coming away from the mêlée concussed, after being struck over the head by a blunt instrument. It was not the only fight he got himself mixed up with either, and gave the make up artist plenty of overtime as his bruised face was disguised.

Gibson took a great deal of care over his portrayal of Christian, delving deep into his researches. It could not be just pure coincidence that one of his twin sons born during the making of *"The Year Of Living Dangerously"*, the film he starred in immediately prior to *"The Bounty"* (therefore during a period when he could possibly have begun putting out tentative investigations into his next role), was named Christian. Now there are two pretend Fletchers (him and Brando) each with a real child called Christian! Mel Gibson wanted to play the mutineer unlike anyone else, and strove to give a taste of the real man, so much so that he visited a London psychiatrist with details of Fletcher to find out as much as he could about his personality. His final filmed version provides an insight into a very silly, spoilt and sulky young man, whom he describes with a mixture of Australian irreverence and American disrespect as, 'just a loyal office boy who sort of flipped out at work one day and tossed the boss off the ship!' He wanted to dispel the myth that Christian was the hero, likening him to, 'a kid with a few problems' and stressed that the whole idea of the film was to show both Fletcher and Bligh's point of view.

It is a grand film, using details straight out of Bligh's own log, though based upon the book *"Captain Bligh And Mr Christian"* by Robert Hough, an excellent, enjoyable and basically truthful publication, which has since been renamed *"The Bounty"* and has a cover adorned with stills from the film. The only main fault I can find with both book and movie is the perpetuation of the love affair between Christian and Mauatua, and perhaps to take that away from the story is like denying the existence of Robin Hood's Maid Marion. Other slight imperfections are overwhelmed by the incredible attention to detail, especially the copies of the white ceremonial dresses worn by the island girls that Bligh wrote were so 'becoming and pretty'.

By the time *"The Bounty"* was released in 1984, the stage musical *"Mutiny"!* was well into its two years preparation, which its mentor and star, David Essex, had to endure before getting this production underway. He raised the backing, composed the music, co-wrote the lyrics with Richard Crane (who was once resident dramatist at the National Theatre), cast himself in the role of Fletcher Christian, even though he was a good fifteen years older, and sometime during the year and two months it ran at the Piccadilly Theatre, followed Marlon Brando's example by bedding his leading lady. In a seven minute postal interview (I sent the questions and tape, he recorded the answers) obtained after fourteen months of constantly harrassing his agent, Essex economically explained that because he considers himself a writer of music which was a factor so inherent in work on the ship, he was drawn toward the credible transition of having music in the show without it needing to be a bit superfluous. Also he was very interested in the story, even though he was originally worried that with three well-known films around, it had already been done to death. His conscience was soothed by the first two films being, as he said, 'a bit skew-wiff, a bit Hollywood', and the last one he felt was pretty accurate, from the Bligh point of view. As his version was to revolve solely around his portrayal of Fletcher Christian, he had nothing to fear from going ahead.

Once the money side of matters was settled, they got down to the serious planning; William Dudley went back to the drawings of the orginal *Bounty,* and working from them designed and built a stupendous masterpiece, masquerading as a fully moving stage set. Despite being a bad sailor Essex found seasickness no problem as his mind was so focused (especially in the storm sequence) that he did not have time to start feeling queasy. The worst aspect of performing on a constantly tilting surface at the beginning was getting used to manoeuvring it correctly; lots of lights would cascade down on actors in rehearsals! Six weeks were spent practising in all, before they actually opened, a very strenuous, very physical period for everyone involved. Even Frank Finlay (who was Bligh) clambered up and down the ropes as they strove to get the feeling of working very closely together as a crew.

The perfected programme presented to the paying audience was a strange affair, visually colourful and stunning, burning with energy, wistfully romantic, bristling with highs and lows, good and bad, but unfortunately full of inconsistencies and terrible song lyrics. 'The Emerald Isle set in a sapphire sea' made me instantly think of Ireland instead of Tahiti, and the sentimentality contained in the ballad *"Friends"* (plus the enforced dragging out of the word 'material-i-i-ise' to make it fit with the tune) left me desperately embarrassed for Frank Finlay who was forced to utter part of the text, as well as be on the receiving end of some of it. It was quite nice to be able to sing along with the more well known songs, such as *"Tahiti"* and *"Fallen Angels Riding"*, and the folksy, sea shanty rhythms in the *"Prologue"* and *"Lash"* bobbed along beautifully. Also a true taste of eighteenth century hornpipe music seemed to be contained in the raucous *"Saucy Sal"* and surely the Tahitian welcome could not be surpassed. All in all *"Mutiny!"* passed muster by doing exactly what every theatrical production endeavours to do, it provided an excellent evening's entertainment and left a very firm initial impression, which set me on the road to discover exactly where they have gone wrong.

I do wish I had been present at the performance when the stairs leading between the decks collapsed as the cook went down, just at the moment a funeral procession passed by on the top deck, and all the mournful sailors struggled to remain serious. Even the corpse witnessed what happened and the Union Jack that was shrouding him began shaking as he succumbed to a fit of the giggles. Luckily the only casualty was a set of broken stairs, the cook was fine.

Out of all the possible endings, they chose to let Fletcher Christian finish his days out in his cave (although the whole show was rounded off with the arrival of the *Topaz* at Pitcairn and a quick résumé of the final fates of the remaining men), because the image of Christian by himself, alone, and in disarray mentally seemed more powerful than the probably most accurate theory, that he was killed by a Tahitian and then eaten by pigs, which did not appeal as a very good close to a musical.

During the last six months of *"Mutiny's"* run, Simon Horrill, an excellent, classically trained ballet dancer who has toured the world and worked in Wayne Sleep's *"Dash"*, joined the company and played Thomas Ellison – as a midshipman. He had no sympathy for the character he was playing, because he knew he was nowhere near portraying the actual person who fully paid the price for his insubordination, thinking of him as 'a bit of a toe-rag, because he was the one with the cushy life, getting all the nice drinks and meals downstairs and then he goes and does a bit of the old dripping off to the baddies', as Simon thought they were in the end. These loyalist tendencies stemmed from a deep respect for Frank Finlay's phenomenal acting, which petrified him first of all, coupled with borrowing a facsimile of Bligh's notebook, from which he sensed that Bligh genuinely did everything for the right reasons. He sensibly noted, 'You have got to be a hard task master to achieve anything in any walk of life – like the production itself, there's no way the show was going to get on if people didn't shout and scream at us to sing in key. You can't just say, "Oh get on with it and sing any key you like", you have got to sing in the same key, and people had to toe the line on the boat'.

Simon was inclined to disagree with David Essex's point of view concerning working on board the ship. He had to take seasickness tablets for the first week he was there because of the way the boat rises completely out of the stage and tilts and turns. As for the storm sequence, he would go to the edge and look down into a fifty foot drop straight into the basement. With absolute conviction he said, 'I felt really ill in my first week, I was terrible, I didn't need any reality. Oh, it was awful'. He likened it to being on a constant merry-go-round, and even at the end of the evening, when he was finally at home, he would be merrily chatting and suddenly, with profuse apologies, disappear quickly to bed explaining he could see three of them, because he was still swirling around.

The boat (both Simon and David Essex referred to their *Bounty* as 'the boat') caused other problems as well. Being used to large areas in which to dance, Simon had to work hard at getting used to such a confined space. Two huge central masts, a steering wheel, grids where they clambered down to the lower level, and an ever present awareness of being close to the edge of a sheer drop restricted their performance. Also having been used to 'hundreds of feet' clear above his head on a normal stage, suddenly he was confronted with diagonal rigging hampering his movements which, together with the upright masts, gave the impression of being inside a small tent.

The whole ship revolved on an incredible cogs system housed below the stage run by hydraulics, with lots of wheels to guide her – they quite literally had to steer a proper course. William Dudley had engineered some incredible mechanics, because she not only revolved and could be raised and lowered, she also split straight down the middle to reveal the inside of the cabins downstairs. It gave Simon the fright of his life when, during a dress rehearsal, he stepped onto the wrong half and started going down instead of up so, knowing he was not meant to be down with the officers, he scrambled madly with one foot on one deck and one foot on the other and was slowly being separted in two. In all his years as a dancer, he had never moved so quickly to get onto the top level! Initially the whole movement was disorientating and he was not able to discover which end he should be facing for ages, all sense of direction failed completely. When he first joined the cast, as part of his studies he was sent out into the audience with his script and music to try and plot his movements, but of course he was watching a mirror image and once he tried to put it into practice, found himself up the wrong end of the boat and moving in an opposite direction from everybody else. When it got too much like 'patting your head and rubbing your tummy', he gave up and watched from the wings.

From the auditorium side of the stage he was able to appreciate the full effect of the tightly woven net veil they placed across the stage at certain parts of the proceedings to help emphasise the stormy weather. It had clouds painted on it and yet more swirling clouds were projected upon it together with clever lighting effects, which combined to produce some brilliant, evocative sights, but from the performer's side they may as well have acted to a brick wall. It was very unnerving for them, not being able to immediately see the audience (searching to see if there was an empty seat or whether Mum was in), but the atmosphere of being cut off in the middle of the sea was greatly enhanced, especially as all the wings and backdrop were black.

Simon's role consisted of one solitary line ('Is it true what they say about the Tahitian women?'), joining in the general volume of the singing (even when off stage during the natives' war dance he had to sit in a booth and provide the backing grunts) and producing the most stylish footwork possible. The second act opened with a delightful, romantic ballet dance where four of the sailors, including Simon, wooed four Tahitian girls. It looked delightful, starting out slow and building up very fast with lots of high lifts, some around the neck, but even the beauty of that was only reached after a great deal of hard work. The men had to be so careful about lifting their partners without becoming tangled in the sarong costumes which had lots of spare pieces of material in which fingers could become tangled. Rehearsals would suddenly degenerate into a muddled pile of dancers with a wig one way and a costume the other. More serious was the stage area on which they had to dance, because, although the boat was packed away, it did not fall flush into the basement, leaving slight ridges they had to be careful not to trip over. The whole area was so tilted it was like a sheer precipice. The exaggerated angle caused a great deal of discomfort for the musicians as well, because should anyone drop one of their props or part of their costume came adrift, the offending article rolled straight down into the orchestra pit. Due to the terrifying amount of damage a spear from the warriors' dance could cause, as the actors moved at alarming speeds, the sight of a broom handle with a dangerous, though blunted, tip hurling towards them, warranted a safety net positioned right across the pit.

Safety was always uppermost during *"Mutiny!"* much more than in many other productions, simply because of the fantastic amount of dangerous equipment they had around. Anyone who climbed the rigging had to wear a safety wire, and a member of the stage management was always on the ship. He was the one with the strategically placed scarf to hide an earphone, and a mircrophone belt round his waist complete with a hand microphone, so he could relay any problems to the backstage crew. The first introduction the audience are given to the ship is when the hull rises up out of the stage and the masts and rigging lower from the ceiling, and, as they twirl round, there comes the moment when the two elements line up and drop into place. On one occasion, the person responsible for overseeing the alignment had to speak quickly into his microphone for the management to fly the rigging out, because it had not married up properly and could not be bolted together. An American actor who saw the show told Simon that in the States they would have demanded danger money everytime anyone had to walk a plank or climb a piece of rigging, because it could be so very treacherous.

They were backed up by a large backstage crew, who crept around dressed entirely in black, including balaclavas. The stage management provided all the props and made sure everything was in its proper place at the right time (especially the Ribena-filled decanter), and the wardrobe people were really kept busy. The worst thing they had to deal with was the Tahitian king's head-dress; a high cone of about two or three feet smothered in quills, with tiny orange feathers stuck on the end of them. The first time this king was seen was as he rose in a canoe from below the stage (to give the impression of it sailing in by the side of the boat) and these delicate little feathers would invariably get caught or they would bend and break. So between almost every performance wardrobe would be frantically repairing them. Another major problem were the wigs, which tended to be balding after a while, and for characters who were supposed to be in the region of 17 to 24 years old, they seemed to be going thin on top very early. Simon replaced two other Ellison's so his had already had a great deal of use – he remembered he had to be very careful the way he parted his wig. This part of his costume initially tended to be a bit of a nuisance, until he got used to a plait flapping into his face, something he had never had to contend with before.

The show closed on 20th September, 1986, on a memorable note. During the course of so long a run, they had gathered a regular following of devotees who came back time after time, and often knew the plot a lot better than some of the new cast members! At the final matinee, the mutiny had just taken place, Bligh had been set adrift and David Essex inquired, 'Who's coming with me?' to which the entire audience replied, 'WE ARE!' The whole cast was won over, having to face upstage as they dissolved into hysterics.

The sheer, pure, romantic magic of the *Bounty* had proved fatally attractive yet again!

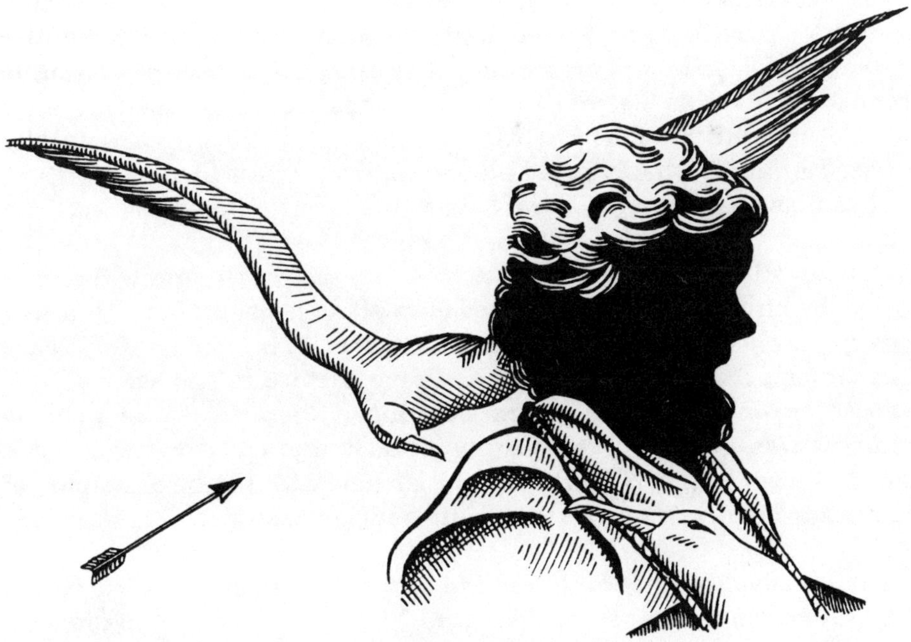

CHAPTER TEN

Man, Myth and Miscellaneous

The Isle of Man is inexorably entwined with *Bounty's* story, so much so that any man on the island with the surname Christian will bear the nickname 'Fletcher'. A fiercely independent small dot in the Irish Sea, Man's influence seems to somehow bubble beneath the surface at odd moments during the whole of *Bounty's* tale. For centuries the island had been an entirely separate empire from the British mainland, ruled over by its own Parliament, Tynwald (which still exists), until the passing of the Revestment Act in 1765, when George III took on the extra title of King of Man. It did little to quell the autonomous spirit of the

Manx people, who were still presided over by Deemsters (over which post the Christian family had built an almost immune inheritance system) and even to this present day they continue to declare legislation from Tynwald Hill. Fletcher's decision to hold so many meetings after the mutiny with his fellow rebels on *Bounty* and Pitcairn now makes sense. To him, it was Tynwald all over again, with a Christian still at its head, as Deemster; he *knew* how to make such situations work for him.

One tradition to which the Isle of Man desperately clung was the right to use the birch as a legally accepted form of punishment; in truth it was a very rarely used deterrent. Inhabitants of Man could safely leave their front doors open, with a gold dinner service in full view if they wanted, without fear of anyone stealing it, because to be publicly whipped was not only extremely painful, it was embarrassing and a dreadful disgrace. This is why I feel Fletcher, with the birch as part of his background, was so worried about the ignominy of tasting the Navy lash.

The Common Market outlawed the continued use of the birch during the 1970s, interference which greatly angered the Manxonians, although they were forced into accepting this hierarchical judgement. Australian actress Magda Palmer, a beautiful lady with flaming, rich red hair you would kill for, visited Man during all the uproar to make a programme in a series of small documentaries detailing many different aspects of Britain for the Central Office of Information, which syndicated the finished ten minute films around the Commonwealth countries. For four and a half years she travelled the length and breadth of Britain to give the far-flung, scattered members of the Commonwealth a sense of togetherness and unity with the mother country. On one occasion she went down in a diving bell in Scotland, another subject was a book factory – this time her attention was turned on Tynwald.

At five o'clock one morning she was sitting in a hired bus with the rest of the film crew, travelling to the site of Tynwald Hill to set up the equipment ready for filming at the historic site; behind them was a big silver truck full of the necessary apparatus. Suddenly, as they approached a bridge, their driver, a defrocked cleric, announced that before they crossed the bridge they were all to say, first to the left, 'Good morning, little people' and then repeat it to the right . They were about to enter the Little People's territory and if they were not treated with respect, unknown calamities could befall these humans. Magda, being a polite lady, obliged but she was a lone voice in the bus. The driver was having none of this and hit the breaks with an almighty crunch, forced the big silver truck to reverse, backed-up himself, demanded the occupants of his bus did better this time and tried again. All the ladies present greeted the little people; only four voices in total.

The driver was not taking the risk of offending the wee folk; he slammed on the brakes again, back went the big silver truck, back went the bus and once more he insisted that *all* his passengers acknowledged these mythological inhabitants of ivy (an old superstition of Man is never to take ivy inside a house, a little person might be on one of the leaves and they do not appreciate being locked in human homes). The camera crew, described by Magda as, 'tough men who had been knocking around a bit' and were sporting t-shirts with the slogan 'Birch Me Baby' boldly emblazoned across their chests, were fed up with this cleric, especially as they knew the sooner the shoot was completed the sooner they would be in the pub, so on this third attempt to cross the bridge a loud chorus of 'Good morning *** little people' 'Good morning *** little people' rang through the bus. The driver was content and carried on over the bridge. For the rest of the day Magda was to hear about nothing else except 'little people'; the crew were so annoyed at being bullied into saying good morning to them. The cleric later explained there had been two nasty motor bike accidents near that bridge and, looking very harshly at the film men, declared that both bikers were not the type to pay their respects to the little people, who therefore decided to teach them some manners the hard way.

William Bligh does not seem to have been the type to recognise the evidence of the little people either, whereas Fletcher Christian, coming from a family so steeped in Man's traditions, probably would have.

Whilst on the island Magda visited Onchan Church, and was shown the parish records regarding William and Betsy Bligh's marriage. Therefore curious about Fletcher Christian, she asked to see his records and was shown an entry for a Christian which only gave the mother's name and stated 'baby born', which has given rise to the rumour that Fletcher was born the wrong side of the blanket. My personal feelings are (so long as the dates tally) that when Ann Christian lived on Man with her two youngest, Fletcher and Humphry, she did indeed have another baby, and it could have been the social castration from this that finally drove Fletcher to sea. A myth of my own devising to add to the confusion that already abides.

However, Glynn Christian (New Zealand born, seventh generation descendant of Fletcher's, via Norfolk Island) has some very viable views on the circumstances surrounding the mutiny. He backs up the point that Fletcher was extremely ambitious, saying, ' to be so called in Georgian days was very, very, very, very extraordinary; yes, that many verys because ambition simply did not exist. You were born into a place in society and you did well in it. To climb upwards, which is what ambition would have been then, was not only unthinkable, it was impossible – with one exception. The Navy. In the Navy you got promoted according to your ability and thus you could be the illigitimate son of a publican, but an admiral. So, somebody who went into the Navy and was described as ambitious would be the equivalent of one of our great high flying moguls today; it was a very special and accurate description, but people of the twentieth century just do not seem to realise that'. In his excellent book, *'Fragile Paradise'*, Glynn has delved deep into the background of the Navy, Georgian society and the Bligh and Christian families to give an authentic picture; it is a well researched tome, though only for the dedicated reader being somewhat heavy going. I enjoyed it though.

When I talked to him, he also picked up on the Isle of Man's influence over Fletcher's decision to take *Bounty* in the first place. It was a snap resolution, and one he regretted a great deal, but Fletcher Christian was only doing what the rest of the Christian family, his antecedents from the Island of Man, had done for generations and that was to take the lead, particularly when a group of people felt they were oppressed. The Christian Deemsters had protected the island's special spirtual independence for over a thousand years, and Glynn is able to trace back twenty-five grandfathers, to 1380, who were law givers and can be seen time and time again standing up for the rights of lesser people, so he says, 'Fletcher was only being a perfectly ordinary Christian, which is important to see in context against Bligh whom he felt, rightly or wrongly (probably rightly), was not doing his job properly and being beastly unkind'.

Although Bligh was technically a superb sailor, his basic character fault was he was not, as they would so charmingly put it nowadays, 'a people's person'; he could not manage people. Glynn explained the only time Bligh was in control was when there was a problem, he simply was not somebody with whom to sit round a table with. He would emasculate the men by taking their powers from them and would grossly and deeply insult them; there is nothing more untrue than 'sticks and stones can break my bones, but names will never hurt me', names hurt and wound far more, and Bligh was a great master at being brutal with his tongue. The combination of insensitivity plus that very wounding tongue, is unquestionably something which aroused a unique collection of adventurers, and something was bound to happen. He feels the most interesting thing about *Bounty's* mutiny is that *we* know about it. Such occurences were happening virtually every day, but no one was left to tell the tale; captains nailed to masts were flayed alive, their skins peeled bit by bit over the days, officers chopped up and thrown through port holes – both were perfectly ordinary, bloody incidents. *Bounty's* victims, of course survived and when the story became common knowledge through them, it was easy (and still is) for people to associate themselves with it romantically; because there was no blood it does not sound really nasty.

As he had found fame in Britian as a modern-day Fanny Craddock, I sought his professional opinion as to why the breadfruit, once delivered, established and matured in the West Indies, was rejected by the slaves. Was it, I wondered, too revolting to taste? No, he assured me, it can be rather delicious and is now a basic part of West Indian food, but two hundred years ago many of the serfs were first generation Africans, who had been transported on the slave ships, and the style of food they were used to was totally different. They had been living on bananas, but the banana tree (which Glynn explained intriguingly is not a tree at all, but a herb – it actually does not have a trunk) is fragile and will blow over in a decent storm, making them incredibly expensive to propagate, but a breadfruit tree can feed something like ten people for a year; much more economical, but initially the slaves did not like it, being much too bland for their tastes, though they were forced into accepting and devouring it eventually.

Magda Palmer was covering an auction at Christies in 1976, again for Central Office of Information, and on the agenda that day was the notebook William Bligh used as his log in the long boat. Magda is a very psychic lady who can pick up some uncanny senses and when invited to flip through the log before the filming of the auction began, she was initially very gentle with it. Her director soon complained, saying, 'Come on, you're an actress, how would you thumb through it?' Thinking, 'My goodness gracious me, it's old, is it sort of strong?', she touched her finger with a little bit of tongue and flicked her way though, but when it came to re-wetting her finger she was stunned – she could taste salt.

This taste suddenly took her right into the book and her eyes really focused on the perfect penmanship and she recalled thinking, 'I would be terrified if I saw such handwriting from anybody, I think they'd be looking if I had one hair out of place'. Going through the log she could not see one deviating movement, the same slope, every letter was always precise, a fine line going up and a heavy line going down and the thought crossed her mind, 'In a long boat, at sea? How did he do it? What a perfectionist this man must have been and how he must have kept his mind on it. Can you imagine that man wavering one little bit in his decision about anybody whether he was right or wrong?' It is this precise hand writing of Bligh's that made me decide to branch away from the norm in calling *Bounty's* sailmaker Leboque; if you are already familiar with the crew members you may know this character as Lebogue, but I am convinced Bligh spelt his name with a 'q' and not the generally accepted 'g' found in print. William's 'g's are consistently written differently from the thirteenth letter found in Lawrence Leboque's entry in the muster list.

Catching a flavour of salt was not the only physical experience Magda picked up from this book, she also felt an awful pain deep in the bone of the right arm, which struck her as strange when the writing was so perfect (usually, she felt, when you have a sore arm you are going to let up somewhere or another), accompanied by a terrific ache in her head, a hard, heavy pain that was exploding, wanting to open the lid and move off. The idea has been put forward that Bligh had a brain tumour, which gave him slightly schizophrenic tendencies; what look like manic attacks of outrage against people were basically because he was in great pain. Nothing was ever proved, but, put together with Magda's experiences, it certainly makes sense.

At Christies, Magda was treated like a V.I.P. for the day and given a reserved seat in the second row of a very packed auction room. They had to sit through well over a hundred lots (old masters that were treated like your ordinary, run-of-the-mill paintings) until the one before Bligh's notebook was knocked down. Suddenly the tension started to mount, all the lights blazed as though a heavy sun had just entered the room and everybody, dressed to the nines, sat bolt upright, eyes gleaming and popping. The place became so crowded nobody could move. Magda ran the gauntlet of emotions, she wanted to laugh and scream and be sick and sit and hide in a corner because the atmosphere was so totally, wonderfully electric and taut. All of a sudden it struck her, how the argument between these two men could still affect people. That is really what the sale of the log was all about, getting the characters of these fellows straight; they were both so strong in the tension, nobody in the room was important anymore, they were one great big electric field. The bidding began, and quickly settled between two people – though everyone in the room was mutely joining in – until the biggest climax of all, at 73,000 Australian dollars, the hammer fell to conclude the sale, and no one knew who had bought the notebook or where it was going. A beautifully exquisite boxed facsimile of it has since been published, telling us the original was acquired for the National Library of Australia.

Other facsimilies of manuscripts and documents with *Bounty* connections have appeared from publishers Genesis. They have reproduced the most breath-taking, refined, hand bound in leather, limited editions of both logs of *Bounty* and *Providence,* and John Fryer's narrative, *"The Voyage Of The Bounty Launch"*. Unfortunately, the 500 copies of *Bounty's* log were completely sold out long ago, though it is little wonder with a signed foreword by Earl Mounbatten of

Burma accompanying each one. There are plans for yet more titles to join this collection: *"The Trial Of Peter Heywood, Mutineer. A Fight For His Life"* by Nessie Heywood; the 1790 classic *"An Account Of The Mutinous Seizure Of The Bounty With The Succeeding Hardships Of The Crew To Which Are Added Secret Anecdotes Of The Otaheitan Females"* – thank goodness Genesis have reduced the title to *"The Mutinous Seizure Of The Bounty"* and *"The Journal Of HMS Bounty"* by James Morrison – my local library scoured the country for this book to discover only two copies in existence, one in the British Museum Library and another at Reading University. In fact, there is a third in the National Maritime Museum, Greenwich.

One final book in the Genesis collection is *"The Letters of Fletcher Christian"*, a publication which first appeared in 1796 with, naturally for those days, the ridiculously over long title of *"Letters From Mr Fletcher Christian Containing A Narrative Of The Transactions On Board His Majesty's Ship Bounty Before And After The Mutiny, With His Subsequent Voyages And Travels In South America"*. This volume tells the story of how Fletcher supposedly made his way to Chile and was employed by the Spanish Government, in gratitude for saving their shipwrecked Major General. The authenticity of this work is less credible than that greatest of twentieth-century hoaxes, the *Hitler Diaries*, because Fletcher is reputed to disclaim any hatred of Bligh as being the cause of the uprising, rather it was the lure of Tahiti. Sounds just the sort of idea William Bligh would like to perpetuate.

If the theory that Fletcher was alive in South America in 1796 is acceptable, it will be relatively easy to believe Peter Heywood's yarn of how, when he was in Plymouth in 1808, he noticed something familiar about the outline of a man walking ahead of him. His step quickened as he attempted to catch him up and the man, obviously hearing the increased footfall, turned. Heywood was convinced Fletcher Christian had seen him and hurried even more, but the stranger fled. With mounting eagerness, Peter gave chase but was eventually outstripped and the man disappeared. Puzzled, Peter decided to keep quiet, concluding Fletcher did not want to risk being discovered, even by an old friend, and this story did not materialise until after his death in 1831, when it was revealed by Lady Belcher, his step-daughter. If the man was not Christian, he must have been most relieved to out distance the footpad who later became an admiral.

The rumours continued that Fletcher had returned to England and the popular conjecture was of him being hidden on Belle Island in the middle of Lake Windermere. This island, with its pepperpot folly of a house right in the middle, was the property and namesake of his probable first love, Isabella Christian Curwen. The theory was expounded upon because of the density of trees on Belle Island, which conceal the house and would have provided ample cover for Fletcher to move around comfortably without detection. Glynn Christian subdued this theory, by discovering the bulk of foliage was not planted until 1802, and from little shrubs mighty trees do not grow in just six or seven years.

In 1798 a collaboration of poems by Samuel Taylor Coleridge and William Wordsworth appeared under the collective title of *"Lyrical Ballads"*; one of Coleridge's contributions was the *"The Rime Of The Ancient Mariner"* – thought by many to be inspired by contumacious Christian. Under the influence of opium, Coleridge possibly lapped up Wordsworth's reminiscences of when he lived in Cockermouth during the same period as Fletcher and how he even attended the same school, though at six years the mutineer's junior they would not have shared the same classroom. However, Wordsworth's father was an attorney and with the Christians so ensconsed in the law, the families paths must surely have crossed. A little hero worship may even have crept in on the poets side, stirring Coleridge's furtive, stoned mind to hallucinate over Fletcher's feelings, and perchance resulted in him hanging an albatross round his neck. The hypothesis is taken even further. If Christian *was* living on Belle Isle, Wordsworth, with his family connections, might have been aware of the secret, and taken Coleridge to visit him. Coupled with the fact that Coleridge elaborated and enlarged his original version of the *"The Ancient Mariner"* into the famous poem known today, and reprinted it in 1817, it is quite feasible to conclude that his first attempt was purely imaginative, whereas he revised and added to it after meeting its progenitor. All depends on what renderings are considered true in the first place.

Over the next few decades stories came tumbling out of Pitcairn, each telling a different version of Fletcher's death. The general confusion thrown up by John Adams' smokescreens could not be accurately verified by the rest of the island's occupants, because they only knew what they were told by Adams; as in the case of Thursday October Christian who was firmly of the opinion that his mother had also passed over, while constantly addressing Isabella as, 'Mrs Christian'. It is thought that Adams was so vague because he had actually been the one to kill Fletcher, after he had survived the massacre by the Polynesians, crawled off to his cave with his head severely dented, nursed his wounds (aided and abetted by his wife) and then attempted to leave Pitcairn. To prevent him going, Adams is supposed to have shot him, then deliberately wove a tissue of misleading lies around him to cover up his action.

Dr James Cerini from Victoria, Australia has come up with the most intriguing explanation of all; Fletcher Christian was alive and well and masquerading under the name of John Adams. The learned conjecture pulls together little obtuse details, such as Adams' insistence on always revering Fletcher as '*Mr* Christian'. He would sometimes refer to him in the first person, then revert to the third, and the second generation Pitcairner's naturally called him father. The decider though would be in the phenomenal difference between two signatures credited to John Adams; one is the shaky autograph of the newly taught illiterate, whereas the other is in a flowing, fluent, scholarly style. Adams was not taught to write until late in his life, so there is always the possibility that Ned Young wrote one as an example for Adams to copy, as part of his lessons. That is if the coaching really did take place; if it was Fletcher and not John, schooling by a dead man would be a very convenient explanation of his mastery with a pen. So if Alexander Smith had been slaughtered by the rampaging natives, and Christian knew of his alias, what could be simpler when Pitcairn was discoverd than to take on this deceased comrade's identity; rather than ringleader he could now act the duped follower.

Unfortunately Dr Cerini has discounted the events at the time of the massacre. One of the murderous men was apparently heard to apologise to Ned Young for the close brush with death to which Adams, alias Smith, had been subjected, bringing forth the thought that Young had engineered the whole situation; he was after all the only one to pull through totally unscathed. And this is not the only incitement of which the swarthy native of St Kitts, in the West Indies, with rotting and gaping teeth, 'and rather a bad look', was accused; many think he first put the idea of mutiny into Fletcher's head, while others feel it was George Stewart when he roused Christian to relieve the watch that fateful morning. It seems that Young, perhaps in league with Smith, manipulated Christian and, having used him to gain his own ends, promptly devised a method of getting rid of him when he had finally outlived his usefulness. The others, who had tilled the land and built the houses, were also superfluous, and all were annihilated in one successful onslaught. The outcome suited Young admirably – more women for him, less aggravation for the eternally indebted Polynesians.

On the coast of Pitcairn is an area named Oh Dear, supposedly the final words spoken by Fletcher Christian. When I met Terry Jones (of *"Monty Pythons Flying Circus"*) in connection with an interview for my charity HOPE, he caught sight of a map of Pitcairn which sits in the front of the book we ask all our 'victims' to sign. His Python-esque sense of humour was instantly aroused when he found Oh Dear; 'Oh dear,' he chuckled, his dry wit coming readily to the fore as he exclaimed, 'there's really a place called Oh Dear!' He might be interested to know there is also somewhere on the island called Oo-Ar-Oo; Thursday October Christian's daughter was fishing around some rocks, using her skirt to scoop the catch up in, when Edmund McCoy crept up behind and touched her on the backside. The frightened woman jumped and yelled, 'Oo ar oo', and so that clump of rocks has been known ever since. Other names to capture the imagination are John Catch A Cow (by all accords John, whoever he was, chased a cow all round the island before finally overcoming his bovine prey), No Guts Captain, Ugly Name Side, Bitey-Bitey and Wandering Jew.

This last, although being slightly in land, must surely be connected with a ship of the same name as, in either 1881 or 1882 the *Wandering Jew* harboured at Albert Dock, Hull, carrying the first Pitcairners who left the island for this country. A gentleman on board a neighbouring ship distinctly heard strains of *"Blow The Man Down"* floating over the waves from them.

This first step towards becoming involved with life outside their small environment has gradually developed, and the perfect answer to their desire to join in with world events came on Sunday 11th September 1988; as the rest of mankind ran Sports Aid's 'Race Against Time' for the benefit of third world countries, they were determined to contribute as well and the whole community pounded round and round their island until they had completed a six mile course.

Television has brought up a few instances where *Bounty's* tale has helped the humour of a programme along. One was on *"The Two Ronnies"*; a very affable mutiny was taking place between Ronnie Corbett as Christian and Ronnie Barker as Bligh. Eventually a worrying point was raised, the name of the ship was something like *Sunflower*, and for the sake of posterity they wanted to change it into something more powerful. Corbett's Christian suggested they take on the name of a stock of chocolate bars he had in his cabin, and so they agreed for history to record 'the mutiny on the Crunchie'! Another instance was when Dennis Nordon, on his compilation programme of film out-takes, *"It'll Be All Right On The Night 5"*, cited a director in one of his clips, who almost melted the bleep machine, as the ultimate example in vexation when explaining 'He could have given irritability lessons to Captain Bligh'.

William's honour has constantly been discredited, yet nothing can be as disparaging, not only to his good name but also Fletcher's, as the degradation put forth by Madge Derby in 1965, that Bligh and Christian indulged in a homosexual affair. In the interest of accurate research, I put the question of whether it was possible for a sexual relationship to have existed between the two men to Anthony Hopkins, who withered me with a very definite, mortifying 'No'. Arguments which could convince about chagrined lovers feuding have been put forward, but they were trapped on a tiny ship for two years and could never had kept such an affair secret. No one ever alluded to it afterwards, whereas somebody with a grievance against Bligh (Fryer and Purcell spring instantly to mind) could have damned his career in an instance, with such explosive information. Even if a deliberate code of silence was protecting at least Fletcher Christian's memory, William Purcell might well have unwittingly remarked about it when languishing in his asylum. Finally let us remember William Bligh was born under the zodiac sign of Virgo who are very faithful; they are not called virgins for nothing!

He has turned out to be quite a typical Virgo in many respects, especially the list-making perfectionist who cannot leave the smallest detail out. His clear and exact record containing specific notes about the men left on *Bounty* serves as an excellent example of this. So nobody at the European settlements to whom he forwarded copies, in case *Bounty* called in at one of them for help, would be in any doubt as to whom they were dealing with, Bligh wrote this about Christian; 'His knees stands a little out and may be called a little bow legged He is subject to violent perspiration and particularly in his hands so that he soils anything he handles.' Considering the steps and ladderways on board a ship it is no wonder Fletcher was bow legged. Magda Palmer is certain Bligh also mentioned that Christian was particularly hairy in the notebook she scanned at Christies, though if he had been overly hirsute it is doubtful the Tahitian's possibly would not have respected him so completely as they had a hatred of bodily hair, which they plucked out.

It is interesting to note that Christian was a Libran, the ones who balance the scales of justice, which it would seem he did, fighting a long, emotional battle against Bligh's prejudices until taking action to redress the equilibrium. In the East the Chinese way of analysing someone's character and future is by looking at one of twelve animals which rule over any one given year. Therefore you return to the same sign after twelve years rather than every twelve months. Christian was born in the year of the Monkey, which the more charitable might link to his behaviour, while William Bligh's sign is that of the Dog, and he did bark a lot. At one time, Fletcher was treated rather as William's pet and there is another famous Virgo mixed with the Dog who is renowned for his pet chimpanzee (which, for the purposes of poetic licence, has to be close enough to a monkey) – Michael Jackson. If a Jackson fan had lived two hundred years ago he could well have found himself sympathising with Bligh.

The latest *Bounty* has completed her voyage to Australia as part of their Bicentennial celebrations and is planning a re-enactment of the mutiny in the Pacific. Ken Rosebery, along with thirty other incurable romantics (including Ron Ware, Bligh's descendant who re-ran the open boat voyage), owns and runs the ship, and is the Australian adventurer I met in Portsmouth. Overcome by the beauty and romantic appeal of sailing a replica of Bligh's *Bounty* around the world, he instigated the buying of her from the film makers when she became surplus to their requirements. She has made a second appearance on film by doubling as *Resolution* in the magnificent Revcom/ABC series *"Captain James Cook"*, which brought us the disquieting experience of witnessing Bligh aboard his own ship as master; many and varied are the strange consequences to be gained from suspending realism.

When Ken first took possession of her she was in excellent order having been beautifully maintained by the crew, who were inspired by the magic of *Bounty* to stay with her through thick and thin. So the fully rigged ship which is 133 feet long over all, including the bowsprit (the pole that sticks out in the front to take more sails), with the highest of three masts measuring 97 feet, carrying 7000 square feet of sail and eleven *miles* of rope, was in immaculate mock-18th century condition. She can even be propelled by sail alone, within the constraints of the sailing characteristics of a ship from the 1700s; they do not perform as ably as a modern sailing vessel, yet they handle very well down wind (the wind has to come from behind the ship for it to set the square sails) therefore they do not beat up wind like a modern fore and aft vessel can, but apart from that she sails admirably – in a reasonable wind of fifteen or twenty knots, she can be making up to eight knots. Not that they have to rely on the weather as the original crew did because, although the top half is fairly authentic, down below decks is an entirely different world, a complete living village.

She is an entirely steel hulled, Lloyd's 100 A1 twin turbo charged, diesel powered modern vessel, with satellite navigation, computers, comfortable accommodation and air conditioning; very sea worthy and in line with modern maritime regulations. Not that such stringent details prevented an eerie latter-day sea yarn unfolding. As *Bounty* crossed the vast seas from her birth place in New Zealand to the film set at Tahiti, her engines stopped during an horrendous storm and she was nearly lost. When the damage was later surveyed, a clock was found to have stopped at 5.00 am on 28th April, the exact time of the mutiny – on its anniversary. It crossed my mind to wonder how a repetition of the mutiny is to be avoided as Ken is running *Bounty* as a solid business venture, inviting people to pay for the prerogative of living in the same cramped amount of space, however luxuriously and comfortably furnished. All possibilities have been well thought through and dealt with, for instance they only carry thirty eight people instead of rivalling the forty six originals. Thirteen of these are permanent, professional crew members, starting with the captain, who is a fully qualified foreign going class one master mariner. Next are three officers, who are the first, second and third mates, and are each in charge of a watch, during which period they are in full control of the ship. Three engineers are headed by the Chief Engineer, who is actually the second highest ranking officer on board, and between them they look after the complete running of the mechanical side of things, an extensive, mammoth task including the care of the engines, generators, fresh water systems, sewage systems, electrical systems and navigational equipment. The final six full-timers are made up of the boatswain, a cook and assistant, and deck hands who help out with the general work. That leaves room for just twenty-five paying adventurers euphemistically referred to as the 'trainee crew'.

Ken admits that room is tight, although they have the extra capacity for accommodation where once the nursery was housed, so fewer bodies and increased room immediately amounts to more comfort. The running of three watches of course means that not everyone is on the same time schedule or routine, which helps a great deal to spread the facilities of the ship around so, with everyone evenly distributed (at any one moment during the day or night, as many as eighteen people could be on deck; those on watch working, others asleep or relaxing, swinging in their hammocks), it comes as a pleasant surprise how uncrowded it can be. While everyone else is enjoying doing exactly what he first fell for, the excitment of sailing *Bounty* around the world, he is remaining in the office or meeting bank managers in an effort to keep the ship a feasible concern, but one pleasure he will not forego is the undertaking proposed for 1989/90 when they plan to sail out to

Norfolk Island, across to Tahiti and finally end up at Pitcairn to celebrate the two bicentenaries connected with the story; the anniversary of the mutiny itself on 28th April and the founding of Pitcairn Island on 15th January.

I started this book with everything clear cut and well defined; Fletcher Christian was cruelly victimised, William Bligh his sanctimonious assailant, with everyone else slotting in on one side or the other. Now I have come to the end of this highly fascinating, eventful and enjoyable, though sometimes very long and weary, adventure in my life, I have discovered everything revolves around the warm, greyish areas in the middle. William was not a terrible megalomaniac; he was an upright, law abiding, pious Protestant who could perhaps have done with a bit less mouth and a deal more imagination. On the other hand, Fletcher was no hard done by saint. He comes across as a spoilt, morose, aspiring, feckless youngster who needed to do a lot of growing up, rather than trust in an inate charm to see him through life, without having to worry about any consequences. For me, they have met halfway; neither is better nor worse than the other, they just had very different ideas on the same subject, and those differences exploded into rebounding repercussions which I hope you now realise were so far reaching, they still affect us today.

THE FATE OF THE CREW OF THE BOUNTY

BLIGH	William	Commander	Died 6 Dec 1817 aged 63
BROWN	William	Assistant Botanist	Murdered on Pitcairn 1793
BURKITT	Thomas	AB	Hanged on HMS *Brunswick* 30 Oct 1792
BYRNE	Michael	AB (Blind Fiddler)	Acquitted at court martial
CHRISTIAN	Fletcher	Master's mate to 2 Mar 1788 then Acting Lieutenant	Possibly murdered on Pitcairn 1793
CHURCHILL	Charles	Master-At-Arms	Murdered on Tahiti 1789
COLE	William	Boatswain	Survived launch voyage
COLEMAN	Joseph	Armourer	Acquitted at court martial
ELLISON	Thomas	AB	Hanged on HMS *Brunswick* 30 Oct 1792
ELPHINSTONE	William	Master's Mate	Died of malaria in Batavia
FRYER	John	Master	Died 26 May 1817 aged 64
HALL	Thomas	AB	Died of malaria in Batavia
HALLET	John	Midshipman	Drowned with HMS *Penelope*
HAYWARD	Thomas	AB to 1 Dec 1787 then Midshipman	Drowned during typhoon in China
HEYWOOD	Peter	Midshipman	Conviction at court martial quashed
HILLBRANT	Henry	AB	Drowned aboard *Pandora*
HUGGAN	Thomas	Surgeon	Died 10 Dec 1788
LAMB	Robert	AB	Died of malaria in Batavia
LEBOQUE	Lawrence	Sailmaker	Survived launch voyage
LEDWARD	Thomas Denman	AB to 11 Dec 1788 then Acting Surgeon	Lost at sea going home from Batavia
LINKLETTER	Peter	Quarter Master	Died of malaria in Batavia
MARTIN	Isaac	AB	Murdered on Pitcairn 1793
MCINTOSH	Thomas	Carpenter's Mate to 31 Dec 1787 then Carpenter's Crew	Acquitted at court martial
MCKOY	William	AB	Fell to death from cliff on Pitcairn
MILLS	John	Gunner's Mate	Murdered on Pitcairn 1793
MILLWARD	John	AB	Hanged on HMS Brunswick 30 Oct 1792
MORRISON	James	Boatswain's Mate	Drowned with *Blenheim* in 1807
MUSPRATT	William	AB	Conviction at court martial quashed

NELSON	David	Botanist	Died of fever in Coupang
NORMAN	Charles	Carpenter's Crew to 1 Jan 1788 then Carpenter's Mate	Acquitted at court martial
NORTON	John	Quarter Master	Stoned to death on Tofua
PECKOVER	William	Gunner	Survived launch voyage
PURCELL	William	Carpenter	Died in an asylum, 10 March 1834
QUINTAL	Matthew	AB	Executed on Pitcairn by Young 1796
SAMUEL	John	Clerk and Steward	Survived launch voyage
SIMPSON	George	AB to 14 Oct 1787 then Quarter Master's Mate	Survived launch voyage
SKINNER	Richard	AB	Drowned aboard *Pandora*
SMITH	Alexander (alias ADAMS John)	AB	Died on Pitcairn 5 March 1829
SMITH	John	AB	Survived launch voyage
STEWART	George	Midshipman	Drowned aboard *Pandora*
SUMNER	John	AB	Drowned aboard *Pandora*
THOMPSON	Matthew	AB	Beaten to death on Tahiti
TINKLER	Robert	AB	Survived launch voyage
VALENTINE	James	AB	Died 9 Oct 1788
WILLIAMS	John	AB	Murdered on Pitcairn 1793
YOUNG	Edward	AB	Died of asthma on Pitcairn 25 Dec 1800

Acknowledgements

I am indebted to the following people and organizations for their invaluable help with the compiling and completion of this book:

Colonel John Blashford-Snell, Ben and Irma Christian, Glynn Christian, David Essex, Charles Higham, Anthony Hopkins, Simon Horrill, Magda Palmer, Richard Robinson, Ken Rosebery, Hedley and Olive Rundle and Jim Russell, all of whom have such varied, interesting and unique thoughts, feelings and tales to tell of the *Bounty* story, and I thank them for sharing them with me. Also I am beholden to Connie Moore and Dr Roger Morriss for their time and efforts on my behalf.

BOUNTY REPLICA
Twickers World Ltd
22 Church Street
Twickenham TW1 3NW
01–892 7606/8164

You can sail the South Pacific on the *Bounty* Replica, as part of her trainee crew, for a holiday that promises to be different from most others.

GENESIS PUBLICATIONS
9 Pilgrim House
Quarry Street
Guildford, Surrey
0483–37431

Genesis have published limited edition facsimilies of several original manuscripts in their *Bounty* Collection, coupled with interesting introductions especially written by Stephen Waters.

HOSPITAL ORIENTATED PROGRAMME ENTERPRISES (H.O.P.E.)
28 Overdale
Ashtead
Surrey, KT21 1PW
0372–272841

A charity formed especially to supply hospital radio stations around the country with exclusive interviews and book, film and TV reviews, it welcomes all volunteers with some spare time to donate to a very worthwhile organization.

NATIONAL MARITIME MUSEUM
Greenwich
London SE10 9NF
01–858 4422/5265

Everything about the British Navy is to be found in this famous museum. From 28th April 1989 they will be celebrating the mutiny's bicentenary with a special exhibition. Included in the displays will be John Fryer's narrative, which they house, along with an extensive collection of books, papers and manuscripts on the subject.

OPERATION RALEIGH
Alpha Place
Flood Street
Chelsea
London SW3 5SZ
01–351 7541

Operation Raleigh encourages young people to join in many varied adventures on both sea and land and in so doing gives them a unique opportunity to discover hidden talents and team spirit, as they lend muscle power to needy causes around the world.

THE PUBLIC RECORDS OFFICE
Ruskin Avenue
Kew, Richmond
Surrey, TW9 4DU
01–876 3444

All ships logs, plus numerous other Naval documents (including muster lists) are kept here, along with material relating to the Army and RAF. They are open 9.30 a.m. – 5.00 p.m., Monday to Friday, except on public holidays and during the annual stocktaking (usually the first two full weeks in October). Admission is by reader's ticket only, which will be issued on production of proof of identity.

TOWN DOCKS MUSEUM
Victoria Square
Hull
0482–222744

A small display in this museum in *Bounty's* birthplace contains a copy of Robert Dodds' painting of the launch being set adrift, a portrait of Bligh, his chart of the Humber, a model of the *Bounty* and a picture of the breadfruit, plus detailed notes.

WILLIAM AND BETSY BLIGH'S MARRIAGE
Onchan Parish Church
Isle of Man

The Manx Museum has an array of *Bounty* related exhibits including portraits of both Peter and Nessie Heywood and examples of wood carvings from Pitcairn.

WILLIAM BLIGH'S TOMB
St Mary-at-Lambeth
Next Lambeth Palace
Lambeth Palace Road
London SE1 7JU
01–261 1891

This church was closed in 1972 and rescued from demolition by the Tradescant Trust, which has founded the first Museum of Garden History there, plus a centre for lectures and exhibitions related to this theme. Bligh's tomb is fenced off from the rest of the graveyard and can only be reached through the building, which is open Monday – Friday 11 a.m.–3 p.m. and Sunday 10.30 a.m.– 5 p.m., March to second Sunday of December.

Lastly, but not, of course, least, my sincere and grateful thanks to Alastair and Sharon Cannons, Colleen Doyle, Christina, Janice, Julian, Louise and Thomas Freke, Bill and Thelma Pearson, Albert Stoakley, Roy Stockdill, David and Vicky Warren, Marian White and everyone at the SPA for all their unstinting help, love and support behind the scenes.

Bibliography

Books:

A Guide To Pitcairn
Published for the Government of the Islands of Pitcairn, Henderson, Ducie and Oeno, by the British Consulate-General, Auckland

Australian Cinema, First 80 Years by Graham Shirley and Brian Adams
Angus and Robertson

"Beloved, Respected And Lamented" by J E Chandler
Tradescant Trust

Brando, The Unauthorised Biography by Charles Higham
Sidgwick and Jackson

Captain Bligh by Richard Humble
Arthur Barker (a subsidiary of Weidenfeld)

Captain James Cook by John Hooker
Penguin

Fragile Paradise by Glynn Christian
Hamish Hamilton

Hell and Paradise by Peter Clarke
Viking

Heritage Of Britain
Reader's Digest

International Encyclopaedia Of Film by Dr Roger Manvell
Michael Joseph

John Fryer Of The Bounty, Notes On His Career, Written by his Daughter Mary Ann. Introduction by Owen Rutter
Golden Cockrell Press

Lloyds Maritime Atlas, 7th Edition
Lloyds

Mel Gibson by Keith McKay
Sidgwick and Jackson

Niven's Hollywood by Tom Hutchinson
Macmillan

Talking Pictures by Barry Norman
BBC Books: Hodder and Stoughton

The Bounty by Richard Hough
Corgi

The Cambridge Guide To English Literature by Michael Stapleton
Book Club Associates

The Court-Martial Of The Bounty Mutineers (edited by Owen Rutter)
Wm. Hodge

The Films of Errol Flynn by Tony Thomas, Rudy Behlmer and Clifford McCarty
Citadel Press

The Journal Of James Morrison by James Morrison (edited by Owen Rutter)
Golden Cockrell Press

The Mutiny Of The Bounty by John Barrow
Blackie

The Mutiny On Board HMS Bounty by William Bligh
Airmont

The Oxford Illustrated Dictionary, 2nd Edition
Book Club Associates

The Story Of The Isle Of Man, Volume 2; 1406-1964 by C. W. Airne, M.A.
The Norris Modern Press Ltd

Twentieth Century Thesaurus
Chambers

Uffa Fox's Second Book by Uffa Fox
Peter Davis

War In the Falklands by The Sunday Express Magazine Team
Weidenfeld and Nicolson

Who Caused The Mutiny On the Bounty? by Madge Darby
Angus and Robertson

Magazines:

National Geographic
Article on the *Pandora,* October 1985 issue

Programme of stage musical, *Mutiny*!

Weekend
Article on Mel Gibson, 19-25 August 1987 issue

Woman's Own
Article on David Essex, 18 May 1985 issue

Manuscripts:

John Fryer's Narrative by John Fryer (Ref: RUSI/NM/46)
National Maritime Museum, Greenwich
Kind Permission to quote from this document given by the Trustees of the National Maritime Museum.

Log of HMS *Bounty* (ref: ADM 55/151)
Public Record Office, Kew

Log of HMS *Brunswick* (ref: ADM 51/112)
Public Record Office, Kew

Log of HMS *Duke* (Ref: ADM 51/265)
Public Record Office, Kew

Logs of HMS *Providence*
Public Record Office, Kew

Muster List of HMS *Bounty* (Ref: ADM 36/10744)
Public Record Office, Kew

Newspapers:

The Hull Daily Mirror, Tuesday, 6 October, 1936

The Times, Friday, 9 March, 1790